AMERICAN HISTORY BEFORE 1877

Jason H. Silverman, Ph.D.
Winthrop College

An American BookWorks Corporation Project

McGraw-Hill Book Company

New York   St. Louis   San Francisco   Auckland   Bogotá   Hamburg
London   Madrid   Mexico   Milan   Montreal   New Delhi   Panama
Paris   São Paulo   Singapore   Sydney   Tokyo   Toronto

To Susan, with love

Jason H. Silverman is Associate Professor of History at Winthrop College, Rock Hill, South Carolina. He received his B.A. degree from the University of Virginia, his M.A. from Colorado State University, and his Ph.D. from the University of Kentucky. Before joining the faculty of Winthrop College, he taught at the University of Kentucky and Yale University. He is the author of *Unwelcome Guests: Canada West's Response to American Fugitive Slaves, 1800–1865*, and the forthcoming *Beyond the Melting Pot in Dixie: Immigration and Ethnicity in Southern History*, as well as numerous articles and essays in scholarly journals and anthologies. He is also a coeditor of volumes 2 and 3 of *The Frederick Douglass Papers*. Dr. Silverman is a past recipient of Winthrop College's Outstanding Junior Professor Award, and was also honored by the freshman honorary society Alpha Lambda Delta as one of the school's exceptional teachers of freshmen.

Editor, Vicki L. Eaklor, Ph.D., Alfred University

American History Before 1877

1 2 3 4 5 6 7 8 9 10 11 12 13 14 15 16 17 18 19 20 FGR FGR 8 9 2 1 0 9 8

ISBN 0–07–057539–8

Library of Congress Cataloging-in-Publication Data
Silverman, Jason H.
    American history before 1877
        1. United States—History.   I. Title
E178.1.S583 1988 973   88-12709
ISBN 0-07-057539-8

Preface

This volume is intended to serve two purposes. First, it is itself a synoptic history of the United States to 1877, and in that regard may stand independent of all other texts. Second, it is also a review text which can be used in conjunction with most of the major, comprehensive American history texts. While it follows no one textbook in particular, the chapter organization corresponds as closely as possible to that of many other volumes.

Because brevity was a major concern, no attempt has been made to cover the major interpretive or historiographical debates that pertain to this period of American history. Rather, the reader is encouraged to consult the "Recommended Reading" section that follows each chapter. In this section readers are directed to detailed studies of topics, events, and personalities mentioned in the chapter about which they wish to know more. The emphasis here is on recent, easily obtainable books. Unless a book is considered a classic in its field, only the more recent works are included. Readers wishing detailed maps in addition to the ones included here are directed to *The American Heritage Dictional Atlas of U.S. History* and Kenneth T. Jackson's and James Truslow Adams's *Atlas of American History*.

Another primary concern was that the information in this volume be readily accessible. Since it is a review volume, readers must be able to use this book quickly and successfully in conjunction with their primary textbook or secondary readings. Since it is also an introduction to the history of the United States from the period of European discovery and colonization to the end of the Reconstruction era, the reader must be able to use this book comprehensively. The time lines preceding each chapter will succinctly indicate, in chronological order, the key events that will be covered. A quick look at a few pages will indicate the material covered there; the subheadings will turn the reader's attention to the chapter organization.

This volume, then, is at once a brief history, an outline, and a review guide. Careful use, I hope, will help make the study of American history a more easily understood and enjoyable experience.

Acknowledgments

In many ways, this book has been a labor of love for me, and I am delighted to acknowledge those people who selflessly helped along the way. Thanks must first go to my chairman, Bert Viault, for recommending me to do this volume and then providing me with a little released time to work on it and other projects. Too, his frequent friendly inquiry "Well, what chapter are you working on now?" always motivated and encouraged me when my energy faltered. My colleague and friend Jim Casada read every chapter with a keen editorial eye. In the process, he saved me from many errors and made the manuscript more readable. I also thank my students at Winthrop College for making the teaching of American history always an exciting and enjoyable experience. Mr. Fred Grayson, president of American Book-Works Corporation, has been a pleasure to work with throughout this project, and I am thankful for all his help and good words.

I am deeply grateful to Jon Safren, my close friend for over twenty years. Our semiweekly (sometimes more frequent) telephone conversations, either postgame or postdate, never failed to remind me that there was a very important world existing beyond my academic one. Tom Appleton and Paul Doutrich have been good and loyal friends since graduate school. As always, their friendship was sustaining during the writing of this book. My in-laws, Jim and Eloise Riel, two of the most generous people it has ever been my pleasure to know, never ceased to provide encouragement, support, and anything else that was needed. For this I am truly appreciative.

My greatest debt, though, is to my wife, Susan. Patient and comforting, intelligent and wise, she has given me immeasurable assistance on this project, as with all of my undertakings. The dedication of this book to her is but small acknowledgment that without her, it would all be meaningless.

J.H.S.
Rock Hill, S.C.
June 1988

Contents

CHAPTER 1

America Becomes the European Frontier

Time Line

c. 38,000 B.C.	The Indians, America's first settlers, begin to cross a land bridge between Siberia and Alaska
c. 1000	Leif Ericsson and the Norse discover Vinland in North America
c. 1400	Improvements in navigational science, technology, cartography, printing and shipbuilding increase possibilities for global exploration by Europeans

1492	Columbus makes voyage of rediscovery to America
1513	Balboa claims the Pacific for Spain
	Ponce de León explores Florida
1519	Cortés begins conquest of Mexico
	Magellan begins circumnavigation of the globe
1531	Pizarro begins conquest of Peru
1580s	Gilbert and Raleigh attempt colonization for the British
1606	James I gives London and Plymouth Companies the right to colonize in America
1608	Champlain founds Quebec for the French
1609	Hudson explores in North America for the Dutch

It is all too frequently believed that Christopher Columbus discovered America in 1492. In truth, Columbus was not the discoverer of America, if by that we mean the first person to encounter the New World—the two continents which lie between Europe and Africa, to the east, and Asia, to the west. At least two other groups of people reached the Americas before Columbus. Between 40,000 B.C. and 12,000 B.C. people from northeast Asia reached the New World from across the Pacific and settled the two continents. Truly deserving to be called native Americans, the descendants of these people are known as Indians. Then, around A.D. 1000, the Norse, or Scandinavians, from northern Europe, reached North America from the east.

Accepting the fact that Columbus followed in other's footsteps, we shall begin our brief history of America with a generation of adventuresome, ambitious Europeans seeking their destiny and wealth in the New World. Progress in navigational science, technology, cartography, printing, and shipbuilding all made long-distance discovery and colonization not only feasible but potentially profitable as well. By the time of Christopher Columbus's sail to America, Europe was ready and eager to attempt to tap the resources of a truly new world.

The Norse (Vikings) and Early Attempts at Discovery

The Norse were technically the first Europeans to discover North America, and they attempted to colonize it between 986 and 1013. Their attempts at colonization were unsuccessful, though, and in time the discovery was forgotten. In contrast, the rediscovery of North America by Christopher Columbus in 1492 had far-reaching historical consequences for that part of the world.

Medieval Europe did not respond vigorously to the Norse discovery because it did not have the resources, energy or strong, centralized political institutions to do so. Generally, Europe during the Middle Ages was poor, politically disunited, constantly beset by local wars and chronic disorder, and its people were largely illiterate and unfree.

The fifteenth- and sixteenth-century explorations and conquests of new lands were activated by the growth of trade with the East (Asia), the organization of towns, and development of nation-states. These forces were accelerated by revolutionary developments in printing, navigational science, shipbuilding, and weapons technology. Between 1000 and 1500, Europe was transformed into a dynamic society well equipped for trans-oceanic expansion. Expeditions and conquests could now be financed by monarchs and the wealthy merchants of the new nation-states.

Led by Prince Henry the Navigator (1394–1460), the Portuguese launched voyages along the African coast. Prince Henry established a school for seamanship, navigation, and exploration, and his activities put the Portuguese at the forefront of the age of exploration. Such activities impressed Christopher Columbus, a young Italian seaman and geographer trained in Portugal. His discovery, or rediscovery, of the New World (including the Bahamas, Cuba, and Haiti) in 1492, financed by Ferdinand and Isabella of Spain, stimulated the Spanish explorations and conquests of this area in the sixteenth century. Before long though, the profitable Spanish monopoly in the New World was being challenged by the French, Dutch, and English who established their own colonies.

New Spain

Spain's biggest task was to govern what Columbus had discovered. Through warfare, overwork, random cruelties, land encroachment, and diseases incidental to unsanitary labor encampments, native Indians were nearly exterminated. Primarily at fault was the insatiable Spanish demand for labor.

The Spanish Crown granted colonists the rights to the labor of the Indians in a particular village. The recipient promised to protect and Christianize "his" Indians. The Indians could not be legally enslaved because, insisted the Crown, they were royal subjects, potential Christians, and therefore freemen. But this was difficult to enforce, and the colonists often used the Indians' refusal to embrace Christianity as an excuse for waging war against a tribe, frequently reducing prisoners to slavery.

Between 1492 and 1519, Spain's achievements in America seemed moderate at best. The Caribbean's meager gold supply began to dwindle after 1518; mining yielded to cattle and sheep raising as the chief occupation of the area. The islands taken by the Spanish did provide an excellent base for further explorations. The most notable of such explorations and the Spanish adventurers, or conquistadors, who made them were these: (1) Vasco de Balboa in 1513 crossed the Isthmus between North and South America to the Pacific Ocean and founded Panama; (2) in the same year Juan Ponce de León explored the Florida coast; (3) Ferdinand Magellan sailed around the world between the years 1519 and 1522 and claimed the Philippine Islands for Spain; (4) Hernán Cortés conquered the Aztec empire in the Valley of Mexico between 1519 and 1521 and overthrew Montezuma; and (5) Francisco Pizarro overran the Inca civilization high in the Andes Mountains beginning in 1531.

Because they had acquired incredible sums of gold and silver from their victims, Cortés and Pizarro inspired many more Spanish colonists to seek their wealth in the New World. By 1575, there were almost 175,000 Spaniards taking advantage of the resources of both North and South America, Christianizing and exploiting the natives, and sending tremendous amounts of wealth back to Europe.

Merging with the Portuguese

In 1580, King Philip II of Spain, rather than risk conflict with his neighbor and nearest competitor, united his empire with that of the Portuguese to create a colossus unlike anything the world had ever seen. Portuguese possessions in the East (Africa and India, for example) and Spanish possessions in the Americas had finally united East and West.

Spain's wealth in the New World was considerable. However, the extravagant success Spain achieved in empire building tempted its maritime neighbors. The threat of the Dutch, French, and English (much intensified by the religious rivalry between Catholics and Protestants) increased the cost of protecting Spain's overseas empire and decreased its profit margin until it reached zero. By the 1640s this sustained pressure had reduced the Spanish empire to chaos and rebellion. The world giant emerged from the crisis as a second-class power.

The Dutch

As long as they could obtain products directly from Spain, Dutch ships remained in European waters. When Spanish ports were closed to the Dutch (because of their insistence on maintaining Calvinism) and Spain began confiscating their ships, the Dutch spread across the seas in the 1590s, and enjoyed an explosive growth in trade. Dutch trading and resistance to the Spanish began to effectively erode Spanish commercial power.

The Dutch founded the colony of New Netherland on the Hudson River, the strategic heart of North America. After Henry Hudson explored the river for the Dutch in 1609, a trading post was erected. Calvinist families began to settle, and in 1626 Governor Peter Minuit founded New Amsterdam on Manhattan Island. It didn't really prosper and attracted little support from the home government. The colony barely survived several disastrous Indian wars and foreign encroachments. Yet under the leadership of a fierce one-legged Calvinist soldier, Peter Stuyvesant, New Netherland began to grow at last in the 1650s.

By then, the Dutch had turned their efforts against Spanish domination over them in Europe—a turning that gave France and England a series of opportunities in the New World.

New France

For most of the 1650s, France was so badly divided by religious civil war—the Huguenots (Calvinists) against the Catholics—that it played no significant role in overseas competition.

Nevertheless, two early efforts do deserve mention. The

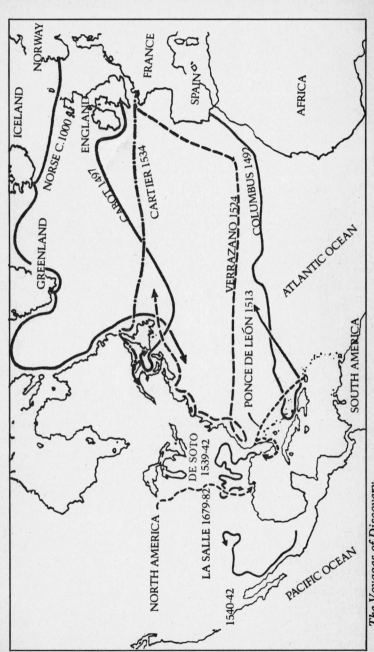

The Voyages of Discovery

first was by Giovanni Verrazano, who in 1524 explored along the coast of North America, and the second by Jacques Cartier, who tried unsuccessfully to establish settlements along the St. Lawrence River between 1534 and 1535.

After 1600, attention of the French was mostly focused on the Caribbean, where they attacked and plundered Spanish colonies. Other Frenchmen, fewer in number and mostly Catholic, followed Samuel de Champlain to the St. Lawrence River, where he founded Quebec in 1608. There Champlain hoped to establish a profitable fur trade. He also believed in the conversion of Indians through complete assimilation. Indians, he thought, could only become good Christians if they first became good Frenchmen and -women.

Catholic missionaries soon joined the fur traders among the Indians. But little progress in colonization occurred before 1627, when, in the middle of a civil war, the French Crown took time to charter a militant Catholic company which obtained jurisdiction over Canada.

The company agreed to provide four thousand settlers for Canada, all of whom had to be Catholic. They would receive full rights as French subjects, as would Indian converts. The company was also empowered to issue feudal land grants within its extensive claims. In short, Canada would become what France itself was not: a perfect hierarchical Catholic society.

However, the demands of European wars thwarted attempts to settle the colony. Even after the founding of Montreal in 1641, growth was slow. Canada contained only approximately five hundred Europeans in 1649 and approximately twenty-five hundred when the French Crown finally assumed direct control of its affairs in 1663.

The English

Throughout the sixteenth century, the English had no more

success than the French at threatening Spain's New World empire. John Cabot claimed North America (which he believed to be China) for the English in a voyage of 1497 that was soon all but forgotten. Later, the exploits of Captain John Hawkins, the leader of the "sea dogs," who raided Spanish ships in the 1560s, and similar activities by Sir Francis Drake in the 1570s won special recognition from Queen Elizabeth I.

For the most part the English largely ignored the New World for the next seventy years. In this period they expelled most foreign merchants from English soil, won control over their own foreign commerce, and created respectable trade relations with various parts of the world. Largely because these activities brought decent profits, London's wealthy merchants avoided riskier American adventures.

The true pioneers of English colonization were Sir Humphrey Gilbert and his half brother Sir Walter Raleigh, though neither of them succeeded in founding a permanent colony. Both were friends of Queen Elizabeth I. Gilbert insisted to the queen that English bases in America would give greater opportunities for sapping the power of Spain. In 1578 he obtained from the queen a patent conferring upon him for six years the exclusive "right" to "inhabit and possess at his choice all remote and heathen lands not in the actual possession of any Christian prince."

Gilbert and Raleigh then, with seven ships and four hundred men, set out in that year to establish a base in the New World. Storms, however, turned them back before they had crossed the ocean.

Gilbert waited five years while he sought to raise enough money to try again. In 1583, he sailed with a second and smaller expedition and reached Newfoundland, taking possession of it in the name of the queen. He proceeded southward along the coast looking for a good place to build a military outpost that eventually might grow into a profitable colony, of which he would be proprietor. Once more a storm defeated him; this time his ship sank and he was lost at sea.

The next year, 1584, Raleigh secured from Elizabeth a six-year grant similar to Gilbert's and sent out men to look over the American coast. They returned with two Indians and with glowing reports of an island the natives called Roanoke and of its environs (present-day North Carolina). With her permission, Raleigh named the area Virginia in honor of Elizabeth, the "Virgin Queen."

In return, Raleigh expected financial aid from the queen but was informed that she could not afford it. He had to raise the money from private investors to finance yet another voyage to Roanoke.

Raleigh sent out two more expeditions, going as far north as Chesapeake Bay and carrying approximately two hundred settlers who lived on Roanoke Island for a while. When a relief ship, delayed three years by the hostilities with the Spanish, arrived in 1590, it found the island utterly deserted. What had become of the "lost colony" is still a mystery.

The colonizing efforts of Gilbert and Raleigh did teach lessons and set examples for future and more successful promoters of colonization. After his ill-fated attempt, Raleigh again sought financial aid from merchants, to whom he sold the rights of trading with his proposed colony. He realized that the undertaking was too big for the purse of one person alone. And some of the colonizers who followed him would raise funds for their ventures by forming companies and selling stock.

When James I became king of England in 1603, Raleigh was accused of plotting against him and was deprived of his monopoly, imprisoned, and eventually executed. From then on, nobody would receive grants so vast and undefined as both his and Gilbert's had been. Thereafter the Crown, in theory the owner as well as the sovereign of lands to be occupied by Englishmen, granted and regranted territory to companies of proprietors on terms that imposed varying conditions and set boundaries, which were, however, often vague and conflicting.

A group of London merchants to whom Raleigh had assigned his charter rights planned to renew his attempts at colonization in Virginia, which still consisted of an undefined stretch along the Atlantic seaboard. A rival group of merchants was also interested in American ventures. In 1606, King James I issued a new charter which divided America between the two interested groups. The London Company was granted the exclusive right to colonize between present-day Cape Fear in North Carolina, and close to what is today New York City. The Plymouth Company received the same right to colonize from the New York area north to present-day Bangor, Maine. Neither company was allowed to start a colony within 100 miles of where the other had already put a settlement. Each company, as soon as it had begun actual colonization, was to receive a grant of land 100 miles wide and 100 miles deep. The settlers themselves were to retain all the "liberties, franchises, and immunities" that belonged to the English at home.

Through the efforts of the London Company the first enduring English colony was about to be planted in America. The merchants intended from the outset to found not an agricultural settlement, but rather a trading post. To it they expected to send English manufactures for barter with the Indians, and from it they hoped to bring back American commodities procured in exchange or produced by the labor of their own employees.

Mercantilism

England's ventures in the New World of course were not terribly different from those of its European neighbors. All nations at this time undertook colonization schemes basically for one reason: wealth. Colonies would increase the wealth of the mother country, such as England, and lessen its dependence on other nations.

According to the mercantile theory, the mother country would prosper and grow strong by exporting more to foreigners and importing less and less from them. Colonies, on the other hand, would assist by providing a market for the mother country's manufactured goods and a source of supply for raw materials that the mother country could neither obtain nor produce at home. In theory, the colonies stood to prosper as well, because they could exchange their crude products for finer goods manufactured most economically by the mother country, which had more capital and skilled labor than the colonies.

As we shall soon see, the mercantile system did not work exactly this way between England and its colonies. And this provided the origin for conflict that would ultimately culminate in a revolution.

While Spain and Portugal achieved great success early on in the European race for an empire in the New World, maintaining that empire proved to be a different story. Their success spawned intense competition from their European neighbors, each of which attempted not only to sap Spanish and Portuguese wealth but to create bases of their own as well. French, Dutch, and English attempts all served to erode the Spanish-Portuguese empire. Though they entered the competition somewhat late, the English, by the early seventeenth century, were on the verge of creating the most sustained New World colonial venture.

Recommended Reading

James T. Axtell, *The Invasion Within: The Contest of Cultures in Colonial North America* (1985)

Charles R. Boxer, *The Portuguese Seaborne Empire* (1969)

Paul H. Chapman, *The Norse Discovery of America* (1981)

Alfred W. Crosby, *The Columbian Exchange: Biological and Cultural Consequences of 1492* (1972)

Richard Drinnon, *Facing West: The Metaphysics of Indian Hating and Empire Building* (1980)

W. J. Eccles, *France in America* (1972)

Charles Gibson, *Spain in America* (1966)

Francis Jennings, *The Invasion of America: Indians, Colonialism, and the Cant of Conquest* (1975)

Alvin M. Josephy, Jr., *The Indian Heritage of America* (1968)

Karen O. Kupperman, *Settling with the Indian: The Meeting of English and Indian Cultures in America, 1580–1640* (1980)

James Long, *Conquest and Commerce: Spain and England in the Americas* (1975)

Samuel Eliot Morison, *Christopher Columbus, Mariner* (1955)

Samuel Eliot Morison, *The European Discovery of America: The Northern Voyages, 500–1600* (1971)

Samuel Eliot Morison, *The Southern Voyages, 500–1600* (1974)

Wallace Notestein, *The English People on the Eve of Colonization, 1603–1630* (1954)

J. H. Parry, *The Age of Recognizance: Discovery, Exploration, and Settlement, 1450–1650* (1963)

J. H. Parry, *The Spanish Seaborne Empire* (1966)

Frederick J. Pohl, *The Viking Settlements of North America* (1972)

David B. Quinn, *North America from Earliest Discovery to First Settlements* (1977)

Alfred L. Rowse, *The Expansion of Elizabethan England* (1955)

Wilcomb E. Washburn, *The Indian in America* (1975)

Eric Wolf, *Sons of the Shaking Earth* (1957)

CHAPTER 2

Britain's Empire in North America

Time Line

1607	London Company settles Jamestown
1612	John Rolfe introduces tobacco to Jamestown
1619	First group of black Africans arrives at Jamestown
	The House of Burgesses is established as Virginia's legislature
1620	Pilgrims arrive at Plymouth Rock

1629	Massachusetts Bay Company chartered for the Puritans
1630	Massachusetts Bay colony, under the leadership of John Winthrop, establishes Boston
1632	George Calvert, Lord Baltimore, is granted a charter to settle Maryland
1636	Thomas Hooker establishes colony of Connecticut
	Anne Hutchinson is banished from Massachusetts Bay Colony
	Roger Williams establishes colony of Rhode Island at Providence
1649	Maryland Toleration Act passed ensuring religious freedom for all Christians
1664	New York, formerly the Dutch settlement of New Netherland, becomes a British colony
1679	New Hampshire becomes a separate colony under the leadership of John Wheelwright
1681	William Penn receives a charter to found the Quaker colony of Pennsylvania
1701	Delaware becomes a separate colony
1719	South Carolina becomes a separate royal colony
1729	The proprietors of North Carolina surrender their governing rights to the Crown

1732   General James Oglethorpe obtains a charter
               to found Georgia as a refuge for English
               debtors

---

*Though England entered the race for New World colonies later
than Spain or Portugal it nevertheless achieved greater success
than any of its European neighbors. The colonies that were established under the British flag were motivated by the desire to
seek financial gain or religious freedom or to establish a political stronghold in the New World. In the end, all British colonies
persevered to form that foundation which would ultimately become the United States of America.*

Virginia

The London Company's first expedition sailed into
Chesapeake Bay and up the James River in the spring of 1607
with about one hundred men. The men had instructions from the
company to avoid the mistakes of Roanoke and pick an easily
defended site well inland and on high ground. They selected an
area and called it Jamestown, naming it, like the river, for their
king.

The area they picked was surrounded by thick woods, which
were hard to clear for cultivation. Soon, the colonists were
threatened by the neighboring Indians who resented the arrogant
encroachment of the settlers. The colonists, too many of whom
were adventurous gentlemen and too few of whom were willing
laborers, ran into serious difficulties from the moment they
landed. They faced an overwhelming task in trying to sustain
themselves, and the promoters in London complicated the task
by demanding a quick return on their investment. When the men
in Jamestown ought to have been growing food, they were required to hunt for gold and to pile up lumber, tar, pitch, and iron

ore for export. By January 1608, when ships appeared with additional men and supplies, all but thirty-eight of the first arrivals were dead.

Jamestown was saved from extinction by the leadership of twenty-seven-year-old Captain John Smith. Leadership in the colony had been divided among several members of a council who quarreled continually until Smith, as council president, exerted his will. He imposed work and order on the community. During the winter of 1609, fewer than a dozen in a population of two hundred died. When Smith left in the summer of 1609, the colony was showing true signs of survival.

Promoters in London were making a concerted effort to build up the Virginia colony. To raise money and men, they sold company stock to "adventurers" remaining at home, gave shares to "planters" willing to migrate at their own expense, and provided passage for poor men agreeing to serve the company for seven years.

A new plan was set up whereby the company would hold all land and carry on all trade for a seven year period. The settlers would contribute their labor to the common enterprise and draw upon a company storehouse for their subsistence. At the end of the period the profits would be divided among the stockholders. The London merchants obtained a new charter (1609) which increased their power over the colony and enlarged its area.

In the spring of 1609 the company sent off to Virginia a "fleet" of nine vessels with about six thousand men, women, and children aboard. But disaster followed. One of the ships sank in a hurricane, and another ran aground on the island of Bermuda. Disease, fatigue, and hunger plagued the settlers who did reach Jamestown. The winter of 1609–1610 was the worst "starving time" for the colonists; food was so scarce that one report even spoke of cannibalism. When spring came, many were ready to abandon the colony for good.

Under the guidance of men like Thomas Dale and Thomas

Gates, however, strong leadership formerly supplied by John Smith was restored. New expeditions with hundreds of settlers began to arrive. The colony spread, with new settlements lining the river above and below Jamestown.

The turning point in the colony's history came in 1612. In that year Jamestown planter John Rolfe began to experiment with the growing of tobacco. He found it grew well in Virginia soil, and more importantly, he found ready buyers in England. Soon tobacco cultivation spread up and down the James River.

When the London Company's seven year communal period was up in 1616, the company had no profits to divide, but only land and debts. Still, the promoters were optimistic due to their success with tobacco. In 1618 they launched a last great campaign to attract settlers and make the colony profitable. Under the "headright" system, 50 acres of land were offered to anyone who paid his own or someone else's passage to Virginia, plus 50 more acres for each additional migrant whose way he paid. Thus, a wealthy man could send or take servants to work for him and receive, in turn, a sizable plantation in the New World.

The company expected to add to its income by charging the headright landholder a small rental on his property. Old investors and settlers were given grants of 100 acres apiece. To make life in the colony more attractive, the company promised the colonists the rights of Englishmen, an end to strict and arbitrary rule, and even a share in self-government.

In 1619 two events occurred in Virginia that were to have a profound effect upon the subsequent course of American history. First, delegates from the various communities met as a lower house (House of Burgesses) to consider, along with the governor and his council (appointed by the London Company), the enactment of laws for the colony. This was the first example of an elected legislature, a representative assembly, within what was to become the United States. Second, approximately twenty blacks arrived, not as slaves, but as "servants" to be held for a term of years and then freed. Yet even though their initial status was similar to that of the white servants with whom planters already were familiar, the blacks were almost immediately set apart in subtle but racially discriminatory ways. Thus a start had been made toward the enslavement of blacks, a problem which would ultimately culminate in civil war.

In the meantime, the colonists were attempting to survive. A peaceful coexistence was maintained with the surrounding Indians until 1622. In that year colonists and Indians, led by Opechancanough, warred over the colonists' territorial encroachments, and the result was a massacre on both sides.

The massacre came as a final blow to the London Company, which soon faced bankruptcy. In 1624 King James revoked the company's charter and took control of the colony. By that time the white population of Virginia was less than thirteen hundred; thousands more had come over, but most of these had died and many had gone back to England.

Still, the remaining colonists had a cash crop, a representative government (which was to continue), and a hope for future growth and prosperity. Though a failure as a profit-making enterprise, Virginia was at last succeeding as a colonizing venture.

Plymouth Plantation

While the London Company was starting the colonization of Jamestown, the Plymouth Company attempted to found a colony far to the north, on the coast of what is now Maine. The attempt lasted only a year and then the surviving colonists returned to England. The Plymouth Company sent Captain John Smith to chart the area for further colonization and he named it "New England."

Their motivations were different from those of the London Company. They were religious dissenters who had met with much opposition in England. From time to time they had been imprisoned and even executed for defying the government and the Church of England.

Though it was against the law to leave England without the consent of the king, a group of these "Pilgrim separatists," as they were called, escaped to Holland, across the English Channel, where they hoped to worship as they pleased.

In Holland they were allowed to meet and hold religious services, but they encountered prejudices in other areas, especially jobs, since they were not Dutch citizens. Too, the Pilgrims did not want to raise their children under the Dutch flag. So, they looked to the world across the Atlantic for salvation.

Leaders of this group got permission from the London Company to settle as an independent community with land of its own in Virginia. The king, though not guaranteeing religious freedom, assured them that if they conducted themselves peacefully they would not be molested. This historic concession opened English America to settlement by dissenting Protestants.

The voyage was financed by English merchants on the condition that, as at Jamestown, a communal plan be set up where the merchants would share in the profits after a seven-year period. When they arrived in the New World, time and the elements forced them to land in an area outside the London Company's territory, near Cape Cod, an area John Smith had referred to as "Plymouth."

Since their territory lay outside the London Company's, they would be without a government once on shore. On board then, an agreement was signed on November 21, 1620–the Mayflower Compact, named for their ship. It established a civil government under which the colonists would create congregations and profess loyalty to the Crown. The majority would rule under their agreement. On December 21, 1620, these Pilgrim separatists landed at Plymouth Rock.

During their first winter the colonists suffered terrible losses due to disease and exposure. However, among the neighboring Indians, whose military power had been weakened by a recent plague, the Pilgrims discovered friends who showed them how to obtain seafood and cultivate corn. After the first harvest, the settlers invited the Indians to join them in an October festival, the original Thanksgiving.

The Pilgrims could not aspire to rich farms on the sandy and marshy soil, but they soon developed a profitable trade in fish and furs. More settlers began to arrive and the population slowly grew.

The people of the colony, named Plymouth Plantation, elected their own governor, William Bradford, and for thirty years they continually reelected him as their leader. Though they had problems over their charter and over finances, they never forgot that their mission was a godly one. Compared to other contemporary religions, Plymouth orthodoxy was never intolerant or obsessive, but religion did govern the Pilgrims' conduct of their daily affairs and remained a vital part of their lives.

Massachusetts Bay

Religion played almost as important a part in initiating the settlement at Massachusetts Bay as it had at Plymouth.

The Puritan dissenters within the Church of England were more numerous and socially more prominent than the Pilgrim separatists. They remained hopeful until the 1620s that they could reform the established church by removing the remaining vestiges of Catholicism. By the middle of that decade some began to despair and look to the New World as a potential refuge.

Due to the oppressive religious policies of King Charles I, who censored Puritan books, prevented the Puritans from lecturing, and attempted to impose Anglican beliefs on all dissenters, the Massachusetts Bay Company was chartered in 1629. The charter was different from all previous ones. It omitted (due to the religious persecution) the provision that the governor, assistants, and freemen (stockholders) of the company had to remain in England to conduct the business. In 1630, they sailed under the leadership of the company's governor, John Winthrop, a gentleman of means with a university education, a deep but narrow piety, a cool and calculating way, and a remarkably forceful and stubborn character. The expedition of seventeen ships and one thousand people was the largest of its kind in the seventeenth century. These colonists founded a number of towns, among them Boston, which was the colony's capital.

At first, only those who were stockholders could participate in the local government, elect officials, and pass laws for the colony. However, power eventually spread to the freemen, that is, elected voters or citizens.

To become an elected voter was no easy chore. To participate in colonial government, a man first had to be a member of the Puritan Church. In England, the Puritans had required for church membership only that a person profess the faith, sign the covenant, and live an upright life. In Massachusetts, the Puritans began to limit membership to "visible saints," those who could demonstrate that they had received God's saving grace and hence belonged to the elect, the group whom God had chosen for eventual salvation. Whether admitted to membership or not, everyone in the community was part of the congregation and was required by law to attend religious services.

Unlike the Pilgrims at Plymouth, the Puritan founders of Massachusetts had come with no intention of breaking away from the Church of England. They only wished, at first, to save the church from what they saw as the evil influence of Rome. Nevertheless, they soon acted as if they were religiously independent. Each congregation chose its own minister and regulated its own affairs, and thus was created what came to be known as the Congregational Church.

John Winthrop and other founders saw Massachusetts as a

holy commonwealth, a model for the corrupt world to see. The problem was to keep it holy. In this effort the preachers and the politicians worked together. The ministers did not run the government, but they supported it and exerted great influence upon the church membership, who alone could vote or hold office.

The government in turn protected the ministers, taxed the people (members and nonmembers) to support the church, and enforced the law requiring attendance at services. In Massachusetts, then, dissenters to Puritanism had no more freedom of worship than the Puritans themselves had in England.

Massachusetts, however, was a success. After the first severe winter, when two hundred died and others decided to leave, the colony prospered. The neighboring Pilgrims assisted with food and advice, and many prosperous colonists arrived with necessary supplies for subsistence and trade. As religious persecutions escalated in England under Charles I, the number of Puritans leaving England increased rapidly, so that by 1643 the colony had a population of approximately fifteen thousand. Eventually Plymouth Plantation would merge with Massachusetts, in 1691.

Connecticut, Rhode Island, New Hampshire, Maine

Because of its strict religious policies, an outpouring of people from Massachusetts Bay colony to various places in New England had begun. Not all the incoming settlers were "saints," and as the population increased, the proportion of those who could vote or hold office declined. To the Puritan authorities, opposition to their church seemed like a threat to the government—both heresy and treason. The independent thinkers had little choice: give in or get out.

The first of these was Thomas Hooker, a minister who questioned the fairness of the Massachusetts government. He wanted a government chosen by all for the welfare of all. Coming in direct opposition to John Winthrop and the leaders of Massachusetts Bay colony, Hooker and his followers decided to leave. They journeyed beyond the established frontier to the rich and fertile Connecticut Valley.

In 1639 they adopted a constitution known as the Fundamental Orders of Connecticut. This provided for a government similar to that of Massachusetts Bay but gave a larger proportion of the men the right to vote and hold office.

Rhode Island had its origin in the religious dissent of Roger Williams, a young minister of Massachusetts Bay. Williams was an extreme separatist who first advocated not religious freedom but rather a church made even more pure and strict. He made friends with the Indians and concluded that the land belonged to them rather than the king or the Massachusetts Bay Company.

The colonial government considered Williams a dangerous man and ordered him deported. But he escaped and found refuge with a neighboring Indian tribe. He bought a tract of land from them and in 1636, with a few friends, established the town of Providence on it.

By that time another menace to the established order appeared in Massachusetts Bay. Anne Hutchinson, the wife of a substantial Bostonian, attracted many followers with her belief that the Holy Spirit dwelled within and guided every true believer. Winthrop feared if this was so, the Bible would have no more authority than anyone's personal revelation and both the church and government would be exposed to anarchy.

Mrs. Hutchinson's followers were numerous and influential. Ultimately, though, she was tried and convicted of heresy and sedition and banished from the colony. She and her followers moved to a point not far from Williams's town of Providence.

In time, other communities of dissidents arose in that vicinity. As Williams matured, he modified some of his views on religion and began to advocate complete freedom of worship and absolute separation of church and state. In 1644 he obtained from Parliament a charter authorizing a government for all the combined dissident settlements.

New Hampshire and Maine were founded in much the same way. No one was interested in settling in these regions until religious dissenters began to arrive in them. New Hampshire, under the leadership of John Wheelwright, a disciple of Anne Hutchinson, became a separate colony in 1679. Maine remained under the jurisdiction of Massachusetts Bay until it was admitted as a state in 1820.

Maryland

In Maryland the situation was much different than in New England. One of the stockholders of the London Company, George Calvert, Lord Baltimore, after taking part in the promotion of Virginia, conceived the idea of undertaking a new colony on his own. Himself a convert to the Roman Catholic faith, he had in mind the establishment of a refuge for Roman Catholics, who were victims of political discrimination in England.

Obtaining a charter from the king, Calvert located his territory north of the established Virginia. He died before the grant became official (1632), and his son, the second Lord Baltimore, administered the domain as proprietor.

Maryland's charter contained some curious provisions which revived the long dead concept of feudalism. Calvert and his heirs were to hold their province as "true and absolute lords and proprietors," and exercising within Maryland a power comparable to the king of England, they were allowed to subdivide the land into parcels to men who would become their vassals.

With assistance from the Indians and from neighboring Virginians, the early Marylanders knew no massacres, no plagues, no starving. The Calverts drew on the experience of Virginia. To early arrivals they offered land on generous terms for a

modest rent.   Protestant settlers outnumbered the Roman
Catholics, who were not too inclined to leave England.

A representative assembly, the House of Delegates, basing
its proceedings on Parliament, was allowed. By the 1650s
Maryland had a two-house legislature, with the governor and his
council comprising the upper house. The governor was appointed by the proprietor. This was similar to the government
that was developing in Virginia, except there the governor was
appointed by the king.

Political turbulence marked the early history of Maryland,
as Protestants were hostile to the Catholic minority and the
Catholic proprietor. As an appeasement, a Protestant governor
was appointed and freedom of worship was assured to all who
believed in Jesus Christ. This was passed in 1649 as part of the
Maryland Toleration Act which included a series of strict penalties for religious offenses, including death for cursing God.

The Carolinas

After Lord Baltimore settled Maryland, no new colonizing
effort took place for thirty years. After 1640, the struggle between King Charles I and Parliament distracted attention from
colonization. The English Civil War (1642–1651) and the
period of Oliver Cromwell's Protectorate (1653–659) resulted in
the struggling colonies' being left pretty much to their own
devices. King Charles I was executed. The monarchy was rees-
tablished by the Restoration (1660), when his son, Charles II, acceded to the throne. Then, this new English monarch began
rewarding his faithful with truly regal gifts of American land.
The Carolinas, New York, New Jersey, and Pennsylvania, like
Maryland, were founded by proprietors rather than companies.

By the 1660s, companies had lost interest in colonization and
had turned to more profitable ventures. Charles II, in 1663 and
1665, awarded eight proprietors joint title to a vast territory south

from Virginia to the borders of Spanish Florida. Like Lord Baltimore they were given almost kingly powers over their grant.

These proprietors expected to profit as landlords and land speculators, reserving tremendous estates for their own development, selling or giving away the rest in smaller tracts, and collecting annual payments as rents from the settlers.

Though committed to the Church of England, the Carolina proprietors welcomed all Christian customers. Indeed, their charter guaranteed religious freedom to all who would worship as Christians. The proprietors also promised political freedom—at least as much of it as was to be found anywhere else in America—with laws to be made by a representative assembly.

The proprietors also had an investment in the African slave trade and intended to introduce slaves into the colony so as to profit both from selling them and from using their labor. Early settlers were offered a bonus of extra land for every black bondsman or -woman they brought in. Thus black slavery existed from the outset in the Carolinas with no transitional period of temporary servitude as in Virginia.

The colony developed along two natural but quite different lines in its widely separated areas of settlement. The northern part, the first to be settled, suffered in the early years from geographic handicaps—swampland and lack of natural harbors, for example. Many who settled here had a primitive, backwoods existence: they had no roads, few villages, churches, or schools.

The southern part was favored with an excellent harbor. The city of Charleston was soon established, with its wharves, fortifications, fine houses, and wide streets. The settlement grew quickly, and with it came a stratified society. Many of the early inhabitants had come from declining sugar plantations in the West Indies, bringing with them their African slaves. Wealthy plantation owners came to dominate the region's economy, social life, and politics as ordinary farmers were mostly located inland. Charleston became a center for trade and became capital of Carolina in 1690.

After the eight noblemen discovered their enterprise was not profitable enough, they surrendered their governing rights to the king, who in 1729 divided the colony into North Carolina and South Carolina.

New York

A year after making his first Carolina grant, Charles II bestowed in 1664, upon his brother, the Duke of York, a large tract of land south of the Massachusetts Bay colony. Though the territory had been colonized by the Dutch and it took three Anglo-Dutch wars to secure it, New York, formerly New Netherland, was firmly under British control in 1664.

The Duke of York was given absolute power over his domain but since the inhabitants of his province included Anglicans from England, Puritans from New England, and Calvinists from Holland, he found it wise to be broad-minded with regard to religion and politics.

Like other proprietors before him, instead of going to America he delegated powers to a governor and council. The duke's laws provided for the election of some local officials and the gubernatorial appointment of others. There were to be a variety of established churches and the residents were to be taxed to support them.

With generous land estates the colony grew rapidly. Wealthy English and Dutch landlords, shipowners, and fur traders along with the duke's political appointees dominated the colonial government. Though the colony had become predominantly English in both customs and population, there still remained Dutch traditions to give a distinctive regional flavor.

Pennsylvania, New Jersey, Delaware

The Society of Friends originated in mid-seventeenth century England in response to the preachings of George Fox, whose followers came to be known as Quakers (from his admonition to them to "tremble at the name of the Lord"). The essence of his doctrine was the Inner Light, the illumination from God within each soul, the divine conscience, which when rightly heeded could guide human beings along the paths of righteousness.

Of all the Protestant sects of the time, the Quakers were the most democratic. They had no church government except for occasional meetings. They had no traditional church buildings, only meeting houses, and they had no paid clergy. They treated women as equals and disregarded class distinctions of the day as well. They refused to take oaths of any kind or to participate in any wars.

Because of these unpopular practices Quakers were jailed from time to time. Like the Puritans, many Quakers looked to America for asylum. Some settled in Rhode Island and Carolina, but they longed for a colony of their own.

However, as head of a sect despised in England, Fox found it difficult to get a grant. Then he met William Penn, son of an influential admiral in the Royal Navy. Penn converted to the doctrine of the Inner Light and with Fox purchased New Jersey (formerly part of New York) in 1682.

Penn inherited Pennsylvania (which King Charles II insisted on naming for Penn's father) in 1681. Penn was to have the rights to this vast territory as both landlord and ruler. Through informative and honest promoting, Penn made Pennsylvania the best-known and most cosmopolitan colony. He called Pennsylvania a "Holy Experiment," and he closely supervised its planning, devising a liberal frame of government with a representative assembly.

He personally oversaw the construction of Philadelphia

("the city of brotherly love"), which, like Charleston, was a carefully planned urban environment and thus served as a pattern for most later cities in America. Like Roger Williams, Penn believed the land belonged to the Indians, and he was careful to see that they were reimbursed. The Indians, in turn, honored him as a rarity, an honest white man. Thus his colony had no trouble prospering. Thoughtful planning, favorable climate and soil, affluent and well-equipped settlers, and assistance from neighbors all spelled success for Penn's colony.

Delaware was treated as part of Pennsylvania but was given the privilege of setting up its own representative assembly. It did so in 1701 and thereafter was considered a separate colony, though until the Revolution it continued to have the same governor as Pennsylvania.

Georgia

The last colony to be founded was Georgia, and it was unique in its origins. It was founded by neither a corporation nor a proprietorship, and its guiding purpose was neither to make a profit nor to create a sectarian refuge.

In the beginning the work was done by trustees serving without pay. Their purposes were (1) to provide a new start in life for Englishmen imprisoned for debt, and (2) to erect a military barrier against the Spaniards on the southern border of English America.

Constant conflict existed between the English and Spanish over the area. General James Oglethorpe, military hero of one war with Spain, realized the serious need for a buffer colony between South Carolina and Spanish Florida. As head of a Parliamentary committee investigating English prisons, Oglethorpe knew firsthand the plight of honest debtors rotting in confinement. He conceived the idea of solving both problems at once by resettling such prisoners as farmer-soldiers on the distant frontier.

Oglethorpe obtained a charter in 1732 which stipulated the need for military security. Landholdings were limited in size to keep the settlement compact. Blacks, free or slave, were excluded, as were Roman Catholics, to forestall the danger of wartime insurrection or of collusion with the enemy. Indian trade was strictly regulated, with rum prohibited.

Only a few debtors were released from jail and sent to Georgia. But hundreds of needy tradespeople and artisans from England and Scotland and religious refugees from Germany and Switzerland were brought to the colony at the trustees' expense.

Many others, however, chose not to settle in Georgia, but rather in South Carolina where there were no laws against big plantations, slaves, and rum. Therefore the restrictions were ultimately repealed and after 1750 Georgia developed much like South Carolina.

While the American colonies had been founded for basically religious or economic reasons, all were to some degree transformed by the New World environment. Most had become more liberal in their policies than they might have initially intended. One, Massachusetts Bay, became stricter and more authoritative. All, however, embarked on a course that would soon take them from being merely transplanted Englishmen and –women to becoming truly American.

Recommended Reading

Charles M. Andrews, *The Colonial Period of American History* (1934–1937)

P. L. Barbour, *The Three Worlds of Captain John Smith* (1964)

Emery Battis, *Saints and Sectarians: Anne Hutchinson and the Antinomian Controversy in Massachusetts Bay Colony* (1962)

Daniel J. Boorstin, *The Americans: The Colonial Experience* (1958)

Carl Bridenbaugh, *Jamestown, 1544–1699* (1980)

Carl Bridenbaugh, *Vexed and Troubled Englishmen, 1590–1642* (1974)

Thomas J. Condon, *New York Beginnings: The Commercial Origins of New Netherlands* (1968)

Wesley F. Craven, *The Southern Colonies in the Seventeenth Century, 1607–1689* (1949)

Michael Kammen, *Colonial New York* (1975)

Allan Kulikoff, *Tobacco and Slaves: The Development of Southern Cultures in the Chesapeake, 1680–1800* (1986)

George Langdon, *Pilgrim Colony: A History of New Plymouth, 1620–1691* (1966)

Peter Laslett, *The World We Have Lost* (1965)

Hugh Lefler and William S. Powell, *Colonial North Carolina* (1973)

Perry Miller, *Errand into the Wilderness* (1964)

Edmund S. Morgan, *American Slavery/American Freedom: The Ordeal of Colonial Virginia* (1975)

Edmund S. Morgan, *The Puritan Dilemma: The Story of John Winthrop* (1958)

Edmund S. Morgan, *Roger Williams, the Church, and the State* (1967)

Gary B. Nash, *Quakers and Politics: Pennsylvania, 1681–1726* (1968)

John E. Pomfret and Floyd M. Shumway, *Founding the American Colonies, 1583–1600* (1970)

M. Eugene Sirman, *Colonial South Carolina* (1966)

Paul Taylor, *Georgia Plan: 1732–1752* (1972)

Alden Vaughn, *American Genesis: Captain John Smith and the Founding of America* (1975)

Clarence Ver Steeg, *Origins of the Southern Mosaic* (1975)

CHAPTER 3

The "Americans": A New People

Time Line

1619   The first Africans arrive in Jamestown as indentured servants

1619–1776   Approximately 350,000 Africans brought to America by slave traders

1636   Harvard College is founded, the first college in the British colonies

1662   Half-Way Covenant is enacted by Massachusetts Bay Puritans

1692–1693	Salem witch trials result in executions of twenty people
1720s–1740s	Great Awakening occurs in the colonies, led by such ministers as Jonathan Edwards, George Whitefield, and John Wesley
1732–1757	Benjamin Franklin publishes *Poor Richard's Almanack*

Although many of the colonizing ventures described in the previous chapter were led by noblemen, rich businessmen, and merchants in pursuit of wealth and honors, the truth is that most of the colonists had no such reasons for leaving their homelands. We must now consider the lives of the majority of immigrants who came to the New World and built the foundations upon which their new country would be based. We also must examine how and when these European emigrants ceased being Old Worldish and commenced being American. In so doing, we will seek to answer the question posed by the French gentleman J. Hector St. John de Crèvecoeur, who, after settling in the colonies, asked in 1782 the poignant question, "What, then, is this American, this new man?"

Eager Immigrants

Most immigrants to America in the seventeenth and eighteenth centuries came willingly. This does not necessarily mean they came wisely. Many were misinformed by promoters recruiting colonists for their plantations or by brokers who received a fee for each prospective immigrant they enlisted. These men advertised in print or spread their message by word of mouth; like the hucksters of our own day, they were not always scrupulous about the truth.

Nevertheless, ordinary people could hope to make significant gains in America. Those who were willing to work hard could expect to make greater gains than if they stayed behind in Europe. In the New World, where land and other resources were abundant, the scarce and hence valuable commodity was labor. Those who could supply it were in an enviable economic position.

For men and women of the colonial era, America's wealth and relative emptiness meant high wages and cheap land. Most Europeans of this period were farmers, and to them cheap land was an incomparable attraction. This was well understood by colonial promoters, and thus the establishment of such systems as the headright, where settlers were given many acres of land for paying either their way over or that of another person.

If land was not given away, then it was sold very cheaply. William Penn, for instance, in recruiting for his own colony sold 15,000 acres of land to a group of Germans for the paltry sum of 5 cents an acre. Even those not interested in land per se, such as laborers and artisans who came for higher wages, were swayed by the cheap price of land. Accordingly, these groups eventually sought some wealth in the accumulation of land.

Indentured Servants

America attracted some very poor peasants and laborers, but the Atlantic passage cost about $100, far more than they could possibly afford. Their solution lay in contracting their labor, or agreeing to an "indenture." The would-be immigrant, in return for having the cost of passage paid by a ship captain or potential employer, agreed to work for a specified period of time at a specified wage. The employer also often agreed to some sort of "freedom dues" at the end of the indenture period.

There were several kinds of indentured servants. Those who possessed skills that were needed had the best leverage, for they could negotiate favorable terms even before leaving Europe. The indenture for such a servant would often last less than the average four years. It would also frequently specify the trade at which the servant would work and define what were considered acceptable working conditions.

There were many other less fortunate indentured servants, however. In particular, the "redemptioners" who fled Europe in the eighteenth century in the wake of war, famine, and poverty were among the worst off. First, they moved as families, unlike the typical single bondsman. Second, the redemptioners arranged for merchants to advance them their fare and agreed, in turn, to reimburse their sponsors when they arrived in America. If, upon arrival in America, they could not immediately repay their debt, they had to allow the merchant to "sell" their services in payment. This arrangement unfortunately often led to the separation of families as children might be "sold" to one master and their parents to another.

Indentured servants' lives were hard. Masters had the authority and the right to beat and to whip them. They could not vote, marry, or participate in trade. Their indenture could be transferred freely from one master to another, and if servants ran away, their terms of servitude could be extended.

Many failed to survive their indenture period, but a substantial minority did achieve success in America. By the end of the colonial period, a large portion of the population from Pennsylvania south were descendants of servants who came to America with little more than the clothes on their backs and whatever skills they possessed.

Less Fortunate Newcomers

Many who came to America did so without their free consent. Some were victims of kidnappers who enticed the young, naive, or intoxicated aboard a ship to collect a fee from the captain, who would sell the captives as indentured servants in the colonies.

More numerous were convicts given a choice of going to America as seven-year indentured servants or facing the executioner at home. Those who went were pardoned and turned over to merchants who would assume the expense of the trip in exchange for the right to sell the felon's labor to the colonists. Although the colonies did not necessarily want them, some twenty thousand convicts were sent over during the eighteenth century, most of them to Virginia and Maryland, where their labor was used on the great Chesapeake plantations.

African Laborers

By far the most important form of labor was black labor. Between 1619 and 1776 some 350,000 Africans were brought by slave traders to America. Coming mainly from the west coast of Africa, these blacks were anything but primitive savages. Their skills in agriculture, weaving, metal work, pottery making, and wood and ivory carving made them very valuable laborers. In government, too, the West Africa peoples revealed great talent. Many of their nation-states had imposed order and had brought prosperity to large areas of the "dark continent."

Though the slave-trading raids on Africa dated back to ancient times, it was the Portuguese explorations of the fourteenth and fifteenth centuries that soon popularized the practice beyond previous limits. With the advent of plantation agriculture in America, the slave trade took on great dimensions. Greed and the need for cheap labor led many entrepreneurs to look toward Africa. Indeed, in the Spanish empire black Africans were used with great success in replacing the Indians who insisted on running away.

African slaves at first were taken from their homes by white slavers, but when this proved to be impractical, the Europeans began to rely on the African chieftains themselves for their supply of human chattel. Chained together and marched overland for hundreds of miles to the coast, African prisoners of war, victims of slave-raiding parties, or indigenous African slaves soon found themselves barter for guns, powder, cloth, and rum.

Taken aboard filthy, crowded vessels for their journey to the New World, these Africans experienced the hideous "middle passage" where many died en route. Kept below deck and chained together in stifling temperatures as they were brought across the Atlantic, even many of the young and strong among them were severely weakened, fatigued, and diseased by the time they reached the Americas, .

The first Africans arrived in English America (Jamestown) as indentured servants in 1619. Their legal status at this time was ambiguous at best. These first arrivals were not distinguished clearly from other indentured servants. However, it did not take long for their status to change and be clarified. Largely, the change in their status came as a result of racism. From the beginning the English were prejudiced against the physical characteristics of Africans which they contrasted unfavorably with those of Europeans. Blackness, to the Englishman, seemed to suggest evil.

The vulnerability of the newly arrived Africans added to their exploitation as well. Being away from all that was familiar and unable to communicate even with other Africans of different tribes, black slaves were incapable of protecting themselves. Without friends to champion their rights or protect them from oppression, they were easily reduced to permanent bondage and treated as mere physical property.

European prejudice and black unfamiliarity made it possible to reduce the Africans to permanent slaves but did not supply the motive. Profit supplied the motive to create a system that placed blacks in bondage in perpetuity. English planters in America needed only to look to the Caribbean islands, where slaves had been used on the larger sugar plantations for quite some time and with considerable profit, to see that the system could and did work. It was also evidenced on these large sugar plantations that slaves were more controllable and cost-effective than were indentured servants, who, in the planters' eyes, often created more trouble than they were worth.

Yet in English America the black population grew slowly. Sugar could not be grown in Virginia and Maryland, and the tobacco planters could not afford huge investments in slaves. In 1649, blacks comprised only 2 percent of Virginia's total population.

This soon changed, though. Indentured servants' labor was proving impractical for profit. They became difficult to recruit, their terms of service were short (about four years), and they did not remain on the plantation when their tenure had expired. Instead, former indentured servants established themselves as independent farmers or planters or went off to work in the towns. In addition, indentured servants proved difficult to manage. They complained about the food and working conditions, or they simply ran away. Worse still, they brought their masters before court magistrates on charges of violation of contracts.

Obviously, slaves did not present these problems. By law they were not to be brutally mistreated, but those who were abused or exploited had no recourse in the courts. Their bondage was permanent, and their offspring became part of their master's ever-growing property.

English America, lacking the wealth of the Caribbean's sugar plantations, never became a major importer of slave labor. In fact, the Caribbean and Latin America imported ten times the number of African slaves that the English colonies in America did. But the colonists in America did nurture carefully the health of those they acquired, and through modest importations and natural increase the black population grew rapidly after 1650. By 1700, there were sixteen thousand slaves in Virginia and three thousand in Maryland. Fifty years later, Virginia had more than one hundred thousand slaves, Maryland almost forty-five thousand, and South Carolina fifty-seven thousand. By 1750 more than 20 percent of the inhabitants of English America were black slaves. By the eve of the American Revolution, blacks comprised a majority of the population of South Carolina and fully 40 percent of that of Virginia.

Other "Americans"

Besides Africans, other non-English peoples came to America, particularly after 1700. Having recovered in the 1630s from a sustained economic depression, England began to dissuade, if not prohibit, the emigration of skilled laborers to the New World. As the numbers of English immigrants began to dwindle in the early eighteenth century, considerable numbers arrived from France, Switzerland, Ireland, and Scotland.

The earliest, though not the most numerous, among these were the French Calvinists, or Huguenots who fled the religious and political persecution after Louis XIV revoked the Edict of Nantes in 1685. Under the edict (1598) the Huguenots had enjoyed liberties and privileges that enabled them to constitute practically a state within the state in Roman Catholic France. They became successful merchants and craftspeople in such growing American port cities as Boston, New York, and particularly Charleston, South Carolina, where their influence was keenly felt.

Others, such as the German Protestants and German Catholics, sought relief from religious persecution in their homelands by emigrating to the English colonies. Many of these hard-working German peasants located in Pennsylvania, the Shenandoah Valley, and the Piedmont regions of North Carolina and Virginia, where they created fine schools and newspapers.

The most numerous of the newcomers were the Scotch-Irish,

who left Ireland to escape difficulties with their English landlords and with the Anglican Church. The Scotch-Irish were distinct from the Scots who came directly to America from Scotland. In the early 1600s King James I, to further the conquest of Ireland, had seen to the peopling of the northern county of Ulster with his subjects from the Scottish lowlands, who as good Presbyterians might be relied upon to defend their ground against Irish Catholics. These Ulster colonists, or Scotch-Irish, eventually were forced to seek refuge in America after the English government destroyed their prosperity and outlawed their religion. Primarily they settled on the colonial frontiers in America, where they demonstrated a remarkable degree of resourcefulness, rugged individuality, and self-reliance.

All of these immigrants contributed to the rapid growth of the colonies. At the beginning of the eighteenth century the population of the colonies was approximately 250,000; by the eve of the American Revolution it was nearly ten times greater. The rate of growth of the American colonies was twice that of Europe during the same period.

Besides the steady flow of European immigrants to America, the growth of the colonial population could also be attributed to natural increase. Marrying earlier and having more children, colonial Americans experienced a mortality rate that was half that of Europe. Colonial Americans were also quite able to tap the abundant crops, plentiful land, and great quantities of wood that existed for house building, heating, and cooking fuel.

Forms of Livelihood

Most Americans were farmers or engaged in related agricultural pursuits. On the frontier, the farming was of the subsistence variety with little more grown, or wild game caught, than the family needed for survival. In New England, the typical farm was small enough to be worked by the farmer, his sons, or perhaps a hired hand. The farmer, however, could count on the assistance of his neighbors at harvest time or for barn raisings. In the middle Atlantic colonies, wheat became the primary crop, and the people of the region became known as the "breadmakers" by their countrymen. Though there were small farms in the South, the region came to be dominated by the larger tobacco plantations with thousands of acres and many slave laborers. Besides tobacco in the Chesapeake, in the lower southern colonies rice and indigo became staple crops in the monolithic agricultural system of the region.

Until the early eighteenth century most Americans produced all of their necessities within the home. This began to change, though, as Americans became able to purchase manufactured goods in shops in the new burgeoning cities. The growing urban environments of Philadelphia, Boston, and Charleston, for example, encouraged such skilled artisans as carpenters, chandlers (candle makers), coopers (barrel makers), tailors, weavers, cordwainers (shoemakers), and wheelwrights to display their wares to an eager marketplace.

Women artisans also found a niche in the colonial urban workplace. Female dressmakers and milliners (makers of women's hats) were a common sight. After the death of her husband, a woman frequently assumed his former work of cobbler, tinworker, or blacksmith.

Lumbering, fur trading, and fishing became big businesses by colonial standards. Colonial Americans, relying on nature and its resources for their livelihoods, seldom if ever were concerned about conservation. As such, ideas like crop rotation, preservation of trees and wildlife, and quotas for fishing and hunting were many years in the future.

These industries spawned other profitable businesses. New England enjoyed a very healthy shipbuilding industry. With the harnessing of waterpower, mills for grist and for fulling cloth (treating and beating cloth to clean and thicken it) became common sights. The use of mills also encouraged the colonial production of iron in a crude form. By the time of the American Revolution, in fact, colonial iron makers accounted for 15 percent of the world's iron supply.

The Americanization of the Colonists

When and how did the colonists cease being European in their perspective and practices? How did a unique American culture and society emerge? We must now examine the colonists' most important institutions to understand the process of Americanization.

Religion

One fundamental institution that the Europeans carried with them to America was their religion. The colonists brought with them English variations on a number of religions. However, in the unique conditions in America, the practices of many of these groups began to change from their original European character.

In New England, for example, the American environment affected church structure. The sparseness of population and the isolation of settlements encouraged church government by individual, autonomous congregations. Instead of having bishops, as in the Church of England, or a council of church elders, as in Scottish Presbyterianism, most groups of Christians led by their ministers developed completely independent of other congregations, creating the system known as Congregationalism.

The Puritans made strong distinctions between members of the congregation and members of the church. All were required to attend services but only a few "elect," chosen by God, were members of the church. As in the cases of Roger Williams and Anne Hutchinson, dissenters were treated harshly. The Puritans, then, used their American environment to create a stronger, more elite, more demanding church structure than had existed previously in England.

As long as the zeal that had developed in the charged religious atmosphere of early-seventeenth-century England continued to exert its influence on people's minds, all was well. Young men and women could expect to have the required religious conversion experience and could expect to be admitted to the community as full religious equals. But as time passed, the feelings that had once come easily for many ceased to come at all. Before long, many children of church members could not be admitted. This left most without normal civil rights and threatened the church with a much-decreased membership.

This problem was partially resolved in the Massachusetts Bay colony in 1662 with the Half-Way Covenant, which allowed the children of church members to become nonvoting members themselves without the conversion experience. The children merely had to show that they understood, believed in, and would obey God's will as revealed in the Bible.

This policy eased the crisis, but it did not prevent the further erosion of orthodoxy in the Massachusetts Bay colony. As the years passed, the numbers of immigrants dwindled and more and more of the old faith wore away. Increasing numbers of New Englanders ceased to obey religious sanctions. By the mid-eighteenth century New England was ripe for a great religious revival.

The same was true for the southern colonies. In Virginia and Maryland the dispersion of settlements, the distances between tobacco plantations, and the absence of cities made it hard to practice Old World religion (Anglicanism).

In isolated communities like those of North Carolina there were few churches of any kind. Low salaries, isolation, absence of towns, and strong-willed colonists all dissuaded people from accepting clerical positions.

In the South, then, many colonists completely lost contact

with the church and organized religion. The same occurred in the middle colonies. Worldliness began to replace piety.

The net result of this decline in organized religion had some interesting effects. The multitude of nonchurchgoing colonists and the variety of religious sects made it impossible for England to impose any religious conformity upon the colonists. The British recognized this and strongly supported religious toleration in the colonies. Americans enjoyed freedom to worship as they pleased and dissenters from the dominant religion paid a much smaller civil price for their dissent than did almost any other people in the Christian world.

Whatever its benefits, the general decline in orthodoxy created a vacuum that was filled by the renewed religious fervor of the Great Awakening. Beginning in the 1720s as a series of revivals among the Presbyterians and Dutch Reformed in the middle colonies, the movement soon spread across the entire nation.

Ministers such as Jonathan Edwards and George Whitefield in emotional and fiery speeches called people back to God and threatened them with eternal damnation for sin. Edwards, a Yale graduate, was appalled by the decline of orthodoxy that he observed all around him, and he resolved to do something about it. In 1729 he began to preach the old Calvinist doctrine of predestination, in an attempt to demonstrate the omnipotence and splendor of Calvin's God. Unlike the Calvinist Edwards, Whitefield, borrowing from John Wesley, the English preacher who founded Methodism, believed that sinners might earn salvation and that God did not confine his grace to a small elect. These Methodist revivalists were largely indifferent to the Calvinist idea that salvation was God's gift alone. People could earn their own salvation if they purified their hearts and lives and accepted Christ with love and sincere conviction.

Although this was nothing new, Whitefield, Edwards, and the other revivalists presented their religious messages so simply and so emotionally that they called thousands back to religion. Tremendously popular with the common people, the revivalists were attacked by the educated. Yet the revivalists presented further religious diversity to America and added to the already numerous religious choices in the colonies. The religious environment was becoming truly American.

Government

Government was another institution altered by the American environment. Colonists carried with them the political ideas of the mother country. On the local level the "town" in New England and the "vestry" in the South were transplanted English governmental units. The sheriff and the justice of the peace were fashioned after English models as well. And there were parallels between Parliament and the legislatures of each colony. Beginning in 1619, settlers created legislatures in each colony, and they always resembled the upper and lower houses of Parliament.

Each colony had a chief executive who was analogous to the Crown. Whether appointed by the king or the proprietor or elected by the citizens (only in Connecticut and Rhode Island), the governor normally exercised the right of veto over the legislature much as, in theory at least, the sovereign did in England.

Britain regarded the colonial legislatures as inferior. At first the colonial legislatures, when they met, resembled corporate stockholder meetings. Encouraged by the growing colonial population and aided by distance and by British indifference, they soon expanded their powers.

In the early eighteenth century the colonial lower houses (1) won the right to initiate bills having to do with provincial finances; and (2) forced the governor to permit them to debate openly without executive interference, to determine the qualifications of their own members, to prevent representatives of the crown from attending their deliberations, and to meet when and for however long they wished.

By the end of the colonial era, these representative assemblies had gained control over (1) taxation, expenditures, and salaries of officials, (2) military and Indian affairs, and (3) everything that affected religion, education, and general welfare.

At first the English government did little to restrain colonial assemblies; only after 1763 did Britain seriously try to limit colonial self-government. And that would end in disaster for the empire.

American political life was more democratic and political power more widely diffused in the colonies than in Britain. Upper houses in colonial legislatures were appointed and were composed of prominent landed gentlemen, lawyers, and merchants. They were not hereditary positions as in England's House of Lords.

Lower houses were more democratic than England's House of Commons. Slaves, women, and indentured servants could not, of course, vote. There was a property requirement for free white males, but since property was so easily acquired and widely held, this disqualified few from voting. Religious requirements were maintained in most colonies, but due to the diversity, these were relaxed and disqualified very few potential voters.

All told, the colonial voting public included a very large part of the population of free white men. Artisans, yeoman, slave overseers, tradesmen, and even free servants voted. Deference—political submission to one's superiors—was not as prominent in America as it was in England. Candidates could not act aloof or undemocratic, or ignore the wishes of their constituents if they expected to be elected or remain in office. They had to remain in contact with the voting public.

Yet the colonial governments did retain some elements of the Old World aristocracy. In both the northern and the southern colonies, rich, influential members of the community maintained most power. Affluent planters in the South and successful merchants and lawyers in the North were the focal points of power.

Thus, colonial government was a unique blend of democracy and aristocracy. Compared with modern democratic governments, the colonial systems were deficient. However, at that time complete democracy really did not exist, and if people thought about it, it was generally associated with anarchy. Most believed that the best government was one that mixed democracy with monarchy and aristocracy. Democratic rhetoric would not come until later.

Nevertheless, the transfer of political institutions from England to America produced a tendency toward greater popular freedom and democratic self-determination.

Education

Americans placed a great premium on education. In 1636, just six years after the establishment of the Massachusetts Bay colony, the first college was created, Harvard College in Cambridge, Massachusetts. Although limited at first to humanistic studies and theology, the curriculum soon expanded to include natural sciences as well.

Massachusetts' example was soon followed by other colonies, and by the time of the Revolution, there were eight other institutions of higher education including William and Mary College in Virginia (1693), Yale College in Connecticut (1701), the College of New Jersey, later to become Princeton (1746), King's College, later Columbia, in New York (1754), the College, Academy, and Charitable School in Philadelphia, later the University of Pennsylvania (1755), Rhode Island College, later Brown (1764), Queen's College, Rutgers, in New Jersey (1766), and Dartmouth in New Hampshire (1769).

Of the six colleges in operation by 1763, all but two were initially founded by religious groups for the training of ministers.

Soon, however, at any of these institutions a male student could take "liberal arts" courses in logic, ethics, physics, geometry, astronomy, rhetoric, Latin, Hebrew, and Greek.

Due to the primary school, Americans were better educated by the end of the colonial period than any other people in the Western world. This still did not prevent such incidences of ignorance as the Salem witch trials in 1693, when passion and emotion overran rationality and twenty people were executed.

The Family

The nuclear family (parents and children) remained the norm in America. With the better nutrition of Americans and the lower rate of infectious diseases that went with dispersed settlements, mortality rates and infant mortality rates, in particular, were below the European average. As a result colonial families had seven to nine members, a household somewhat larger than that of English families of the day.

The family was patriarchal in nature and served to provide not only food and shelter but education to the children. The family was also the producing unit and provided most if not all items needed for survival.

Women had more rights in America than in England and frequently participated in business affairs. Responsible for meals, clothing, comfort, and children, and numerically scarce especially in newly settled regions, women were consistently more able to improve their standing than European women.

They were seldom subjected to the physical abuse suffered by European women, and authorities would interfere in gross cases of wife abuse. Divorce, which was more often an escape for unhappy wives in this period than for unhappy husbands, was easier in America, though not especially widespread. Husbands who deserted their wives were generally forced by the authorities to return to them.

The Arts

The arts were often imitative of Europe rather than fully American. This was especially true of literature and music composition. Arts and crafts flourished as they changed from European imitations to American innovations. Artists such as John Singleton Copley and Benjamin West emerged during the colonial period as truly original, American painters. William Billings and Francis Hopkinson distinguished themselves as prominent colonial composers before 1776.

Newspapers, broadsides, pamphlets, and almanacs proliferated and were read more widely by Americans than Europeans. They informed the colonists on domestic affairs so that they could cast a wise ballot, on weather conditions, and on prices for their products. An almanac like Benjamin Franklin's *Poor Richard's* (1732–1757) sold almost ten thousand copies a year. It was also a piece of creative literature, and in addition to the usual items of interest to farmers—weather forecasts, eclipses, tides, list of religious days—Franklin included witty sayings and proverbs.

Crèvecoeur's question at the beginning of this chapter put it well: the American was a "new man." In the process of traveling to, and acclimating to their new environment, the colonists began to shed many of their English or continental characteristics and assume more American ones. Institutions such as government, religion, and the family all experienced a transformation of sorts in the New World and came to resemble something truly unique, something truly American.

There were differences, then, between England and America. These differences would lead to the divergence of interests and goals between mother country and its colonies. Before long, these British-American differences would be troubling on both sides of the Atlantic. Eventually, disagreements would turn to war.

Recommended Reading

Paul Boyer and Stephen Nissenbaum, *Salem Possessed* (1974)

Timothy H. Breen, *The Character of the Good Ruler: Puritan Political Ideals in New England, 1630–1730* (1982)

Timothy H. Breen, *Puritans and Adventurers: Change and Persistence in Early America* (1980)

Timothy H. Breen and Stephen Innes, *"Myne Own Ground": Race and Freedom on Virginia's Eastern Shore, 1640–1676* (1980)

Carl Bridenbaugh, *Myths and Realities: Societies of the Colonial South* (1952)

Robert E. Brown and B. Katherine Brown, *Virginia 1705–1786: Democracy or Aristocracy* (1955)

J. M. Bumsted and John E. Van de Wetering, *What Must I Do to Be Saved?* (1976)

Richard Bushman, *From Puritan to Yankee: Character and Social Order in Connecticut* (1967)

Verner Crane, *Benjamin Franklin and a Rising People* (1954)

Philip Curtin, *The Atlantic Slave Trade* (1969)

John Demos, *Entertaining Satan: Witchcraft and Culture of Early New England* (1982)

John Demos, *A Little Commonwealth: Family Life in Plymouth Colony* (1970)

Richard S. Dunn, *Puritans and Yankees: The Winthrop Dynasty of New England, 1630–1717* (1982)

David W. Galenson, *White Servitude in Colonial America* (1981)

Jack P. Greene, *The Quest for Power: The Lower Houses of Assembly in the Southern Royal Colonies, 1689–1763* (1963)

Philip Greven, *Four Generations: Population, Land, and Family in Colonial Andover, Massachusetts* (1970)

Philip Greven, *The Protestant Temperament* (1977)

James Henretta and Gregory Noble, *The Evolution of American Society, 1700–1815* (1986)

Richard F. Hofstadter, *America at 1750: A Social Portrait* (1971)

Rhys Isaac, *The Transformation of Virginia, 1740–1790* (1982)

Winthrop Jordan, *White over Black: American Attitudes toward the Negro, 1550–1812* (1968)

Kenneth Lockridge, *A New England Town, the First Hundred Years: Dedham, Massachusetts, 1636–1736* (1970)

Daniel Mannix and Malcolm Cowley, *Black Cargoes: A History of the Atlantic Slave Trade* (1962)

Henry F. May, *The Enlightenment in America* (1976)

Darrett Rutman, *Winthrop's Boston: Portrait of a Puritan Town, 1630–1649* (1965)

Abbot Emerson Smith, *Colonists in Bondage: White Servitude and Convict Labor in America, 1607–1776* (1947)

Patricia Tracy, *Jonathan Edwards, Pastor* (1980)

Robert V. Wells, *The Population of the British Colonies before 1776* (1975)

Peter Wood, *Black Majority: Negroes in Colonial South Carolina from 1670 through the Stono Rebellion* (1974)

Louis B. Wright, *The Cultural Life of the American Colonies, 1607–1763* (1957)

Michael Zuckerman, *Peaceable Kingdoms: Massachusetts Towns in the Eighteenth Century* (1970)

CHAPTER 4

The Road to Revolution

Time Line

1660s	England enacts a series of regulatory measures collectively known as the Navigation Acts
1688	The overthrow of James II begins the Glorious Revolution in England
1699	The Woolen Act passed
1721–1742	The period of "salutary neglect"
1732	The Hat Act passed
1733	The Molasses Act passed

1750	The Iron Act passed
1754	Benjamin Franklin proposes the Albany Plan of Union to the colonies but it is rejected
1754–1763	The French and Indian War
1763	Treaty of Paris ends French and Indian War
	The Proclamation of 1763 prohibits colonists from settling west of the Appalachian Mountains
1764	The Sugar Act passed
	The Currency Act passed
1765	The Quartering Act passed
1765	The Stamp Act passed
1766	Parliament repeals the Stamp Act but replaces it with the Declaratory Act
1767	The Townshend duties enacted
1770	Parliament repeals all the Townshend duties except the tax on tea
	The Boston Massacre occurs
1773	The Tea Act passed
	The Boston Tea Party occurs, led by Samuel Adams and John Hancock
1774	Intolerable, or Coercive, Acts passed
	All colonies except Georgia meet in Philadelphia in the First Continental Congress

1775   Armed confrontation occurs between the
                British and the colonists at Lexington and
                Concord

Why did the colonists revolt? What caused the American Revolution? As long as the American colonies depended upon the mother country, Britain, for their survival, there were few problems in maintaining the empire. However, the stronger the colonists became politically and economically, the more uncomfortable they felt with colonial status. While England was allowing the colonies to grow and prosper, little did anyone realize just how far away from the mercantile system the Americans were traveling. When England attempted to bring the Americans back into the fold, it was too little and much too late.

The American Economy

Agriculture, of course, was the basis of the colonial economy. It employed 90 percent of the working force and was responsible for much of the wealth in the colonies. Most farmers engaged in a diverse form of agriculture—growing corn or wheat, raising hogs and cattle, and planting fruits and vegetables for the family. The southern colonies of Virginia and Maryland formed the great tobacco-growing region.

The farmers were not a socially uniform group. They ranged from laborers (free and slave) to yeoman farmers and the landed gentry. The 10 percent who did not farm were equally diverse, including unskilled laborers as well as wealthy merchants.

The poverty so common in Europe was not the lot of most Americans, and the American poor had a fair chance of rising out of the lower classes. America was uniquely a middle-class society by 1776. About 70 percent of the white population belonged to the urban or rural middle class. In no other country did so large a part of the population achieve middle-class status. Nowhere else was the general level of comfort, even for the lower classes, so high.

At the end of the colonial era, the American average income per person was the second highest in the world, exceeded only by the British. And in America income was far better distributed than elsewhere in the Atlantic world.

Land was an important factor in American colonial prosperity, but that prosperity also depended upon a busy overseas trade. Only by trading the surplus of their fields, forests, and mines for the tropical products of the Caribbean and the manufactured goods of Britain were Americans able to attain the high level of living and comfort they achieved.

England wanted and needed the products of southern colonies: tobacco, rice, indigo, and timber. But northern colonies produced goods that were in competition with British goods (fish, grain, cattle), and as a result northern colonies always bought more than they sold to Britain. To make up for this deficit, the northern colonies sought customers who needed what they produced, and they found the buyers in the Caribbean.

There, the sugar plantations had developed into a booming business, but at the neglect of everything else. This made them excellent customers for the food, livestock, and timber from the northern colonies. By 1700, hundreds of vessels sailed from northern ports each year carrying horses, flour, onions, pork, beef, timber, and codfish for use on the sugar plantations.

Another aspect of colonial trade involved the sale of African slaves. The typical slave trader sent a vessel to the west coast of Africa with a cargo of rum distilled in New England from West Indian molasses. On the African coast he exchanged rum for an English trader's iron, cloth, gunpowder, rifles, jewelry, or beads. With this cargo he bought slaves from middlemen, usually African chieftains.

The slaves, often exhausted and sick from the long trek to

the coast, were then packed aboard small vessels, with little or no room to move, and transported on the agonizing "middle passage" to the Caribbean. The vessels were filthy as well as crowded, and disease often swept through the ship. About 10 percent of the cargo usually died. The survivors were auctioned off in the West Indies and sold for either coin or molasses. The profitable voyage was thus complete.

The slave trade was only one of many variations of the trade involving three or more participants that was known as the triangular trade. The colonies also carried on other profitable but less deplorable triangular trade to help pay for English manufactured goods. Trade, then, was vital to the development and prosperity of the colonies.

Beginning of Restrictions

The economic regulations of the empire did not allow the colonists complete freedom to work out their own economic destiny. Colonial trade from the 1660s on was inhibited by a multitude of nettlesome restrictions.

These restrictions stemmed from the mercantilist belief that the colonies would supply the home country with raw materials and, in turn, would consume its surplus and manufactured goods.

Assuming this, Parliament began in the 1660s to enact a series of regulatory measures collectively called the Navigation Acts. Some of these measures were designed to keep the profits of British colonial trade out of the hands of Britain's European competitors; others confined imperial trade to vessels owned, manned, and built by Britain or the colonists. Still others established lists of "enumerated" articles (including virtually all the most valuable colonial products) that had to be shipped to England first, whatever their final destination. Parliament further required that almost all non-English goods destined for the colonies be shipped to England first.

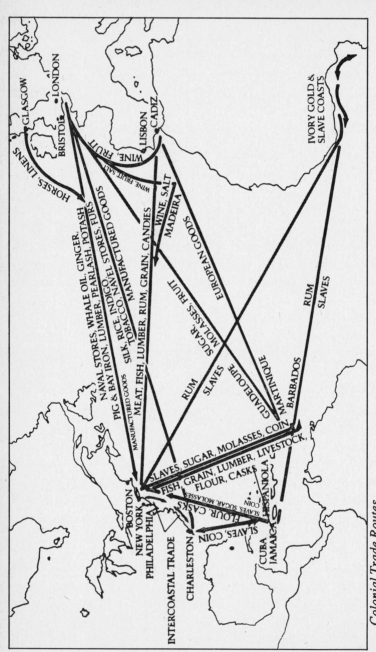

Colonial Trade Routes

These measures, besides excluding foreigners from the imperial trade, were supposed to make Britain the central receiving point for goods imported into, or exported out of, the colonies. Under this proposed system, British merchants would have a major role in the colonial trade and the British government could levy taxes on all goods passing through Great Britain in that trade.

Other pieces of British legislation such as the Woolen Act (1699), the Hat Act (1732), and the Iron Act (1750) sought to restrict colonial industries that competed with the mother country by either prohibiting the industries in question or by limiting their size or their export. To mute the effect of this legislation, Parliament was also careful to establish bounties encouraging the production of items that did not directly compete with English domestic products. It also encouraged the colonists to continue to export those raw materials that were particularly needed in England.

Britain's Justification

Many of Britain's economic regulatory measures were motivated by the cost of maintaining an empire. The major cost was defending the colonies, and the British Army and Navy stood between the colonists and subjugation to Europeans on many occasions.

During the 1600s and 1700s many European wars between England and its neighbors jeopardized the safety of the colonists. The first of a long series of wars between France and England in North America was King William's War (1689–1697). Aided by their Indian allies, the French disrupted English trade and launched attacks on Schenectady, New York, and the New England settlements. The British were aided by the Iroquois. After an unsuccessful attack on Quebec, the British signed the Treaty of Ryswick (1697) with the French. This, however, brought only a temporary lull in the hostilities to gain control of North America.

Queen Anne's War (1701–1713) soon followed. England, the Netherlands, and the Holy Roman Empire fought against France and Spain on the European continent over the succession to the Spanish throne. In America, fighting broke out in the West Indies, the Carolinas, and New England, and again the British opposed the French with both sides employing their Indian allies against one another. The Peace of Utrecht (1713) ceded New-foundland, Acadia, and Hudson Bay to the British. However, in this treaty boundaries were not clearly established between French and British territory on the North American continent and the door was left open for further fighting.

King George's War (1744–1748) followed. Hostilities began when the French sought to seize part of Nova Scotia and when Massachusetts merchants tried to protect their trade and Canadian fisheries against the French. By the time of the Treaty of Aix-la-Chapelle (1748), all conquered territories were returned to their former possessors.

The final struggle in North America between the French and the English, each with their Indian allies, was the French and Indian War (1754–1763). It ended in triumph for the British with the French virtually ousted from the continent. Both sides fought furiously for control of the Mississippi Valley. Early British defeats were reversed when William Pitt became prime minister, as he concentrated British strength on the conquest of Canada and the American interior. With the Treaty of Paris (1763) France's dream of a New France in North America ended.

Throughout all of these wars, the British proved indispensable to colonial security. Though the colonists contributed to the cause in money and men, the greatest cost, by far, was borne by the British. By the conclusion of these wars, the English debt was considerable.

Thus, British attempts at regulating colonial trade were somewhat motivated by the cost of protecting the colonists.

Net Effects of British Legislation

Before 1763, the measures to restrict colonial trade and manufacture insignificantly affected the American pocketbook. Rarely enforced, the Navigation Acts caused little friction. Only the Molasses Act (1733), designed to protect the sugar plantations of the British Caribbean and eliminate colonial trade with the lower-cost foreign (Dutch, French, Spanish) producers, proved troublesome at first. But the colonists responded with a sophisticated system of smuggling, and the law never accomplished its goal. Economically the colonists continued to prosper until 1763.

Political Growth of the Colonies

Politically, the colonists grew prior to 1763 as well. For the most part, British rule and interference were benign. When British monarchs attempted strict rule, the results were usually negligible. When James II reigned (1685–1688) he sought to consolidate the separate northern colonies into one dominion to decrease the costs of maintaining the empire and tighten control over the colonists. The short-lived Dominion of New England included Massachusetts, Plymouth, Rhode Island, Maine, New York, and New Jersey. Appointed by the king as governor of the dominion, Edmund Andros was denounced as a tyrant when he tried to tighten control over the colonists. James II himself was forced to flee to France as a consequence of the Glorious Revolution (1688), and the dominion was dissolved as soon as the news reached the colonies.

In the aftermath, Englishmen on both sides of the Atlantic

assumed more initiative in their self-government and political activism. The English Privy Council, a group of the king's advisers, theoretically had the right to disallow colonial laws, hear appeals from colonial courts, appoint royal governors, and settle disputes among royal agents in the colonial service. Yet after 1700 the influence of the council all but disappeared as a new council of ministers, the cabinet, responsible to Parliament and not the king, emerged. The Privy Council soon became nothing more than an honorary body.

With little interference from England, particularly from 1721 to 1742 during the tenure of Robert Walpole as prime minister, the colonists placed more emphasis on colonial growth and thought less about English control. This period, called the era of "salutary neglect," helped convince the colonists more than ever before that they were autonomous in internal affairs. And indeed, they maintained more control than any other colonial appendage in the mercantilist world.

When the need for united action against the French and their Indian allies became evident at the outset of the French and Indian War, the British government requested that representatives from the colonies meet at Albany, New York. At this Albany Congress (1754), Benjamin Franklin proposed a plan for uniting the American colonies. Under the Albany Plan of Union, the Crown would appoint a president general, and each of the colonies would send representatives to a body that would be empowered to deal with the Indians and provide for the mutual defense of the colonies.

The plan was rejected by the colonial legislatures, which felt it would weaken their powers, and by the English, who felt it would decrease the power of the king and Parliament.

This prompted Franklin to observe, "Everybody cries a union is absolutely necessary, but when they come to the manner and form of the union, their weak noddles are perfectly distracted."

1763: Changes in British Policy

Americans rarely complained about how the empire was run before 1763. After the French and Indian War, American attitudes changed.

At a great cost, England had expanded its empire. The French were eliminated from Canada and were no longer a threat to colonial security and expansion. With the threat gone, the American colonies no longer felt dependent upon the British and began to question the policies of empire.

Many Englishmen felt that the colonies had not contributed significantly to the war effort. In fact, during the conflict the colonists traded with the French. While Britain was expending a great fortune in men and money to protect them, the colonists were making money in a profitable trade with the mother country's enemy.

As a result, British policy toward the colonies changed and the era of salutary neglect was over. The British government began issuing writs of assistance, legal documents that served as a warrant for British customs officials to search private property such as ships, warehouses, and homes for contraband. To the colonists, the writs represented not only a threat to their profitable, albeit illegal, trade but a dangerous encroachment on their rights as private citizens as well.

Though they protested vehemently, the writs were upheld by colonial courts. Under the direction of George Grenville (Britain's secretary of treasury), imperial policy tightened. Due to their behavior during the French and Indian War, Americans would now be more directly subordinate to Parliament, forced to obey laws, and required to pay a larger share of the costs of defending and administering the empire.

Pontiac's uprising (1763–1765), in which the Ottawa chieftain organized an Indian confederation to drive the colonists eastward over the Appalachian Mountains, convinced the British that reaction on their part must be immediate. The first step was the Proclamation of 1763, prohibiting colonists from settling west of the Appalachians and requiring all those already there to remove themselves. The Mississippi Valley, recently obtained from France, was at least temporarily to remain an Indian preserve under British command.

This policy was designed to pacify the Indians and give the British government time to work out a rational policy for colonial expansion. It also made defending the colonists a cheaper endeavor, since British military units would not have to be spread out over large distances. The colonists, who had anticipated lucrative fur trading and land speculating, were, of course, furious.

Distressing the colonists even more were Britain's attempts to raise revenue in America. Acts before had been to regulate trade, but after 1763 they would be designed to extract money from the colonists to pay the imperial debt and provide for colonial defense. The latter would be accomplished by establishing a standing army in America, one for which the colonists would have to pay.

The Sugar Act (1764) and other acts imposing duties on such non-English items as cloth, indigo, coffee, wine, and molasses were to be enforced. Rigid attempts were made to prohibit smuggling, and the profitable West Indies market that the colonists had previously used to negate British policy and taxes was closed.

The Currency Act (1764) prohibited the further issuance of any paper money in the colonies. This meant that American debts to British merchants could only be paid in sterling money of "certain and fixed value." The colonies would now have to raise taxes, something they were loath to do, to pay off their debts from the French and Indian War.

Another Grenville act, the Quartering Act (1765), requiring colonial authorities to provide barracks and supplies for British troops, outraged the colonists. This act provided that in areas in the American colonies where barracks were not available for British troops, they were to be housed in public inns or houses. The person who furnished the quarters was to be paid by the colony in which the troops were stationed. Nevertheless, this act was resented by colonists who opposed paying for the quartering of "foreign" soldiers.

Grenville next passed the Stamp Act (1765), an act that affected all Americans. For example, this required all legal documents, newspapers, private contracts, and college diplomas to bear a British stamp. The stamps were to be paid for in gold and silver and the money raised was to be set aside for exclusive use by the British in the colonies. Violations would be dealt with in court.

The Stamp Act created the greatest furor. It affected two of the most articulate and influential groups in the colonies, lawyers and journalists. It also raised serious questions in the colonies about paying taxes to Britain without equal representation in Parliament. Opposition was widespread and created a rare bond of unity.

Reaction to the passage of this act was swift. The Virginia House of Burgesses, under the encouragement of young radical Patrick Henry, arrogantly stated that since they had all the rights of Englishmen, Americans could only be taxed by their own legislatures.

Virginia's actions excited the other colonies, and soon other colonial assemblies denounced the measure. A colonial congress was called to consider united action in the crisis. As colonists waited for the congress to convene, mob violence sprang up in the colonies, and effigies of British officials were prominently hanged and burned and supporters of the new tax were physically attacked by colonists led by groups like the "Sons of Liberty."

By the time the Stamp Act Congress met in October 1765, the act had no force in any colony except Georgia, where an unusually firm governor succeeded in enforcing it. The congress sent petitions to England which, although moderate, stated once again that Americans could be taxed only by legislative bodies that directly represented them.

The petitions accomplished little in England, and mob violence only exacerbated an already explosive situation. Grenville was ready to use force to implement the law. But pressure from English merchants precluded that. Trade with the mother country had plummeted during the crisis, and some colonies openly practiced nonimportation policies. Pressure from English merchants led to the repeal of the Stamp Act.

Parliament followed its repeal with the Declaratory Act (1766), affirming its right to legislate for the colonies. In essence, Parliament was admitting that it might have made a mistake with the Stamp Act but declaring that it would not accept the argument of "no taxation without representation" used to fight it. Indeed, to Parliament the colonists were represented by Parliament.

Relations between mother country and colonies deteriorated further when Grenville's successor, Charles Townshend implemented his own tax policies. In 1767, the Townshend Acts placed import duties on more goods (glass, lead, paper, tea, paint), authorized colonial courts to issue writs of assistance so customs officers could search private property for violations, and established more regulatory agencies in America.

Americans were outraged and saw no difference between this and the Stamp Act. Again, they boycotted English goods, and again, mob action sprang up rescuing ships and cargoes held for smuggling.

Relations between Britain and America now heated up considerably. In Boston, the center of colonial anti-British feelings, hostility erupted into open violence when a mob attacked a British sentry at his post. Numbers on both sides grew and shots were fired. When the smoke cleared, three colonists were dead and several wounded, two of whom later died. The Boston Massacre (1770), as this was called, served to intensify the feelings on both sides. Only when the British soldiers responsible were arrested was a major uprising averted. Defended by John Adams, five were acquitted and two received light punishment. This incident was the exception to the rule, and the years 1771–1773 were generally quiet.

Economic pressure from merchants in England led to repeal of the Townshend duties in 1770 when trade between the colonies and mother country dropped off considerably. However, British authorities, even those friendly with Americans, now feared the colonists wanted to overturn the basic and established relations between Britain and its colonies. To keep some semblance of British authority, the tax on tea was retained.

Trade with Britain revived and boycotts ended now that the Townshend duties were rescinded. The tax on tea was avoided by smuggling the beverage in from Dutch sources.

The final confrontation occurred when Britain tried to salvage the British East India Tea Company. Almost bankrupt through mismanagement and fraud, the company could not sell its tea due to British taxes and the Dutch tea Americans smuggled. Under the Tea Act (1773), the British allowed the company to sell its tea directly in America through its own agents. In this way, avoiding American middlemen, the company could still pay the tax but sell its tea at a lower price than even the smuggled tea.

Britain's confirming the last vestiges of the Townshend duties by maintaining its control of the tea trade outraged the colonists. They feared Britain might attempt to levy more tax measures and interfere in their colonial trade once more.

This colonial outrage precipitated an explosion that initiated the final step to war. When the first tea-carrying vessels arrived in Boston, a group of colonial radicals led by Samuel Adams and

1732	**The Hat Act**	Prohibited export of hats from the Colonies.
1733	**The Molasses Act**	Eliminated trade with lower-cost foreign producers.
1750	**The Iron Act**	Bar and Pig Iron had to be sent to England for finishing, which was prohibited in the Colonies.
1764	**The Sugar Act**	Duties were imposed on non-English items: cloth, indigo, coffee, wine, and molasses.
1764	**The Currency Act**	Prohibited further issuance of paper money in the Colonies.
1765	**The Quartering Act**	Required Colonial authorities to provide barracks and supplies for British troops.
1765	**The Stamp Act**	Required all legal documents, newspapers, private contracts, and college diplomas to bear a British stamp, to be paid for in gold and silver.
1767	**The Townshend Acts**	Duties imposed on imports: glass, lead, paper, tea, and paint.
1773	**The Tea Act**	Permitted the British East India Tea Company to sell directly in America, avoiding American agents.
1774	**Intolerable (Coercive) Acts**	Designed to punish Boston, it closed its ports until the East India Tea Company had been paid. Limited power of Massachusetts officials, disbanded state legislature, and extended the provisions of the Quartering Act. Also extended the boundaries of British Canada into territory already claimed by Colonies.

The restrictions imposed upon the Colonies by the British in the 18th century.

John Hancock met them. Dressed as Mohawk Indians, the American radicals boarded the ship and dumped the contents of 342 chests of tea into the harbor. Hundreds of people watched and approved of the Boston Tea Party in December 1773.

After other attacks on tea-carrying vessels, Parliament in 1774 passed the Intolerable or Coercive Acts to punish Boston and demonstrate that defiance of the law would no longer be tolerated. Among other things, the laws closed the port of Boston to commerce until the East India Tea Company had been paid for its tea. They also limited the power of Massachusetts officials, disbanded the Massachusetts legislature, and extended the provisions of the Quartering Act so that British troops could be housed in occupied private dwellings. One of the acts, the Quebec Act, extended the boundaries of British Canada into an area previously claimed by other colonies.

The colonists declared the time had come for united action against the Intolerable Acts. Thus, fifty-five delegates representing all the colonies except Georgia met at Philadelphia in September 1774 in the First Continental Congress.

The delegates differed on what action to take. Ultimately, it was decided to withhold taxes from the British, establish an armed militia in Boston, and boycott British goods. In its Declaration of Rights the Congress attacked all British trade legislation since 1763 and vowed to cease trade with the British.

The First Continental Congress was a watershed in the development of American unity. Until then, the colonies had acted independently of one another and in times of crisis had merely cooperated. Now, the first step had been taken toward collective government.

In the following months the colonists prepared for the worst. All over the colonies men joined militia units, collected arms and powder, and began to drill. When the governor of Massachusetts was instructed to enforce the Intolerable Acts, by military action if necessary, and stop colonial preparations for armed defense, the lines were drawn.

At Lexington, Massachusetts, in 1775, British redcoats dispatched to enforce the acts met colonial minutemen, and after someone fired a shot, the imperial disagreement turned into a war. After Lexington, the British moved to Concord, where they again encountered the American patriots. When the fighting ended at both places, about 100 Americans had lost their lives compared to 250 British who were killed or wounded.

Until 1763, Britain's loosely administered empire and the aggressive colonists who lived within it seemed to coexist harmoniously. Whenever Parliament did attempt to exercise its authority, the Americans were particularly adept at circumventing it.

After 1763, the British government, in debt, saw no reason why the British taxpayer should continue to bear the complete burden of American defense. Many Englishmen also believed that the empire need not be so lenient in its relationship with the Americans.

On the other hand, even though the harder policies Britain then adopted were valid in the mercantilist sense, the American colonists, as demonstrated in the previous chapter, had matured and grown independent in thought and economics. To the Americans, British action evoked fears among thousands of people, elite and commoner alike, that they were being subjected to a tyrannical yoke. Fear of oppression and a strong attachment to self-determination in all spheres of life had placed the colonists on a course to revolution. For the next eight years, America would be engaged in mortal combat with the strongest nation on the globe at the time. The result would be the creation of the United States of America.

Recommended Reading

Bernard Bailyn, *The Ideological Origins of the American Revolution* (1967)

Bernard Bailyn, *The Ordeal of Thomas Hutchinson* (1974)

Thomas C. Barrow, *Trade and Empire* (1967)

Richard R. Beeman, *Patrick Henry* (1974)

George L. Beer, *The British Colonial System* (1908)

George L. Beer, *The English Navigation Acts* (1939)

Ian R. Christie and Benjamin W. Labaree, *Empire or Independence, 1760–1776* (1976)

Bernard Donoughue, *British Politics and the American Revolution: The Path to War* (1964)

Lawrence H. Gipson, *The British Empire before the American Revolution* (1936–1970)

Robert A. Gross, *The Minutemen and Their World* (1976)

Merrill Jensen, *The Founding of a Nation: A History of the American Revolution, 1763–1776* (1968)

Benjamin W. Labaree, *The Boston Tea Party* (1964)

Pauline Maier, *From Resistance to Revolution: Colonial Radicals and the Development of American Opposition to Great Britain, 1765–1776* (1972)

Jackson C. Main, *The Social Structure of Revolutionary America* (1965)

Robert Middlekauff, *The Glorious Cause: The American Revolution, 1763–1789* (1982)

John C. Miller, *Origins of the American Revolution* (1943)

John C. Miller, *Sam Adams: Pioneer in Propaganda* (1936)

Edmund S. Morgan and Helen M. Morgan, *The Stamp Act Crisis: Prologue to Revolution* (1953)

Sir Lewis Namier, *England in the Age of the American Revolution* (1961)

Howard H. Peckman, *The Colonial Wars, 1689–1762* (1964)

Arthur M. Schlesinger, *The Colonial Merchants and the American Revolution, 1763–1776* (1917)

John Shy, *Toward Lexington: The Role of the British Army in the Coming of the Revolution* (1965)

Gary M. Walton and James P. Shepard, *The Economic Rise of Early America* (1979)

Hiller Zobel, *The Boston Massacre* (1970)

CHAPTER 5

The American Revolution

Time Line

1775	The Second Continental Congress meets in Philadelphia and declares war on England
	General George Washington is appointed commander in chief of all Continental armies
	Americans are victorious at Bunker's Hill
1776	Thomas Paine's *Common Sense* is published
	The Second Continental Congress approves the Declaration of Independence

	Congress issues paper money in large quantities
1777	The Articles of Confederation are adopted by Congress
	Americans defeat General Burgoyne at the Battle of Saratoga
1778	America and France establish a military alliance
1780	Pennsylvania abolishes slavery
1781	The Articles of Confederation are ratified
	British General Cornwallis surrenders his troops at the Battle of Yorktown, ending the war
1782	America and England sign a preliminary peace treaty
1783	France, Spain, England, and America sign the Treaty of Paris resulting in complete independence for the American colonies

Following the opening of hostilities, the official break with England came swiftly. However, it did not come easily. Ties of memory, habit, and affection and fears of the unknown all acted as deterrents. It was one thing to give voice to revolutionary rhetoric; it was quite another thing to sever ties completely with the mother country. This is what confronted colonists in the aftermath of Lexington and Concord. Still, how could the colonists remain loyal to a sovereign and a government which sent soldiers to subdue and kill them? They concluded, with great agony, that they could not. Deciding to fight for their independence, the colonists entered upon a path that would culminate in the creation of a more open, democratic society than had hitherto existed in the world.

The Second Continental Congress

The battles of Lexington and Concord occurred in the spring of 1775 (April), more than a year before the colonists firmly decided upon independence as a course of action. Shortly after these battles, however, on May 10, 1775, the colonists met again in Philadelphia in the Second Continental Congress. The Congress called upon the states to raise troops for a national fighting force, the Continental Army, with a single commander in chief, forty-three-year-old George Washington. He assumed command in June 1775. Respected throughout the colonies and with impressive military credentials and experience, Washington was the unanimous choice of the delegates to the Second Continental Congress. Also at this meeting, moderates led by delegate John Dickinson set out to try to achieve peaceful reconciliation with England through the so-called Olive Branch Petition, even though fighting had already broken out.

The petition placed the blame for the conflict on the king's ministers and requested that George III prevent Parliament from enacting any further tyrannical legislation. King George refused to accept this petition on the grounds that it was sent by disloyal and seditious colonists. The Americans, he concluded, were in rebellion and should receive no assistance from loyal members of the Crown.

To the members of the Second Continental Congress fell the onerous responsibilities of moving toward a declaration of independence, coordinating the resistance efforts of the newly born states, and seeking support from foreign allies.

Foreign Assistance

Allies would encourage the Americans in their move toward independence. The French regarded Great Britain's difficulties with the American colonies as their good fortune. Still smarting from their defeat in the French and Indian War, the French hoped to see Britain removed from the scene and France restored to a prominent place in North America.

Both France and Spain regarded Britain as a threat to their New World possessions and believed that a weak and powerless, though independent, America would be easier to deal with than Britain. Consequently, both countries soon began to provide the colonists with secret money and supplies. Americans cautiously accepted the foreign support but wisely realized that success was contingent upon their own willingness to fight for independence. Only this would achieve what the two European powers wanted most: a thoroughly defeated Britain.

Thomas Paine and *Common Sense*

Yet there were still many colonists apprehensive about breaking completely with Britain. While they certainly had become disillusioned with Parliament and the king's ministers, they nevertheless clung to their faith in the king himself and hoped he would heed their complaints.

The last illusions were destroyed with the publication of a fifty-page pamphlet entitled *Common Sense* (1776) by Thomas Paine, a recent immigrant from England.

The effect of this document upon the colonists' psyches was immeasurable. In clear and forceful words, Paine denounced King George III and Parliament and insisted the time had come for the colonists to seek their independence. Revolution was justified, he wrote, and the colonists must shed their belief that reconciliation with Britain was possible and desirable. Calling King George a "Royal Brute, a hardened sullen-tempered Pharaoh," Paine stripped away the hesitation and reluctance that many of the colonists maintained.

Widely read throughout the colonies, Paine's pamphlet sold 120,000 copies in three months. It had a profound effect upon the colonists as it confirmed that "nothing but independence" could save America from destruction.

Thanks in large part to Paine's influence, the delegates to the Second Continental Congress agreed to support a declaration of independence. Delegate Richard Henry Lee of Virginia on June 7, 1776, introduced three resolutions stating that (1) the colonies had the right to be free and independent of Britain, (2) the colonies must conclude negotiations for foreign alliances, and (3) the colonies must form themselves into a confederation under a constitution approved by each state. Congress adopted all of Lee's resolutions and appointed a committee that included Thomas Jefferson, John Adams, Benjamin Franklin, Roger Sherman, and Robert Livingston to draft a declaration of independence.

The Declaration of Independence

Drafted primarily by Jefferson and strengthened by Franklin's revisions, the document was completed in draft form by the end of June and submitted to the Congress for its approval in early July. Congress approved the principle of independence on July 2, and formally approved the Declaration on July 4, 1776.

The Declaration had three basic parts. The preamble set forth a philosophy of human rights and dignity in most eloquent fashion. "We hold these Truths to be self-evident," wrote Jefferson, "that all Men are created equal, that they are endowed by

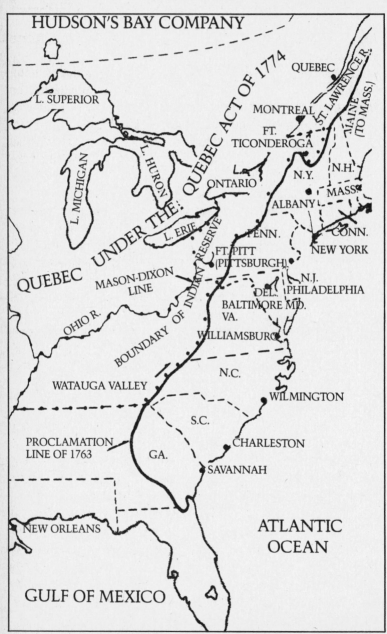

The British Colonies in 1776

their Creator with certain unalienable Rights, that among these are Life, Liberty, and the Pursuit of Happiness. . . ."

The second part listed twenty-seven grievances against King George, his ministers, and Parliament which precipitated the break with England. Among these were the assigning of a standing army in the colonies in a time of peace, disbanding colonial legislatures, prohibiting colonial trade with large portions of the world market, and waging war against the colonists. The conclusion was the announcement of the break with England, in essence, a formal declaration of war.

The Declaration was signed first by John Hancock, president of the Second Continental Congress, on behalf of his colleagues. From August 2 on, the remaining fifty-five signatures were affixed to the official copy of the document. The signers pledged their lives, fortunes, and honor in support of the document they had just approved. The eloquently written document served to crystallize the colonists' cause and inspire their ultimate victory.

With the Declaration of Independence came the need for a permanent structure of government both to conduct the war efficiently and to establish firm congressional authority.

The Articles of Confederation

After much negotiation a plan was accepted. Though they did not provide for a strong central government, the Articles of Confederation, adopted by Congress in November 1777 and ratified by all the states by 1781 so that they could take effect, were an improvement over the old arrangement.

The Articles of Confederation provided for a government not terribly unlike the one in operation at the time but with some increased powers for Congress. The Confederation Congress was to have the powers of conducting war, maintaining foreign relations, and appropriating, borrowing, and issuing money, but not the powers of regulating trade, levying taxes, or drafting troops.

For taxes and troops, Congress would have to petition the states. There was to be no single, separate, powerful executive, but Congress itself was to see to the execution of the laws through a committee of thirteen, made up of one member from each state. There were to be no Confederation courts, and disputes between the states were to be resolved through a very complicated system of arbitration.

The states were to retain their individual sovereignty, and each, regardless of size, was to have only one vote in the Confederation Congress. At least nine states would have to approve any important measure, such as a treaty, before Congress could pass it, and all thirteen states would have to approve the Articles before they could be implemented or amended.

Ratification of the Articles of Confederation was delayed because of disputes among the thirteen states, particularly over the issue of whether Congress or the states would administer the lands in the West. The Confederation came into being just in time to conclude the war and negotiate the peace. Meanwhile, during the years of fighting from 1775 to 1781, the Second Continental Congress served to coordinate and direct the war effort on behalf of the thirteen states. That notwithstanding, the Articles of Confederation were an important milestone in the development of American unity and nationalism.

Americans Mobilize for War

Without the power to tax, Congress had a difficult time financially preparing for the war effort. Americans were able to manufacture only a very small fraction of the war matériel they needed; most was imported from Europe, particularly France. Congress requested that the states contribute significantly to the national effort, but they responded by volunteering only a tiny portion of what was asked of them. Initially, Congress was reluctant to requisition goods directly from the people, but the ravages of war forced Congress to approve of army purchasing agents' commandeering supplies from farmers and paying with certificates of indebtedness.

Congress had little success in raising monies by floating long-term loans at home, since most Americans could not afford war bonds. And those who could preferred investing their capital in more lucrative endeavors such as privateering. The only recourse left to Congress was the issuance of paper money in large quantities. This was added to the already abundant supply of paper money printed by the individual states. With goods and coin (gold and silver) in scarcity and with a plethora of paper money available, it was inevitable that raging inflation would occur. Prices for commodities rose dramatically.

To add to their financial resources, the states confiscated lands belonging to the Crown and to colonial proprietors. In 1777 Congress endorsed the confiscation and selling of the lands of loyalists (those remaining committed to England), with the profits to be donated to the Continental government. While the confiscation and selling were done by eager states, very little of the largess made it to the central government's coffers.

By 1777, after the initial excitement of the war wore off, Americans were increasingly hesitant to enlist in the Continental Army. To man their militias, the states resorted to cajoling by offering bounties, usually in the form of land awards, to those who fought. Recruiting primarily remained on the state level and resulted in thirteen virtually separate armies.

The Fighting

During the first year of the war (1775–1776) no truly decisive battle occurred. On the hills surrounding Boston, British troops under the leadership of General William Howe encountered the Americans in the Battle of Bunker Hill, actually fought on nearby Breed's Hill, and the result was the loss of 40 percent of the British troops. This victory for the Americans clearly demonstrated that they could not, or would not, be easily defeated.

From that point on, the Americans, now under the command of General George Washington, evolved into a trained, skillful, and confident military unit. By March 1776, General Howe concluded that he could not hold the Boston area with Washington's troops dangerously close, and he temporarily abandoned the area to sail to the British stronghold at Halifax, Nova Scotia. Howe's departure, however, did not herald a major American victory. Rather, it indicated that the British were bracing for a major offensive during the second year of the war.

In July 1776, the British commenced the war in earnest. Under the command of Sir William Howe, the greatest military force that Britain had ever sent abroad, thirty-two thousand troops, arrived by ship in New York harbor. In initial confrontations, Washington's army, now in position to meet the British, was greatly outmanned and consequently was driven back into Pennsylvania. Seeking assistance from foreign advisers such as Baron von Steuben and the Marquis de Lafayette, Washington was able to build a force of some eight to ten thousand regular troops. Wisely avoiding the British for a while, Washington waited for the British to cease operations for the winter and on Christmas night 1776 he boldly crossed the frozen Delaware River to surprise the British at Trenton and in early January at Princeton, New Jersey. Though small victories for the American forces, they were nonetheless highly symbolic ones.

During the summer of 1777, the British, under the command of General John Burgoyne and Sir William Howe, launched attacks that resulted in the victory at the Battle of Brandywine Creek. But the patriots persevered, and led by commanders Horatio Gates and Benedict Arnold, they forced Burgoyne to surrender his entire army at Saratoga in October 1777 in one of the most significant military victories of the war for the Americans.

The victory at Saratoga convinced the French that the Americans might very well make good their claim to independence. And, in December 1777, the French recognized the United States as an independent country.

However, the optimism generated by victory at Saratoga was short-lived. The weak central government was proving feeble at coordinating the war effort, and the severe winter decimated Washington's weary, poorly equipped army at Valley Forge. The Americans sought and received foreign assistance and in February 1778 signed a treaty with the French that also brought Spain and the Netherlands into the war against Britain. The Europeans supplied the Americans with personnel and materiel at a crucial time.

Following Saratoga, military activity was at a stalemate for a year. From December 1778 to May 1780, though, the British, thanks to aggressive military leadership, took Savannah, Georgia, Charleston, and most of the rest of South Carolina. When the Americans finally confronted the British general Lord Cornwallis on his northward march, they were soundly defeated at the Battle of Camden in August 1780. Assuming command of the American forces in the South, General Nathanael Greene was able to defeat Cornwallis at Kings Mountain and at Cowpens, South Carolina, and exact a great toll from Cornwallis at Guilford Court House, North Carolina, in 1781. These battles seriously weakened Cornwallis's army, which fled to Yorktown on the peninsula between the York and James Rivers in Virginia in hopes of being evacuated by the British fleet.

It was not the British Navy that arrived, however. With very fortunate timing and much-needed French assistance, Washington was able to march his combined French and American troops down from the North at just the time that the French fleet appeared off the coast of Virginia. Caught between a hostile army and navy, Cornwallis had no recourse but to surrender his forces on October 17, 1781. This defeat finally convinced the British that it would be too difficult and expensive to attempt to subdue the Americans any longer. Cornwallis's defeat at Yorktown forced Lord North to resign as prime minister and be replaced by British officials who were willing to negotiate with the Americans.

Social Effects of the Revolution

An expanding sense of national identity was the most obvious change brought about by the American Revolution. Yet there were other significant ones as well.

Many moderate colonists feared that what had begun as a dispute over the governing of the empire would deteriorate into a social revolution and the established social classes in America would be abolished. Most affected in this regard were the Tories, or loyalists, who remained loyal to the Crown during the war. During and immediately after the war, one hundred thousand of them fled to Canada, to avoid persecution and physical attack, most to Quebec or Nova Scotia in British Canada, leaving their property behind to be confiscated and redistributed. Most covetous of this property were lower-class radicals.

The Revolution, though, did not completely democratize or equalize the nation. Despite the presence of some elements of class conflict during the Revolution, it was scarcely a major confrontation between rich and poor, aristocrat and peasant.

The war created tensions and strained existing institutions and intensified some existing social disputes, but it did not by any means produce class war. Nor did the departure of the Tories from America significantly alter class structure. Their confiscated land did not revolutionize patterns of property holding. Many people, regardless of class, already owned some land, so America was not a society characterized by a large class of landless peasants. Furthermore, the amount of confiscated Tory land was not very large and most of it was purchased by neighboring landholders or by speculators, not the middle or poorer classes.

In some areas the Revolution did liberalize American life. As a result of the war, slavery was destroyed in the North, where it was not as economically or socially significant as it was in the South. In 1775, the first antislavery society was founded in Philadelphia under Quaker influence. Soon, Pennsylvania passed the first law providing for the gradual emancipation of the slaves. Massachusetts abolished slavery in 1783. By 1800 every state from Pennsylvania north was taking steps to abolish slavery. Even in the South, several states passed laws simplifying the process of manumission (the freeing of one's own slaves). All the states there except South Carolina and Georgia prohibited the importation of slaves, and even South Carolina placed wartime restrictions on the slave trade. Nevertheless, slavery would remain a vital aspect of the southern way of life and, in time, would become an even stronger institution.

Women, too, eventually benefited from the liberal ideas encouraged by the Revolution. In New England the rhetoric of freedom led to liberalized divorce laws that placed women on virtually the same plane as men when they sought separation from a brutal or unfaithful spouse. In the absence of husbands and fathers many women became the chief support of their families. And some outspoken supporters of women's rights emerged. Abigail Adams wrote her husband John in 1776 that "in the new code of laws" (the Articles of Confederation) it was important to "remember the ladies and be more generous and favorable to them" than their ancestors had been. "Do not," she implored, "put such unlimited powers in the hands of the husbands."

Political Effects of the Revolution

America's political system also experienced some democraticizing effects of the Revolution. The severing of the ties with England forced most former colonies to write new state constitutions. In some of the new documents the changes were modest, perhaps only the replacing of appointed officials, such as the royal governor or the members of upper legislative houses, with elected ones. Other states enacted vast changes.

Except in Georgia and Pennsylvania, both of which experimented with a unicameral (one-house) legislature, each new state constitution provided for a bicameral (two-house) legislature. All the new constitutions except Pennsylvania's continued the office of governor, though most of them now denied the chief executive many of the powers held previously, such as veto power over laws passed by the legislature.

All the new documents confirmed and expanded upon the notion of popular rule. Most liberalized the franchise, enlarging still further the already sizable voting public, though only in New Jersey were women allowed to vote and soon they were denied the franchise even there. Seven of the new state constitutions had elaborate bills of rights attached, and some had preambles stating that the sovereignty resided in the people. Five of the new constitutions provided for the establishment of public schools, and all of the states soon began to revise and humanize their criminal codes to make the punishment more nearly fit the crime.

One of the most significant manifestations of the new democratic impulses was the development of the constitutional convention, a forum by which the voting public could change aspects of its government when necessary. Such a meeting truly placed sovereignty in the hands of the populace where many believed it belonged. When confirmed by a direct vote of the electors, the actions of a constitutional convention would take precedence over the actions of a legislature. Massachusetts was the first to implement this theory during the Revolution, and its example served the people well when the need to change the basic frame of government reached crisis proportions in 1787.

Foremost, Americans shaped and refined a new form of government after 1776. The Declaration of Independence encouraged republicanism, a representative form of government, in which talent, virtue, and dedication, rather than birth or influence, would qualify a person for high political office.

Even though the Revolutionary leaders opposed the monarchy, hereditary privilege, and aristocratic rule, they still feared the concept of complete democracy which they called "mob rule." Thus, the Revolutionary leaders favored a government in which the popular will and the talent of select leaders were combined.

This preference was reflected in most of the new state constitutions by the bicameral legislature. One house in such an assembly, the lower house, represented the democratic principle, and the other, the upper house, represented citizens of education and ability. Political changes were not intended, then, to create a radically democratic society.

The End of the War

After six long years of war, the British finally laid down their arms and agreed to negotiate with America and its allies in Paris in 1781. Congress appointed John Adams as the American delegate to the peace talks and instructed him not to enter into negotiations unless Great Britain first recognized the United States as "sovereign, free, and independent." Eventually Congress added Benjamin Franklin, John Jay, and other luminaries to the American delegation and encouraged them to remain in close contact with their French allies led by Foreign Minister Count Charles Gravier de Vergennes.

Indeed, France and America had agreed not to negotiate a separate peace with Britain, but America could not resist the

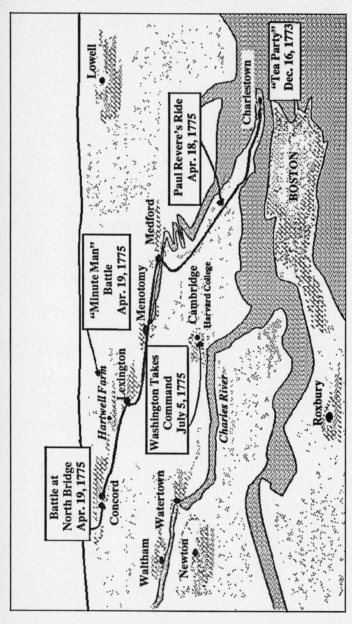

Battle at
North Bridge
Apr. 19, 1775

"Minute Man"
Battle
Apr. 19, 1775

Paul Revere's Ride
Apr. 18, 1775

Washington Takes
Command
July 5, 1775

"Tea Party"
Dec. 16, 1773

Lowell

Concord

Hartwell Farm

Lexington

Menotomy

Medford

Charlestown

Cambridge
Harvard College

BOSTON

Waltham

Watertown

Newton

Charles River

Roxbury

The Boston Area at the Start of the Revolutionary War

temptation to act independently. British emissaries appeared in France to talk informally with Franklin, who suggested what he described as the "necessary" terms of peace, including independence and a western boundary at the Mississippi River, and "desirable" terms, including the cession of Canada.

All of the American negotiators were determined individuals who did not intend to allow either the French or the Spanish to determine America's fate. In November 1782 the Americans signed a preliminary treaty with the English. Under this agreement, Britain recognized the "necessary" terms that Franklin had originally requested—an independent United States with a western boundary at the Mississippi River and a southern boundary at Spanish Florida—but not the "desirable" ones such as the addition of Canada. The treaty did allow the Americans to fish in British territorial waters off Canada, and England promised to evacuate American territory still under British control "with all convenient speed." For its part, the United States promised to repay its long outstanding debts to British creditors and agreed to encourage the states to restore the loyalists' civil rights and property.

Although not happy with the treaty, the French feared that too much opposition would cause the United States to ally with the British, something they dreadfully feared. So France, Britain, Spain, and the United States signed a joint peace treaty on September 3, 1783, approving the previous agreement between America and Britain.

Overall, the peace treaty was quite favorable to the United States. A clear recognition of independence was achieved, as was a generous, if ambiguous, agreement on the borders of the new nation. By strategically playing one European nation off against another, Franklin and his colleagues achieved one of the greatest diplomatic successes in the history of the United States.

The long years of fighting had ended and the United States was now an independent nation. What had commenced as a disagreement within the empire had evolved into a full-blown war. The American colonies had simply outgrown their status as subordinates to Great Britain within the mercantile world. And the colonists were willing to fight and die to maintain their independence.

A new nation with a new government was born as a result. More democratic, more open, and more egalitarian than their European counterparts, the Americans had every reason to be happy and optimistic in 1783. Their jubilation, though, was tempered with concern.

The infant nation now confronted the problems of repairing the damage of the long years of war and learning how to exist as an independent nation in an increasingly hostile world. The obstacles to survival, let alone success, would be formidable. Much physical damage to the countryside had resulted from the war. In the South, the British had carried off thousands of slaves and destroyed property.

More difficult would be the political, social, and intellectual readjustments. The twenty years since the end of the French and Indian War had greatly altered American society. The drift toward religious toleration, political democracy, and social equality had been under way from the planting of the first English communities on the North American continent. The war accelerated these processes.

Republicanism became the dominant ideology and many vestiges of aristocratic privilege were removed. It now remained to be seen how much further these trends would go or whether they would continue at all.

It also remained to be seen if the thirteen separate political and social entities in 1775 had truly become a nation in 1783. Vastness in size and population (900,000 square miles and 3 million people) made it difficult to survive as a unified, independent *nation. In the next few years the Americans would be tested both within and without their borders and, in the process, would determine just how successful they were.*

Recommended Reading

John R. Alden, *The American Revolution, 1775–1783* (1954)

Samuel F. Bemis, *The Diplomacy of the American Revolution* (1935)

Joy and Richard Buel, *The Way of Duty: A Woman and Her Family in Revolutionary America* (1984)

Robert M. Calhoon, *The Loyalists in Revolutionary America* (1973)

Henry S. Commager and Richard B. Morris, eds., *The Spirit of '76: The Story of the American Revolution as Told by Participants* (1958)

Lawrence D. Cress, *Citizens in Arms* (1982)

James T. Flexner, *George Washington in the American Revolution* (1968)

Don Higginbotham, *The War for American Independence* (1971)

Don Higginbotham, ed., *Reconsiderations on the American Revolution* (1978)

James Franklin Jameson, *The American Revolution Considered as a Social Movement* (1925)

Merrill Jensen, *The American Revolution within America* (1974)

Merrill Jensen, *The Articles of Confederation* (1940)

Piers MacKesy, *The War for America* (1964)

Jackson Turner Main, *The Social Structure of Revolutionary America (1965)*

Jackson Turner Main, *The Sovereign States, 1775–1783* (1973)

Jackson Turner Main, *The Upper House in Revolutionary America, 1763–1788* (1973)

Sidney Mead, *The Lively Experiment* (1963)

Edmund S. Morgan, *The Birth of the Republic, 1763–1789* (1956)

Richard B. Morris, *The American Revolution Reconsidered* (1967)

Richard B. Morris, *The Peacemakers* (1965)

Mary Beth Norton, *Liberty's Daughters: The Revolutionary Experience of American Women, 1750–1800* (1980)

Howard H. Peckham, *The War for Independence: A Military History* (1958)

Charles Royster, *A Revolutionary People at War* (1979)

George F. Scheer and Hugh Rankin, *Rebels and Redcoats* (1957)

John Shy, *A People Numerous and Armed* (1976)

Jack Sosin, *The Revolutionary Frontier, 1763–1783* (1967)

William Stinchcombe, *The American Revolution and the French Alliance* (1969)

Theodore Thayer, *Nathanael Greene: Strategist of the American Revolution* (1960)

Willard M. Wallace, *Appeal to Arms* (1951)

Franklin Wickwire, *Cornwallis and the War of Independence* (1970)

William Wilcox, *Portrait of a General: Sir Henry Clinton in the War of Independence* (1964)

Gordon S. Wood, *The Creation of the American Republic, 1776–1787* (1968)

Alfred F. Young, ed., *The American Revolution* (1976)

Arthur Zilversmit, *The First Emancipation: The Abolition of Slavery in the North* (1967)

CHAPTER 6

A More Perfect Union

Time Line

1783   Articles of Confederation Congress flees
            Philadelphia, fearful of attack by unpaid
            Continental soldiers 1784

            Spain closes Mississippi River to American
            use

1785   Congress establishes the Land Ordinance of
            1785, a system of land survey and sale

1786   United States and Spain agree to a treaty
            concerning the use of the Mississippi River,
            but John Jay, the American negotiator,

argues in vain for its ratification by Congress

1787   Shays' Rebellion in Massachusetts

Northwest Ordinance establishes the equality of new states entering the Union and abolishes slavery in the Northwest

Constitutional Convention meets in Philadelphia

State delegations approve the completed draft of the Constitution

1788   Ratification of the Constitution by all states except Rhode Island and North Carolina

James Madison, Alexander Hamilton, and John Jay publish *The Federalist Papers*

1789   George Washington is elected president and John Adams, vice president

The new Congress adopts the first ten amendments, known as the Bill of Rights

North Carolina ratifies the Constitution

1790   Rhode Island ratifies the Constitution

What caused the United States to abandon the Articles of Confederation, the government most Americans wanted in 1781, in favor of the Constitution in 1787? In the previous chapter we concluded by observing that after the American Revolution the happiness of the colonists was tempered by concern for their future. They did not have to wait long for their fears to be realized, for ominous clouds soon loomed on both the domestic and the international fronts. To find out why the need arose for a change in government, we must look first at the immediate postwar years.

The American Economy

The early postwar years of the United States were a time of economic troubles for farmers. Most of the physical damage to rural areas was quickly repaired, but agriculture suffered other ills that were not so easily corrected.

British commercial retaliations hurt American farmers, as they no longer enjoyed the commercial privileges of the empire. The West Indian ports were closed by Britain to American shipping. Furthermore, British bounties, to which American farmers had grown accustomed, were no longer paid on various items. The net result was that the farmers of the new United States could no longer trade their surplus crops; consequently their goods piled up and farm prices fell.

Farmers in the West, beyond the Appalachian Mountains, were also in a very difficult situation. By the mid-1780s thousands of settlers had poured into what are now Tennessee and Kentucky. The goods that these farmers needed, such as salt, guns, powder, farm tools, cloth, and notions, could best be obtained from the East. To pay for their goods the western farmers grew extra grain, tobacco, and corn or accumulated furs, lumber, and livestock for trade.

Their problem came in getting these products to market. To get to the major ports on the Atlantic coast, the farmers had to make, by pack animal, the arduous, slow, and expensive trip across the Alleghenies and the Blue Ridge Mountains. Or they could use the Mississippi River and its tributaries as links to the outside world. By flatboat or raft, they could send their goods down the river and land them at New Orleans to be shipped to east coast ports or directly to Europe.

But the Spanish controlled the mouth of the Mississippi
River and they were not in favor of allowing the Americans access to the port of New Orleans for the purpose of trading and
distributing their goods. The Spanish, of course, had supported
America in its war against Britain. Now, however, they viewed
it as a dangerous example to their own colonies. With this in
mind, the Spanish concluded it would be to their detriment to
help the Americans prosper. They placed the Mississippi River
off-limits to the western American farmers, whose surplus goods
went unsold. When they complained to their national government about their plight, the farmers received only silence in
response.

American trade in general suffered immediately following
the war. Though some improvements were made, most notably
the end of the Navigation Acts and the establishment of new trade
routes, the loss of the British West Indies as a market hurt the
American economy severely. So, too, did European restrictions
on such goods as tobacco and the competition among the Atlantic nations for a piece of the world market.

By the end of the 1780s American overseas trade had partially recuperated from the disruptions of war and postwar, but
the value of trade was still less in 1790 than it had been in 1775.

British competition significantly hurt American trade.
British ships imported goods into the United States, which directly competed with American vessels carrying the same goods.
Although many merchants cried for an American "navigation
act" which would exclude foreigners from importing goods on
any ship except one bearing the American flag, their cries were
in vain.

Craftspeople, artisans, and mechanics, in essence the
manufacturers of the day, were undersold by cheap European imports of cabinets, wigs, hats, silver products, and woven goods.
These people clamored for such legislation as a protective tariff

that would place high duties on imported goods for the purpose of excluding the Europeans from competition.

For the economic ills plaguing the country, merchant, farmer, craftsperson, and creditor alike blamed the feeble national government. If America was to fulfill its economic promise and prosper, something would have to be done with the weak government of the Articles of Confederation.

The National Government during the Economic Crises

The Confederation government had also canceled most of its war debts to the Americans by repudiating hundreds of millions of dollars in Continental currency. With a large domestic debt, the government borrowed heavily from abroad, primarily from the Netherlands. This, of course, only increased the debt even further. When the government requisitioned the states, they responded with only about one-sixth of what was requested from them. This was barely enough to meet the operating expenses of the Confederation government.

In June 1783, Congress, fearful of attack by unpaid and mutinous Continental soldiers, made itself ridiculous by fleeing Philadelphia. Within two years, the Confederation government was virtually an empty shell, with attendance so poor that business could not be conducted. Forced by its lack of effective legislative power to deal with petty problems while major ones clamored for attention, Congress had become a debating society, little respected by outsiders and an object of contempt to its own members.

Congress had not paid the soldiers, nor its debt, because it could not, and this inability was the heart of its domestic weakness. Under the Articles of Confederation, Congress could do little more than assign revenue quotas to the states. The raising and paying of these quotas then became the responsibility of the states, and states were neither especially generous nor efficient in their payments. The government's weakness was also demoralizing to citizens generally, and many feared for the nation's future with such an ineffective national government.

Failures in Foreign Affairs

More disturbing to Americans than the domestic feebleness of their government were its failures in foreign affairs. Virtually everywhere on the globe the new nation was the object of scorn and contempt.

The Treaty of Paris (1783) had in theory recognized the independence of the United States and granted the new nation a vast domain. In practice, however, things were different. Almost immediately the Americans ran into difficulty with the British and the Spanish, and America's French allies proved to be unreliable as well.

Despite previously agreeing to evacuate their forts on American soil, the British defiantly continued to occupy a number of establishments along the Great Lakes. Spain, possessing both the western part of Florida and the Louisiana territories and thus occupying both sides of the lower Mississippi River, chose to close the river to American use in 1784.

In attempts to rectify these problems, Congress sent John Adams to England in 1784 to obtain a commercial treaty with the British (allowing the United States to trade in the British West Indies) and to seek their assurances that they intended to vacate the frontier posts. The British refused to cooperate with Adams, knowing full well that his government did not have the power to retaliate against them. In the 1780s the British even refused to acknowledge the validity of the Confederation Congress by sending a diplomatic representative to the American capital. Continued occupation of military posts by the British was intended, among other things, to embarrass the Americans.

The Americans, for their part, had failed to honor two provisions of the Treaty of Paris. They had not repaid the loyalists for their losses sustained during the war, and they had not paid the prewar debts they owed British merchants.

Britain might have treated Americans with more respect if Congress had imposed economic sanctions that would have crippled English merchants and manufacturers. Such policies had worked before the American Revolution, but Congress now lacked the power to impose these duties and the British knew it.

By contrast, the Spanish government was willing to negotiate with the Americans. In 1786, after months of discussions, John Jay and a Spanish representative, Don Diego de Gardoqui, agreed to a treaty. From the Spanish perspective, the agreement would allow the Americans to trade with the Spanish but not their colonies, set the boundary of Florida according to the American definition, and secretly agree to form an alliance to protect American soil from British encroachments. The Americans would agree to guarantee Spanish possessions in America and forgo use of the Mississippi River for twenty years.

This was not a particularly favorable treaty, and Jay argued in vain for the nine votes necessary for its ratification by Congress. Jay's many months of negotiation, then, went for naught.

The weak American Union suffered from its treatment by the Barbary Coast states (Morocco, Algiers, Tunis, and Tripoli) as well. These North African states traditionally gave refuge to pirates and privateers whose swift vessels preyed on the commerce of Europe. Most European powers either paid a tribute to the pirates in return for safe passage or protected their citizens with their navy. Without the protection of the strong British Navy, American vessels now became fair game. Unwilling to pay a tribute and unable to protect its own shipping, the United States regularly suffered humiliating harassment from the pirates of North Africa.

By 1785, it became apparent that Congress was little more than a shadow, unable to protect American interests abroad or to solve major problems at home. Was it for this, Americans asked, that they had fought and died?

Managing the Lands in the West

Following the Revolution, Americans moved west in unprecedented numbers. At the outset of the war, only a few thousand settlers lived beyond the Appalachian Mountains in the areas of dispute between Britain and Spain. By the 1790s their numbers exceeded 120,000. With so many American settlers now in the West, Congress was implored to provide them with protection from the Indians, access to outside markets for their goods, and courts with systematic processes of law.

In 1780, New York ceded its claims to the western lands, and when Virginia followed suit in 1781, other states followed. As a result, Congress soon found itself in a position to make policy for all of the national domain. The most significant decision made was that the western lands would not be held in permanent inferior status as colonies. Instead, these territories ultimately would be transformed into states on an equal basis with the original thirteen.

The Land Ordinance of 1785 established a system of land survey and sale and became a model for future federal land policy. By its terms, Congress would sell land only after Indian claims had been "extinguished" by treaty. This allegedly would prevent Indian uprisings. After the settling of Indian claims, the government would survey the land and divide it into "townships" of 36 square miles each. Each township would be further divided into "sections" of a single square mile, 640 acres.

The revenue from the sale of four sections of each township was to be reserved for government use while that of one section was for the support of public schools. Congress promised that some land would be set aside for former soldiers. The remaining land would be sold at auction to the highest bidder.

This system was a compromise between people like Thomas Jefferson, who wanted to sell the land as cheaply as possible so that people of little means could purchase small farms, and others who said that land sales were the only asset the Confederation government had and should be used to raise much-needed revenue.

The second installment of the Confederation's land policy was the Northwest Ordinance of 1787. Based on Thomas Jefferson's proposed ordinance of 1784, this law mandated that no more than five nor fewer than three states be formed out of the Northwest Territory and that slavery be forever forbidden throughout the area.

The Northwest Ordinance also established three stages for the evolution of a territory into a state. In the first stage, each territory would have a governor, secretary, and three judges appointed by Congress. In the second stage, when its population reached five thousand free male inhabitants, it could elect a territorial assembly. In the third stage, when its population reached sixty thousand free male inhabitants, the territory could submit a constitution to Congress, and if this was approved, it would then become an equal self-governing state of the Union.

The Northwest Ordinance was a major accomplishment of the Confederation Congress. By excluding slavery from the area, it ensured that the entire North would be free territory. By establishing the precedent that new states would enter the Union on equal footing with the original thirteen, it ensured the continued settlement of the West.

Discontented Americans

Despite the accomplishments of the Articles of Confederation, many Americans considered them a failure and felt they must be abolished or at least amended if the nation was to survive.

Under the leadership of Alexander Hamilton of New York, James Madison of Virginia, and John Dickinson of Delaware, Congress was petitioned to authorize a full-scale meeting in Philadelphia in 1787 to discuss the nation's economic problems and whatever political changes were necessary. Congress, however, merely sat on the proposal, and it appeared nothing would be done.

Shays' Rebellion

Events in Massachusetts soon prompted Congress to act. There, excessive taxes and low farm prices had created a financial disaster. The farmers' debts mounted steadily, and eventually many of them went bankrupt and were foreclosed for tax delinquency.

Mobs of discontented farmers rioted in various parts of New England but posed the most severe threat in western Massachusetts. Led by Daniel Shays, a former captain in the Continental Army, the farmers began to organize and drill as if they once again expected war. On behalf of his fellow farmers, Shays demanded that paper money be issued to mitigate the financial crisis, that tax relief be offered, that a moratorium be established on debts, that the state capital be moved westward from Boston, and that imprisonment for debt be abolished.

In the summer of 1786 Daniel Shays and his followers, in armed bands, concentrated on preventing the collection of debts. In Boston, Shays and his men were denounced as rebels and traitors. Meanwhile, the people of Massachusetts began to panic. In response the governor, James Bowdoin, decided to raise a military force to suppress the disorder.

In January 1787, state militiamen met Shays' troops between

Springfield and Boston, killed several of them, took many more prisoner, and forced the remainder to flee during a raging blizzard. As a military endeavor, Shays' Rebellion amounted to little, but it frightened many people, who feared that a social revolution was close at hand. Shays' Rebellion made the country look even weaker, and the national government at last took heed of the restless mood of the nation. In February 1787 Congress voted to ask the states to send delegates to a proposed constitutional convention in Philadelphia.

A Divided Meeting

The meeting at Independence Hall on May 14, 1787, included many of the nation's most prominent citizens: George Washington, Benjamin Franklin, James Madison, Alexander Hamilton, Robert Morris, James Wilson, James Dickinson, George Mason, Edmund Randolph, John Rutledge, and Charles Pinckney. All states were represented except Rhode Island.

Many of the fifty-five delegates were rich, landed gentry. About half of them were lawyers, and eight of them were signers of the Declaration of Independence. Yet the most important common bond was the belief that the Articles of Confederation had failed as a form of government. Few of the delegates, though, wished to replace the weak Confederation government with a much stronger one if it would be at the expense of individual freedom. The goal of the majority of delegates was to achieve a government of balance, that is, a stronger central government that also would protect local autonomy and local rights.

The Virginians assumed the initiative from the first. George Washington was elected to preside over the meeting. All deliberations, it was agreed, would remain absolutely secret.

Edmund Randolph and James Madison made the first proposal, known as the Virginia Plan. Supported by the larger states, Randolph and Madison encouraged not a revision of the Articles, but a complete new government with separate legislative, executive, and judicial branches. There would be a new bicameral Congress in which representation in both houses would be based upon population. The lower house would elect members of the upper house. The two houses combined would elect an executive and judges for the courts. A council composed of the executive and some judges would have the power to veto acts of the legislature.

This plan was countered by the New Jersey Plan, proposed by William Paterson. Preferred by the smaller states, this plan sought merely to revise the Articles of Confederation rather than discard them. It proposed equal representation of the states in a one-house legislature. Congress was to be given the right to regulate commerce, levy certain taxes, and name the executives and a supreme court.

These two proposals were the basis for many debates during the long, hot summer of 1787. Out of these discussions came a new government. Most significant of all were the compromises that occurred.

The Birth of the Constitution

The new government would have greatly enlarged powers, but they would be specified and not left to Congress to decide. There would be two houses—the Senate, where each state would have equal representation regardless of size and population, and the House of Representatives, where population would determine the number of state representatives.

The delegates chose to compromise on the sensitive issue of defining population. Northerners feared that if slaves were counted in regard to representation in Congress, the South would have too much power. Southerners insisted on some political compensation, since they would have to pay property taxes on slaves if they were not considered people.

It was decided that for purposes of taxes and representation in the lower house, the number of persons to be counted would be "the whole number of free persons" excluding Indians but including indentured servants and "three-fifths of all other persons." With this Three-Fifths Compromise, the Founding Fathers simultaneously defined a slave as property and as three-fifths of a human being.

To avoid the concentration of too much power in one area of government, there would be three branches of government—executive, legislative, and judicial—each with its own independent authority and powers. There would be an elaborate system of checks and balances to prevent one branch from dominating the others.

The vesting of the executive function in a single president with ample authority was a particularly important departure from previous practices in the states and the Confederation. The president was given a veto over congressional legislation (unless repassed by a two-thirds vote in both houses), was to appoint judges and other officials (with the consent of the Senate), was given primary responsibility for foreign relations and the making of treaties (with the advice and consent of two-thirds of the Senate) and was commander in chief of the armed forces, though only Congress could declare war.

The new central government was to have virtually unlimited authority to levy taxes, borrow money, regulate domestic and foreign commerce, conduct foreign relations, and maintain an army and navy. States were forbidden to encroach on national prerogatives in these areas.

The delegates debated every issue, and tempers often flared during the summer of 1787. Under the guidance and leadership of George Washington, the presiding officer, things did not get out of hand. The compromises were largely the work of his fellow Virginian James Madison. On September 17, 1787, the state delegates voted approval of the compromise package and the convention adjourned.

Ratification

The Constitution now had to be adopted by the states. The delegates at Philadelphia had decided that the new government would go into effect when nine states ratified the Constitution.

Delaware, New Jersey, and Pennsylvania almost immediately ratified the Constitution in their state conventions. Indeed, Delaware and Pennsylvania approved by unanimous votes. Early in 1788 Georgia and Connecticut followed suit. For the Federalists, as supporters of the Constitution called themselves, things seemed to start off rather smoothly.

In Massachusetts, the Constitution ran into its first opposition. Such popular leaders as Samuel Adams and John Hancock feared the Constitution, since it lacked a bill of rights. Hancock would not approve ratification unless nine amendments were added to protect the people and their liberties. When he was promised this would occur, Hancock threw his support behind ratification and Massachusetts, in a close vote, approved ratification.

Maryland, South Carolina, and New Hampshire all ratified, and the Constitution had the nine votes needed to establish it among the ratifying states. But Rhode Island and North Carolina had defeated the measure, and Virginia and New York had not acted. If they too rejected, it would be impossible for the new government actually to go into effect.

In Virginia, such notable figures as James Monroe and Patrick Henry opposed the Constitution as dangerous to liberty. The convention ultimately ratified, but thanks to eloquent opposition by Patrick Henry, Virginia too requested that a bill of rights be added to the new frame of government.

Attention was then directed to New York. Without New York the Union would be geographically divided in half and incapable of functioning harmoniously. To persuade New York to ratify, the Federalists flooded the local newspapers with articles written by James Madison, Alexander Hamilton, and John Jay. *The Federalists Papers*, as they were called, were brilliant essays in political theory in support of the new Constitution. Written in support of ratification, the essays defended the principle of a supreme national authority but at the same time sought to reassure doubters that the people and the states had little reason to fear usurpations and tyranny by the new government. In Federalist No. 10, perhaps the most famous essay, Madison argued that the very size and diversity of the country would make it impossible for any single faction to form a majority which could dominate the government.

The persuasiveness of *The Federalist Papers* and Hamilton's emotional presentation of the Federalist position at the state convention ultimately prevailed, and by a narrow margin New York ratified the Constitution.

In 1789 the first national elections occurred as the new Union was secured. Federalist candidates won a majority in the new Congress, and as expected, the electoral college chose George Washington as president and John Adams as vice president. Since they had not ratified the Constitution, Rhode Island and North Carolina did not participate in the elections.

The Bill of Rights

Shortly after the elections, the new government adopted the first ten amendments to the Constitution, known as the Bill of Rights. The first nine limited Congress by forbidding it to encroach upon certain basic rights, such as freedom of religion, speech, and the press, immunity from arbitrary arrest, and trial by jury. The Tenth Amendment, reserving to the states all powers except those specifically withheld from them or delegated to the federal government, strengthened state rights and shifted the emphasis of the Constitution from nationalism to federalism. The nation would now be governed by a system in which states were united under a central authority but remained independent in their internal affairs.

The First Amendment indicates by its own language that it (like the other amendments) is directed only against the federal government, not the people or the states, for it begins, "Congress shall make no law..." The states had their own bills of rights in their constitutions. Virginia was the first state to adopt a bill of rights (1776), thanks in large part to the work of George Mason.

Fearful that if they did not act soon they would be alienated by the other states, North Carolina and Rhode Island reversed their earlier decisions and ratified the Constitution, North Carolina in 1789 and Rhode Island in 1790.

While the Articles of Confederation were a milestone in the development of American unity and solidarity, they were, nevertheless, an imperfect form of government at best. Their weaknesses intensified the growing pains of an infant nation and vividly pointed to the many problems the country was experiencing at home and abroad. Independence, then, brought new fears and anxieties, and many concluded that if the nation was to survive, it would need to revise or discard its central government. Threats of social revolution, such as Shays' Rebellion and the economic crises that spawned it, and disrespect and contempt from the European powers only affirmed the desperate need to do something.

Out of the summer of 1787 came a remarkable document, the Constitution of the United States. Representing compromises of all sorts, the document strengthened the national government while simultaneously protecting the rights of the states and the liberties of the individual. It would be continually tested throughout the ages, but it would endure. The United States was no longer a petty league of thirteen separate states, it was now a nation in more than just name.

Recommended Reading

Charles A. Beard, *An Economic Interpretation of the Constitution of the United States* (1913)

Catherine Drinker Bowen, *Miracle at Philadelphia* (1966)

Irving Brant, *The Bill of Rights: Its Origin and Meaning* (1955)

Irving Brant, *James Madison, The Nationalist, 1780–1787* (1948)

Robert E. Brown, *Charles Beard and the Constitution* (1956)

James McGregor Burns, *The Vineyard of Liberty: The American Experiment* (1982)

Jacob E. Cook, *Alexander Hamilton* (1982)

E. James Ferguson, *The Power of the Purse: A History of American Public Finance, 1776–1790* (1961)

Oscar and Lillian Handlin, *A Restless People: America in Rebellion, 1770–1787* (1982)

H. James Henderson, *Party Politics in the Continental Congress* (1974)

Merrill Jensen, *The New Nation: A History of the United States during the Confederation, 1781–1787* (1948)

Merrill Jensen, *The Articles of Confederation* (1940)

Forrest McDonald, *Alexander Hamilton: A Biography* (1979)

Forrest McDonald, *E Pluribus Unum: The Formation of the American Republic, 1776–1790* (1965)

Forrest McDonald, *We the People: The Economic Origins of the Constitution* (1958)

Andrew McLaughlin, *The Confederation and the Constitution* (1962)

Jackson Turner Main, *The Anti-Federalists: Critics of the Constitution, 1781–1788* (1961)

Frederick Marks III, *Independence on Trial* (1973)

Richard B. Morris, *The Forging of the Union, 1781–1789* (1987)

Jack Rakove, *The Beginnings of National Politics* (1979)

Donald Robinson, *Slavery in the Structure of American Politics, 1765–1820* (1982)

Robert Rutland, *The Birth of the Bill of Rights, 1776–1791* (1955)

Robert Rutland, *The Ordeal of the Constitution: The Anti-Federalists and the Ratification Struggle, 1787–1788* (1966)

Marion Starkey, *A Little Rebellion* (1955)

Robert Taylor, *Western Massachusetts in the Revolution* (1954)

Garry Wills, *Explaining America: The Federalist* (1981)

Gordon Wood, *The Creation of the American Republic, 1776–1787* (1969)

Benjamin Wright, ed., *The Federalist* (1961)

CHAPTER 7

The Federalist Era

Time Line

1789	Congress passes the revenue-raising Tariff and Tonnage Acts
	Congress establishes the various executive departments as well as the federal court system
	The French Revolution begins
1789–1792	Hamilton presents his financial program to Congress
1790	Congress passes Hamilton's Funding Act to pay off the Confederation debt

1791	Congress charters the Bank of the United States
1792	Kentucky is admitted into the Union
1793	France sends Edmond Genêt to America to seek assistance
	Jefferson resigns as secretary of state and is replaced by Edmund Randolph
	The British commence their policy of impressing American seamen and interrupting American trade with the French Caribbean islands
1794	Whiskey Rebellion occurs in western Pennsylvania
	The United States and England sign the Jay Treaty
1795	The United States and Spain sign the Pinckney Treaty
1796	Tennessee is admitted into the Union
	Federalist John Adams is elected president, Republican Thomas Jefferson, vice president
1797	France interrupts American trade on the high seas, resulting in a "quasi-war"
1797–1798	The XYZ Affair
1798	The Department of the Navy is created with cabinet status
	Congress passes the Alien and Sedition Acts

1798–1799   The Virginia and Kentucky Resolutions attack the Alien and Sedition Acts on constitutional grounds

1800   France and America sign the Convention of 1800 nullifying their treaty of 1778

Thomas Jefferson is elected president, Aaron Burr, vice president

Washington, D.C., becomes the national capital

Americans had undergone a destructive war with England followed by a tenuous period of insecurity and instability under the Articles of Confederation. When the new government under the Constitution of the United States was launched in 1789, there was apparent harmony among the Founding Fathers. This rapidly changed, and with the change came the development of political parties. What were the issues that divided the country politically and ultimately led to the first American party system? To answer this, we must first examine the attitudes of America's leaders in the years immediately following the Constitutional Convention of 1787.

Early Differences of Opinion

Initially, there was little substantive disagreement over legislation. In Congress two acts were immediately passed to raise sorely needed money and protect American merchants from foreign competition. The Tariff Act of 1789 placed duties on a wide range of imported items such as hemp, cordage, nails, and glass. The items were selected with the clear intent of stimulating domestic production, and the duties were protective in nature. The major purpose of the tariff, though, was to raise revenue. The Tonnage Act (1789) taxed foreign vessels which docked at American ports.

Congress also established the various executive departments of the new government. Thomas Jefferson was named secretary of state, Alexander Hamilton became secretary of the treasury, Henry Knox was named secretary of war, Samuel Osgood was appointed postmaster general, and Edmund Randolph became attorney general. The structure of the federal court system was put into place as well.

Important differences of opinion soon developed over how to pay the unpaid Revolutionary War debt. The United States owed money to its European allies, and its failure to repay what it owed had damaged the American reputation. Too, it was now very difficult for the American government to borrow more from foreign bankers.

Most of the debt, however, was owed to American citizens. Veterans of the Continental Army, suppliers of war matériel, and those who had lent money to Congress or the states to support the war effort all waited to be repaid.

Hamilton's Financial Answers

To the new secretary of the treasury, Alexander Hamilton, fell the problems of the debt. Hamilton believed the new government could be fortified and made to succeed if he could obtain the support of the wealthy in America. Skeptical of human nature and convinced that people are motivated by self-interest, Hamilton was certain that the best way to curry the favor of the rich was to give them a financial stake in the government. He thus proposed a financial program designed to encourage the propertied classes to look to the federal government for profitable investments and promotion of their interests.

For Hamilton to accomplish his objectives, the government

would first have to pay off its debts and establish some sound financial footing. He proposed that the existing national debt be paid off by exchanging all the miscellaneous certificates of indebtedness for uniform, interest-bearing bonds payable at specific dates. He also suggested that the debts of the states be assumed by the federal government so investors would know to look to the national government for direction in all financial matters. A large and permanent public debt would then be created, with new bonds being issued as the old ones were paid off. Of course, tying the debts of the states to the central government would greatly strengthen the powers of the latter.

To oversee his program, Hamilton proposed the chartering of a national bank. This bank would assist fledgling businesses by providing loans and currency (bank notes) and thus encourage the growth of industries almost in subsidy fashion. A national bank would also provide a place for the deposit of federal funds, facilitate the collection of taxes and the disbursement of the government's expenditures, and generally administer the nation's monetary policies.

A final advantage of the bank, Hamilton believed, was that it was not specifically authorized in the new Constitution. It could be chartered only under a broad reading of that document, and so its chartering would support the doctrine of implied powers. That is, it would establish a precedent for liberally interpreting the powers of the federal government. The doctrine of implied powers is contained in the "elastic clause" to the Constitution (Article I, Section 8, Paragraph 18), which allows Congress "To make all laws which shall be necessary and proper for carrying into execution the foregoing powers, and all other powers vested by this Constitution in the Government of the United States, or in any department or officer thereof."

Hamilton's financial plans would take a great deal of money to implement. To find adequate sources of revenue, Hamilton looked to two forms of taxes and the monies obtained from the sale of public lands in the West. One of the taxes that Hamilton envisioned was an excise tax on alcoholic beverages. The other was a higher tariff on imports. The latter tax would not only raise revenue but also serve to protect and encourage American manufacturing by raising the prices of competing goods coming in from Europe.

Enacting the Hamiltonian Program

Between 1789 and 1792, Hamilton was able to persuade Congress to pass the necessary laws to implement most of his ambitious plans. However, it was only over some formidable opposition. To win congressional support for his program, Hamilton relied on every political tool at his disposal.

The agrarian sections of the country, concluding that they favored the industrial, manufacturing regions, immediately opposed Hamilton's plans. The first objection raised concerned the funding of the Confederation debt. Hamilton prevailed, though, and the Funding Act of 1790 sought to pay off the debt exactly as Hamilton had proposed.

Assumption of the state debts created an even greater furor, especially among states like Virginia, which had already paid off many of its own debts. When the debates stalled on this aspect of the Hamilton plan, he skillfully tied it to the concurrent controversy over the permanent location of the nation's capital. Hamilton convinced prominent Virginians Thomas Jefferson and James Madison that if they would relent in their opposition to the assumption of state debts, he would throw his weight behind a plan to move the capital further south. When Jefferson and Madison agreed, he did, and a plan was struck to move the capital from New York back to Philadelphia for ten years and then permanently to a 10-square-mile tract to be selected by President Washington on the Potomac River between Virginia and Maryland.

Hamilton's revenue proposals encountered their greatest opposition not in Congress, but rather among backcountry farmers, who violently resisted the tax on whiskey, their most profitable commodity. In 1794, this resistance culminated in western Pennsylvania in the Whiskey Rebellion, when frontiersmen took up arms to prevent the collection of the tax. A force of thirteen thousand militiamen, led by Hamilton himself, crushed the insurrection. Although not much money was collected by the tax, this incident helped to establish the authority of the new federal government.

The serious constitutional objections to the creation of a national bank even gave President Washington pause. Hamilton argued convincingly that the Constitution had clearly implied that Congress had the power to create the bank. Jefferson, interpreting the Constitution quite literally, countered that the Tenth Amendment reserved to the states or the people all powers not specifically given to the federal government and that the creation of a national bank was thus unconstitutional. Swayed by the force of Hamilton's argument, Washington signed the bank bill creating the Bank of the United States.

The only portion of Hamilton's financial program that failed in Congress was his proposal for encouraging manufacturing through a higher tariff. The United States was still a land in which agriculture dominated and manufacturing was in its infancy. The fear that high tariffs would adversely affect the country's international trade was simply too insurmountable for Hamilton to prevail.

Although brilliant and quite farsighted, Hamilton's visions for the economic future of the country had engendered much opposition. By 1791, there was already a sizable group in Congress opposed to Hamilton. Led by Jefferson and Madison, a Republican interest was emerging to counter Hamilton and his Federalist interests.

Emergence of Opposition

The Constitution made no allowances for the development of political parties, and some of the Founding Fathers, George Washington, for instance, believed that such organizations were destructive and should be avoided at all costs. Nevertheless, political camps soon centered around the supporters of Hamilton on the one hand and Jefferson and Madison on the other.

Generally speaking, the Republicans shared Jefferson's belief that the farmers of the country were "the chosen people of God, if ever he had a chosen people." A nation of strong, independent yeoman farmers would be an ideal republic, the followers of Jefferson and Madison believed. The artisans, journeymen, and laborers who made up the "mobs" in the cities, however, were "the panders of vice and the instruments by which the liberties of a country are generally overturned."

The Republicans opposed the development of extensive manufacturing and industry on the ground that they would lead to the growth of cities with malcontent, propertyless workers. The Jeffersonian view, then, was a defense of the status quo and in many ways quite conservative.

Federalists and Republicans disagreed as well on the feasibility of democracy. Hamilton and the Federalists tended to be elitists who distrusted human nature and feared democracy for its possible "excesses." To Hamilton, the people were "a great beast." He once told Washington that he had "long since learned to hold public opinion of no value." Other Federalists concurred and believed the best government was a strong one which restrained popular excesses.

Thomas Jefferson and the Republicans generally expressed great confidence in the people. Jefferson regarded the people as trustworthy and safe and stated, "I am not among those who fear the people; they, and not the rich, are our dependence for continued freedom." In this regard he believed the government that governs least governs best.

Political Divisions in Foreign Policy

Many problems still remained with the foreign powers. Spain still controlled the mouth of the Mississippi River and denied Americans use of the port of New Orleans; Britain still restricted American trade within its empire and refused to abandon military posts in the Northwest; and France began to restrict trade with its colonies in violation of a previous treaty.

The French Revolution of 1789 encouraged American partisan politics, since America was closely tied economically to Britain. It was Hamilton's strong belief in the English political system that created these ties. The Federalists were frightened and shocked by events in France and sought to prevent that form of revolutionary spirit from "infecting" the United States. The Republicans applauded the action of the French revolutionaries and admired them for their courage. After the French revolutionary government guillotined King Louis XVI and went to war with Britain and its allies in 1793 over international trade routes, the Washington administration faced some difficult questions. Should the United States recognize the French revolutionary government by accepting its diplomatic minister? Was the United States obliged by its 1778 treaty with France to go to war on the French side?

President Washington decided to recognize the French government, but he was determined to keep the United States at peace and issued a proclamation to this effect in 1793. This proclamation was considered a neutrality statement, even though the word neutral was not used. The following year, Congress passed a Neutrality Act (1794) prohibiting American citizens from participating in the European war and denying use of American soil as a base of operations for either side in the conflict. It was not long before the first test of American neutrality came from the French.

The Genêt Controversy

In 1793, the French sent a bold, young diplomatic minister, Edmond Genêt, to the United States to secure assistance. When Genêt arrived, he immediately proposed that American ports be used to house French warships, American seamen be used as French privateers, and Americans volunteer for fighting against France's enemies. Furthermore, if President Washington did not call Congress into session at once to discuss his demands, Genêt stated, he would take his case over the head of the president and go directly to the American people.

Obviously, Genêt's activities flagrantly disregarded the American policy of neutrality, and President Washington suggested that the French government recall Genêt. However, Genêt's party, the Girondins, had fallen from power in France and been replaced by the still more extreme Jacobins, and Genêt's return to France might mean his execution. Washington generously allowed the arrogant French minister to remain in the United States to ensure his safety, and Genêt settled down to a long, prosperous life with his American wife on a Long Island, New York, farm.

Yet Genêt's visit precipitated great political turmoil in the United States. Hamilton had opposed allowing him into the country for fear it would involve the nation in war. Jefferson had responded by claiming that if America refused Genêt entrance, it in essence repudiated the alliance with France. The Republicans had befriended Genêt and now came under great attack from the Federalists, who despised him. A Federalist newspaper labeled the Republicans the "bastard offspring of Genêt, spawned in hell, to which they will presently return."

Genêt's activities propelled political differences to new

heights and involved the newspapers in the issues for the first time. Federalist and Republican newspapers published scathing criticisms of their opponents, which exaggerated and exacerbated existing differences.

Within Washington's cabinet, the relations between Hamilton and Jefferson had so deteriorated by 1793 that Jefferson resigned as secretary of state and was replaced by a Federalist, Edmund Randolph. This certainly did not end party rivalries, however, as Jefferson still remained the Republican's chief strategist and party mentor.

The Challenge from the British

The British posed even more of a threat to the United States. The British still occupied posts in the Northwest, ten years after they were supposed to leave, and still monopolized the fur trade below the Canadian border. This fact angered the Americans, as they suspected the British in that area had encouraged Indian attacks on American military establishments.

For their part, the British continued to insist that the remaining debts owed English creditors and the unpaid claims of loyalists justified the occupation of the western posts.

The trouble between the two nations turned into a crisis in the fall of 1793, when the British interrupted American trade with the French Caribbean islands. The Royal Navy suddenly started seizing American vessels under a British Order in Council which permitted seizure of neutral cargoes heading for France or French colonies.

Soon over 250 American ships had been boarded by British naval parties, escorted to British ports, and confiscated. Under the pretense of recapturing deserters from the British Navy, hundreds of American sailors were impressed into the British service. These assaults upon their neutrality naturally infuriated the Americans.

Relations became even worse when the British commander in the West began to construct a new military post on American territory. This further expansion of British military power on American soil seemed the last strain on American tolerance, and war appeared imminent.

To avoid a war, for which the United States was not prepared, Washington sent a negotiating party to England headed by the chief justice of the United States, John Jay. Jay's instructions were to be conciliatory, but the British were not inclined to compromise.

For the sake of settlement, Jay was forced to surrender America's claim to trade with the French as a neutral. He also had to agree to a broad definition of contraband that made many goods liable to seizure. The United States government promised to settle all outstanding British claims against American citizens. The British in return agreed to surrender the western posts and pay for the American ships recently confiscated.

In regard to trade within the British Empire, the United States would for the most part be treated as a foreign nation, excluded from commercial privileges normally given subjects of the king. Finally, the British denied liability for slaves they had removed from the South during the Revolution and refused to talk about the Indian problem in the West. The Jay Treaty (1794) said nothing about British interference with American trade or the impressment of American seamen.

Though it made some concessions to the United States, the Jay Treaty was immediately denounced by the Republicans. To France's friends and England's enemies, the treaty seemed a sell-out. Jay was denounced as a traitor by many and hanged in effigy all over the country. Nevertheless, Federalist strength in the Senate ensured the treaty's approval. Fearing the alternative would be war, President Washington signed it into effect in 1794.

The Jay Treaty powerfully reinforced party formation, as Washington came under severe attack by the Republicans. But despite its shortcomings, the Jay Treaty did provide the United States with time to devote to peaceful development and undisputed sovereignty over the Northwest.

The Pinckney Treaty with Spain

With relations settled with Britain, President Washington turned his attention to Spain. Western lands were growing rapidly. The state of Kentucky had been admitted into the Union in 1792, and Tennessee was to enter in 1796. Westerners wanted something done about Spain's refusal to allow the Americans use of the port of New Orleans.

Fearing westerners might take matters into their own hands, President Washington in 1795 sent Thomas Pinckney to Spain to negotiate a treaty. Assuming that the recent Jay Treaty with the British, unpopular though it was, might bind the Americans to the British to their detriment, the Spanish almost immediately signed an agreeable treaty. The Pinckney Treaty with Spain allowed the United States use of New Orleans for a period of three years subject to renewal. The treaty also fixed the northern boundary of Spanish Florida at the 31st parallel where Americans wanted it and obliged the Spanish authorities to prevent the Indians in Florida from coming across the border.

Unlike the Jay Treaty, the Pinckney Treaty was immensely popular and finally settled the nagging problem of navigation of the Mississippi River at virtually no cost to the United States.

The Election of 1796

As the presidential election of 1796 approached, many people urged Washington to run again. Elected twice without a single vote cast against him in the electoral college, Washington could be counted on to keep the Federalist Party together while being elected for a third time. But Washington, weary of the burdens of his office and of the partisan politics that had enmeshed it, longed to retire to his home, Mount Vernon. Consequently he decided to step down after his second term of office.

To make his wishes clear to the American people, Washington, with Hamilton's assistance, composed his Farewell Address, which was published in a Philadelphia newspaper. Leaving office, the president warned against "permanent alliances with any portion of the foreign world." The president also cautioned against political party factionalism and said he feared the loss of national unity if Federalists and Republicans continued to attack one another.

Yet with his departure, party factionalism flourished. To no one's surprise, the Republicans chose as their candidate for the presidency Thomas Jefferson. The Federalists could not decide between Vice President John Adams and Thomas Pinckney, the treaty negotiator. Thus both were chosen.

The election of 1796 centered around the unpopular Jay Treaty and the general direction of America's foreign policy. Electors were chosen by popular vote in half of the states and by state legislatures in the other half.

The two Federalist candidates split many of the votes, resulting in a curious situation. When all of the votes were counted, Adams received the highest number of electoral votes and Jefferson the second highest. Under the existing terms of the Constitution, the two were elected president and vice president respectively. Because the Founding Fathers had not anticipated the development of political parties, the nation now had a president and a vice president with opposing political views.

The "Quasi-War" with France

No sooner had John Adams taken office than he found himself in an undeclared naval war with the French, who considered the Jay Treaty a virtual Anglo-American alliance. The election of the Anglophile Adams further roused the fears of the French, and in 1797 they began to capture American ships on the high seas and, in many cases, imprison the crews.

Adams, following Washington's precedent, chose to negotiate with the French instead of breaking off relations with them. He sent an unofficial delegation comprised of Charles C. Pinckney, John Marshall, and Elbridge Gerry to France to see if they could strike a deal with the French. Received by Charles Talleyrand, the French foreign minister, the Americans were soon given the runaround. Forced to deal with agents of Talleyrand, referred to in diplomatic dispatches as X, Y, and Z, the Americans were told they must first pay a bribe to these French officials, loan France $12 million, and apologize for harsh words spoken by President Adams before negotiations could commence.

The Americans refused these proposals, and when word reached the United States about the French demands, Americans were outraged and insulted.

The XYZ Affair set off a naval war between the United States and France. French attacks on American ships increased, and, over Republican opposition, the Hamiltonian Federalists (now called High Federalists) voted money to triple the size of the Army and Navy. In May 1798, the Department of the Navy was created with cabinet status. Adams cut off all trade with the French and terminated the treaty of 1778 with them. Washington was again called back into service as commander of the Army, with Hamilton placed second in command.

Pressed by his own Federalist Party to declare war formally on the French, the president, aware of American unpreparedness, refused. Still, the United States Navy made a very respectable showing of itself in the "quasi-war," winning a number of conflicts with French vessels and capturing a total of eighty-five ships. Finally convinced that the United States would be a formidable foe, Talleyrand became more conciliatory and formal war was averted.

In 1800, when Adams sent a new three-man commission to France, the Americans met Napoleon Bonaparte, now in power as first consul. The Americans wanted the French to pay for all the damage they had done by interrupting American commerce and to agree to a formal nullification of the 1778 treaty. On the former point Napoleon refused to compensate the Americans, but on the latter point he agreed and signed a new treaty with the Americans, the Convention of 1800. The quasi-war had ended, and the United States had finally freed itself from the perpetually entangling alliance with the French.

Adams and the Curtailment of Civil Liberties

The hostilities with the French had given the Federalists an advantage over the Republicans, and in the congressional elections of 1798 Federalist candidates swept to victory, taking an even greater majority in both houses. Not understanding the concept of a "loyal opposition" or the value of a two-party political system, the Federalists sought to entrench their power further and, in the process, remove all opposition or criticism.

Since many of the Republican critics of the administration were foreigners by birth, especially Irish or French, the Federalists in Congress thought it prudent to restrict the political rights of aliens and make it more difficult for them to become American citizens. To accomplish this, the Federalists attacked the civil liberties of both native-born Americans and immigrants in 1798 in a series of laws known collectively as the Alien and Sedition Acts. Disregarding the Constitution and the Bill of Rights, these acts extended the residence requirement for naturalization from five to fourteen years, sanctioned the deportation of enemy aliens, and established harsh punishment for anyone criticizing the government.

While President Adams neither invoked the Alien Act nor deported any aliens, this law and the new Naturalization Act discouraged more immigration and encouraged many foreigners already here to flee. Under the Sedition Act, the administration did arrest and imprison ten men, all of whom were Republican.

The Alien and Sedition Acts turned into an enormous political blunder for Adams. The administration's flagrant vindictiveness and complete disregard for free speech caused many moderates who were vacillating between political parties to fall fully into the Republican camp.

Until the passage of the Alien and Sedition Acts many Republicans found it difficult to support the France of the XYZ Affair and the undeclared naval war and ultimately sided with the Federalist administration. This now changed rapidly.

The Virginia and Kentucky Resolutions

Republican leaders Thomas Jefferson and James Madison feared that the recent activities by the Federalists constituted a serious threat to civil liberties, including free speech. Further, they saw the Alien and Sedition Acts as a dangerous expansion of federal power relative to the states.

They expressed their views quite eloquently in two sets of resolutions, one written anonymously by Jefferson and adopted by the Kentucky legislature during the 1798–1799 session, and the other written by Madison and approved by the Virginia legislature in 1798. The Virginia and Kentucky Resolutions, as they were called, attacked the Alien and Sedition Acts on constitutional grounds.

The resolutions asserted that the federal government had been created by a "compact," or contract, among the states. And it was a limited government possessing only certain stipulated and restricted powers. Whenever the government exceeded its authority by assuming additional and unauthorized powers, its acts were, in essence, null and void. It was up to the participants in the contract, the states, to determine when and how the central government had usurped its power. When this determination had been made, it was the right and the responsibility of the states to "nullify" the offending actions. Jefferson's and Madison's resolutions urged all of the states to nullify the Alien and Sedition Acts and request their repeal in Congress, but no other state went along with Virginia and Kentucky.

Republican Ascendancy and the Election of 1800

In 1800, the nation faced a bitter presidential election. Washington's death in 1799 had deprived the Federalists of a strong unifying force, and there occurred an open split between extreme and moderate Federalists.

During the nearly dozen years of Federalist rule, the party had made a number of political enemies in the wake of Hamilton's financial program, the suppression of the Whiskey Rebellion, Jay's Treaty, and the Alien and Sedition Acts. Attacking the Federalists on all of these grounds and making states' rights and constitutional liberties their main political platform, the Republicans nominated Thomas Jefferson of Virginia and Aaron Burr of New York as their candidates in the election of 1800.

The Federalists chose President Adams and Charles C. Pinckney to represent them in the election, and they portrayed Jefferson as a dangerous radical who, if elected, would with his supporters bring down a reign of terror on the country comparable to the recent French Revolution. For their part, the Republicans depicted Adams as a tyrant who would be king if allowed. Such modern tactics as printed party tickets, appeals to party loyalty, and public speech making accompanied the election.

When the election was over, Adams had sixty-five state electoral votes and Jefferson and Burr were tied with seventy-three each. According to the Constitution, the decision as to who would be president now rested with the House of Representatives, where the delegation from each state would cast a single vote.

No one doubted that the Republicans intended for Jefferson to be president, but as things stood, the House of Representatives would have to decide the question and the Federalists had the votes to determine the results.

Although the Federalists had savagely attacked Jefferson in the campaign, they detested Burr even more. In fact, Hamilton had stated that Jefferson "had some pretensions to character" but Burr was a complete rogue, a man "bankrupt beyond redemption." After several ballots without a majority for either candidate, Jefferson's assurances that he would not dismantle Hamilton's financial system, decrease the strength of the armed forces, dismiss many Federalists from office, or change the nation's foreign policy of neutrality, swayed the House of Representatives in his favor.

Jefferson, the arch-Republican, was now elected the third president of the United States, with Burr his vice president. The Republicans also won a majority of the seats in both houses of the next Congress.

To Adams, the only branch of government left in the Federalist hands was the judiciary, and the president moved to strengthen their hold on it during the final days of his administration. By the Judiciary Act of 1801, the Federalists managed to increase the number of federal judgeships, and Adams promptly appointed a number of his loyal supporters to the newly created positions. Indeed, it was said that the president stayed up very late his last night in office to complete the signing of his "midnight judges'" commissions. Since federal judgeships were assumed to be appointments for life, Adams believed that Jefferson, the incoming chief executive, would be helpless to remove the new Federalists from the court. Time would prove him wrong.

In spite of bitterness and partisanship, however, the presidential election of 1800 was critical in importance as the first time a modern republic peacefully and constitutionally passed power from one party to another.

In slightly more than ten years, the Americans had laid the foundation of a modern party system. They had discovered, much to their chagrin, that the backbone of their government, the Constitution, needed to be supplemented by political parties.

Jefferson's Republicans had become greater advocates of the individual's personal rights and freedom, and ideologically they would encourage a more open and democratic society. Yet their hopes for the country's social and economic future were naive ones. On the other hand, the Federalists believed that America's potential could not, and should not, be restrained by past practices and values. They had clearly seen that the United States was destined to become an industrial giant as well as an agriculturally self-sufficient one. In the process, though, they had failed to appreciate the fundamental American tenets of equality and personal liberty.

Neither was all right and neither was all wrong. It now remained to be seen if Thomas Jefferson and the Republicans could avoid the excesses of their predecessors and establish a balanced, just, and progressive agenda for the nation.

Recommended Reading

Harry Ammon, *The Genêt Mission* (1973)

Leland Baldwin, *The Whiskey Rebels: The Story of a Frontier Uprising* (1939)

Lance Banning, *The Jeffersonian Persuasion: Evolution of a Party Ideology* (1978)

Richard Buel, Jr., *Securing the Revolution: Ideology in American Politics, 1789–1815* (1972)

William D. Chambers, *Political Parties in a New Nation, The American Experience, 1776–1809* (1963)

Joseph E. Charles, *The Origins of the American Party System* (1956)

Jerald A. Combs, *The Jay Treaty* (1970)

Jacob Ernest Cook, *Alexander Hamilton* (1982)

Noble Cunningham, *The Jeffersonian Republicans: The Formation of Party Organization, 1789–1801* (1957)

Manning Dauer, *The Adams Federalists* (1953)

Alexander De Conde, *Entangling Alliances: Politics and Diplomacy under George Washington* (1958)

Alexander De Conde, *The Quasi-War: The Politics and Diplomacy of the Undeclared War with France, 1797–1801* (1966)

James T. Flexner, *George Washington and the New Nation, 1783–1793* (1969)

James T. Flexner, *George Washington: Anguish and Farewell, 1793–1799 (1972)*

Felix Gilbert, *To the Farewell Address: Ideas of Early American Foreign Policy* (1961)

Paul Goodman, *The Democratic Republicans of Massachusetts: Politics in a Young Republic* (1964)

Richard Hofstadter, *The Idea of a Party System, 1780–1840* (1969)

Reginald Horsman, *The Frontier in the Formative Years, 1783–1815* (1970)

Lawrence Kaplan, *Jefferson and France* (1967)

Richard H. Kohn, *Eagle and Sword: The Federalists and the Creation of the Military Establishment in America, 1783–1802* (1975)

Stephen Kurtz, *The Presidency of John Adams: The Collapse of Federalism, 1795–1800* (1957)

Forrest McDonald, *Alexander Hamilton: A Biography* (1979)

Forrest McDonald, *The Presidency of George Washington* (1974)

John C. Miller, *Alexander Hamilton: Portrait in Paradox* (1959)

John C. Miller, *The Federalist Era, 1789–1801* (1960)

Daniel Sisson, *The American Revolution of 1800* (1974)

James Morton Smith, *Freedom's Fetters: The Alien and Sedition Laws and American Civil Liberties* (1956)

Page Smith, *John Adams* (1962)

Paul A. Varg, *Foreign Policies of the Founding Fathers* (1963)

Patricia Watlington, *The Partisan Spirit* (1972)

John Zvesper, *Political Philosophy and Rhetoric: A Study of the Origins of American Party Politics* (1977)

CHAPTER 8

Jefferson and the Age of Republicanism

Time Line

1802	Congress repeals the Judiciary Act of 1801
1803	The Louisiana Purchase
	Marbury v. Madison
1803–1806	Meriwether Lewis and William Clark explore the trans-Mississippi West
1804	The Twelfth Amendment to the Constitution is ratified
	Jefferson and Burr are reelected

	Hamilton-Burr duel; Hamilton dies shortly thereafter
1805	The Essex Decision by the British restricts American trade with the French even further than under the Jay Treaty of 1794
1805–1806	James Wilkinson–Aaron Burr conspiracy
1806	Congress passes the Nonimportation Act
1806–1807	England and France issue decrees affecting American neutral trade in Europe
1807	The U.S.S. *Chesapeake*–H.M.S. *Leopard* affair
	Congress passes the Embargo Act
1808	James Madison is elected president
1809	Congress passes the Nonintercourse Act
1810	Congress passes Macon's Bill No. 2
	The Shawnees, led by Tecumseh, attack outlying settlements in Indiana Territory
1811	The Bank of the United States is dismantled and closes
	The Battle of Tippecanoe
	The "war hawks" gain control of both the House and the Senate and elect Henry Clay of Kentucky as Speaker of the House
1812	The United States declares war on England
	Madison is reelected

1813	William Henry Harrison's troops win at the Battle of the Thames, and Tecumseh is killed
1814	Andrew Jackson's troops defeat the Creek Indians at the Battle of Horseshoe Bend
	British troops march on Washington and burn the White House, among other public buildings
	Francis Scott Key writes the words to "The Star-Spangled Banner"
	A British invading force is defeated at the Battle of Plattsburg
	The Hartford Convention
	The Treaty of Ghent is signed by the British and the Americans, ending the War of 1812
	Napoleon is defeated in Europe
1815	British forces fall to Jackson's troops at the Battle of New Orleans
1817	The Rush-Bagot Agreement demilitarizes the American-Canadian border

---

As Jefferson assumed office, many people, especially the Federalists, waited to see just how different things would be now with a Republican president. Many years later Jefferson would refer to his victory as the "revolution of 1800." In a sense, it truly was a revolution, since it was the first peaceful transference of power from one party to another in a modern republic. This peaceful change of power eloquently proved the vitality of the

United States Constitution. But overall, there were no major changes, and Jefferson and his successors proved to be far less vindictive or dangerous than their opponents had feared. Indeed, in some areas Jefferson even resembled the strong president that his nemesis, Alexander Hamilton, had long advocated.

Jeffersonian Changes

Jefferson's inaugural address was not a fiercely partisan message that emphasized triumph. Instead, the new president sought to quiet the fears of his enemies. The recent political campaign had been a particularly bitter one, he noted. While it had raised many issues on which Americans strongly disagreed, it was now time for the country to unite.

Trying to be as conciliatory as possible, Jefferson reassured the American people that his party would respect the rights of political minorities. Though the two parties called themselves by different names, he said their members were "brethren of the same principle," and "we are all Republicans, we are all Federalists."

Nevertheless, Jefferson sought to introduce what he called "republican" principles into the government of the United States. Toward this end, he removed many of the formalities that had characterized the Washington and Adams administrations. For example, rather than visit Congress in the royal fashion of his predecessors, Jefferson sent written messages to the legislators on matters of importance. He walked like an ordinary citizen to and from his inaugurations instead of riding in a coach at the head of a procession.

Immediate Changes in Policy

Despite his attempts at conciliation, Jefferson sought to break with the Federalist past in several significant areas. He reduced the national debt somewhat by decreasing the size of the

Army and Navy, which many Republicans considered inessential bodies. In short order, the small Army of four thousand men was reduced to twenty-five hundred. The Navy was scaled down from twenty-five ships in commission to seven, and the number of naval officers was cut accordingly as well.

The Jefferson administration abolished many unpopular taxes imposed by Federalists. Indeed, in 1802 the Republicans in Congress abolished the whole system of internal taxes, leaving only customs duties and the sale of public lands as major sources of revenue. Cutting taxes was made possible only by the substantial revenues that the United States was receiving from import duties during the period of great trade expansion lasting through Jefferson's two terms of office.

The repugnant Alien and Sedition Acts recently passed by the Federalists were repealed or allowed to expire. The national bank created under the Hamiltonian financial plan was gradually dismantled and closed in 1811, two years after Jefferson left office.

Jefferson Becomes a Strong President

Jefferson's changes from the Federalists' principles soon yielded to a more pragmatic approach. Although he earlier condemned a strong central government, he soon saw the need for a powerful executive branch. If it could be used for good purposes, Jefferson concluded, power was not necessarily bad. This, of course, exposed the president to charges of hypocrisy.

Though he wished to reassure his opponents, Jefferson had no intention of allowing them to dominate his administration. Like Washington before him, Jefferson believed that federal offices should be filled with men loyal to the principles and policies of the president. Though he did not attempt a sudden and drastic removal of Federalist officeholders, at every convenient opportunity he replaced holdovers from the Adams administration with his own trusted followers. By the end of his first term, about 50 percent of the government jobs, and by the end of his second term, practically all of them, were held by good Republicans.

To ensure that there would never be another embarrassing situation like the election of 1800, Jefferson encouraged the passage of the Twelfth Amendment to the Constitution, ratified in 1804. By implication, the amendment recognized the existence of political parties as it stipulated that electors should vote for president and vice president as separate and distinct candidates. It was designed to make impossible another electoral vote tie between two presidential candidates of the same party.

Assault on the Judiciary

To Jefferson and the Republicans, the Federalists had used the courts to strengthen their hold on the government and to persecute and prosecute their opposition. Soon after assuming office, Jefferson launched a counterattack on the Federalist-dominated judiciary.

The Republicans first repealed the Naturalization Act, changing back the residence requirement for citizenship of foreigners from fourteen to five years. Next, they repealed the Judiciary Act of 1801 abolishing the new positions President Adams had filled with his "midnight judges."

William Marbury, one of the justices Adams appointed before leaving office, had been scheduled to assume his duties as a new justice of the peace for the District of Columbia. His commission papers, though duly signed and sealed, had not been officially delivered to Marbury by the time Adams had left office. When Jefferson became president, his secretary of state, James Madison, refused to deliver the commission papers to Marbury. Seeing no other recourse, Marbury applied to the Supreme Court for an order, a writ of mandamus, directing Madison to perform his official duty.

The chief justice of the Supreme Court was John Marshall, a dignified Virginian with strong Federalist views. Marshall firmly believed in the process of "judicial review," or the Supreme Court's right to interpret the Constitution as a means of checking the excesses of the other two branches of government.

When Marbury's case came before him, Marshall took the opportunity to assert the Court's power to decide on the constitutionality of laws enacted by Congress. In his decision, *Marbury v. Madison* (1803), the chief justice decided that Marbury had a right to the commission but that the Supreme Court had no power to issue the order forcing Madison to deliver the commission papers. In essence, he declared unconstitutional that part of the Judiciary Act of 1789 which allowed Marbury to sue directly in the Supreme Court without first trying lower courts.

Marshall's decision was an important one. From now on, the power to declare laws unconstitutional would not belong to the elected president or Congress, but to the Supreme Court, an appointive body chosen for life and beyond the influence of popular opinion.

Foreign Affairs and the Louisiana Purchase

In foreign affairs more than anything else, Jefferson realized the need to be a strong president.

As Europe approached war again, the United States once more became embroiled. In the secret Treaty of San Ildefonso, France and Spain agreed that France would be given back the territory of Louisiana, including New Orleans and the mouth of the Mississippi, which it had lost in 1763 as a result of the French and Indian War. To Jefferson, this was a flagrant attempt by Napoleon to reestablish an empire in North America. A strong and arrogant France controlling the mouth of the Mississippi, Jefferson accurately believed, could do serious harm to American prosperity and security.

Even more than before, the United States had crucial interests in keeping the Mississippi Valley open. Hundreds of thousands of Americans now lived west of the Appalachian Mountains. Ohio had over 45,000 people in 1800, Tennessee had 105,000, and Kentucky had 220,000. Over 150 vessels regularly sailed the river transporting 20,000 tons of freight annually.

As Jefferson himself was aware, "There is on the globe one single spot the possessor of which is our natural and habitual enemy. It is New Orleans . . ." If France gained control of it, "from that moment we must marry ourselves to the British fleet and nation."

When word of the French agreement with Spain reached the United States, Jefferson dispatched Robert Livingston to Paris to buy West Florida (sovereignty over which was disputed between France and Spain) and New Orleans. Livingston, however, encountered much difficulty with Foreign Minister Charles Talleyrand, who would not let him see Napoleon. The French were waiting to see the outcome of their efforts to reestablish dominance in the Caribbean. If successful there, they might be able to become a North American power once again.

While Americans waited for Livingston to accomplish something, the Spanish, who had not yet turned New Orleans over to the French, violated the Pinckney Treaty and closed the port of New Orleans to American use. This action, Livingston's lack of progress, and the westerners' growing frustration, forced Jefferson into action. In January 1803, the president sent James Monroe to join Livingston in the negotiations armed with an offer of $2 million to purchase New Orleans and West Florida.

France's attempt to subdue a slave insurrection in Santo Domingo had by now resulted in disaster and it looked as though the French were also about to become involved in a war with the British. With his attention turned to Europe, Napoleon realized that having to defend Louisiana would be a liability. He then resigned himself to the sale of all of Louisiana, a vast region between the Mississippi River and the Rocky Mountains, not just the port of New Orleans, to raise the cash necessary to assist the forthcoming Anglo-French war.

When Monroe arrived, the French were eager to sell all of Louisiana and their offer exceeded American expectations. Livingston, Monroe, and the French signed a treaty on May 2, 1803 (though it was antedated April 30, 1803), awarding Louisiana to the United States for a total of $15 million, or over seven times what Monroe and Livingston were authorized by Congress to spend.

Although delighted with the outcome, Jefferson feared repercussions. Spain had never officially given the area to France and was upset at not receiving its fair share of financial compensation from Napoleon. Trouble could be expected from the Spanish. There were questions concerning the boundaries of the Louisiana territory, since the French had been quite vague about that, and this would anger both the Spanish and the British, whose colonies of Mexico and Canada, respectively, bordered Louisiana.

Most troubling of all to Jefferson was that according to his oft-repeated interpretation of the Constitution, the United States technically lacked the constitutional power to accept Napoleon's offer. In the past, the president had insisted that the federal government possessed only those powers specifically assigned to it by the Constitution. Nowhere did that document deal with the government's authority to acquire new territory. Being persuaded that he did not have the time to propose and then wait for the ratification of a constitutional amendment that would speak to this, Jefferson approved the purchase of Louisiana. In the end, he trusted "that the good sense of the country will correct the evil of loose construction [of the Constitution] when it shall produce ill effects."

The Federalists, of course, attacked this as the assumption

of too much power on behalf of the Republican administration. Opposition notwithstanding, the Senate ratified the Louisiana Purchase treaty, and in December 1803 Louisiana became American territory. The country in one act had virtually doubled its area.

The Lewis and Clark Expeditions

Even before Napoleon had made the startling offer to Monroe and Livingston, Jefferson had prepared to find out more about Louisiana. Now the president sent his private secretary, thirty-two-year-old Meriwether Lewis, and an accomplished Indian fighter, twenty-eight-year-old William Clark, to lead an expedition to explore Louisiana and report on its geography, people, and commercial possibilities.

Leaving their winter camp near St. Louis in May 1804, the expedition reached the Pacific coast in November 1805. At slight cost, approximately $50,000, it accomplished much. Lewis and Clark and their company established important commercial relations with some of the western Indian nations, uncovered strategic passages through the Rocky Mountains, and provided the government with important botanical, zoological, and anthropological data.

In addition to the Lewis and Clark expedition, in 1805 Jefferson sent Lieutenant Zebulon Montgomery Pike, then only twenty-six years old, to explore the Louisiana territory. Leaving from St. Louis and sailing up the Mississippi River, Pike recorded a great deal of useful information about the upper Mississippi Valley.

The Burr Conspiracy

Acquisition of the Louisiana territory now allowed the westerners to send their goods to market through New Orleans. Ironically, it also provoked reactions that seemed to threaten the very existence of the Union. From both the Northeast and the Southwest came secession plots stemming directly from the recent purchase of Louisiana.

A majority of Americans heartily approved of Jefferson's decision to acquire the Louisiana territory, and this manifested itself in the president's overwhelming reelection in 1804. Still, some of the Federalists in New England denounced the acquisition as unconstitutional, as they feared the growth of the West would mitigate their prestige and influence in the country. The most extreme of these Federalists, a group known as the Essex Junto, concluded that to preserve its rightful place, New England must secede from the United States and form its own Northern Confederacy. This plan could not be successful without the support of New York's Federalists, and their leader, Alexander Hamilton, would have nothing to do with any secessionist plots.

Hamilton's fellow New Yorker, Republican Aaron Burr, even though he was still technically the vice president, agreed to run with Federalist support for the governorship of New York in 1804. Rumor had it that Burr was in league with the Essex Junto, and that if he was elected, he would lead his state into secession along with New England. Fearing that the rumors were true, Hamilton during the election cast many aspersions on Burr, even accusing him of treason. Because of the adverse publicity this brought him, Burr lost the election, and seeking retribution, he challenged Hamilton to the satisfaction of a duel.

In July 1804 the two men and their seconds met at Weehawken, New Jersey, across the Hudson River from New York City, for their duel. Hamilton was mortally wounded in the contest and died shortly thereafter. Burr was initially indicted for murder, but the charges were later dropped.

Nevertheless, public outrage followed the death of Hamilton. Presiding over the Senate until the end of his term as vice president, Burr looked to the Southwest to regain his shattered political ambitions. He contacted General James Wilkinson, commander of the United States troops in the West and governor of the Louisiana territory, and the two men sought foreign support for a plan to separate the Southwest from the United States, combine it with parts of Spanish Mexico, and establish an independent nation with themselves as rulers.

Wilkinson betrayed Burr, however, and informed Jefferson that treason was afoot and that an attack on New Orleans might be expected. Burr was then taken into custody and tried for treason before Chief Justice John Marshall. Eventually Burr was acquitted, but he now had gained infamy as a believed traitor. To escape further notoriety, he fled to Europe, where he remained in exile for several years.

Challenges to American Neutrality

The Louisiana Purchase was made possible by European conflict and disorder. Yet these same disruptions began to cause serious problems for Jefferson and the nation.

Almost all of America's troubles after 1803 with the major European belligerents, England and France, repeated those of the 1790s. Controversies over impressment, blockades, neutrality rights, contraband, and Indian incitements plagued America's relations with France and England as they had before.

Following the outbreak of war between France and England in 1803, the British resumed their policy of impressment. Soon, British ships were stopping American vessels on the high seas and forcing American sailors into the Royal Navy.

In July 1805, in the Essex Decision, a British admiralty court declared that American shipping dealings with the French would be restricted even further than under the Jay Treaty of 1794. The ruling stated that the American practice of transporting French West Indian goods first to American ports and then on to France in order to establish the neutrality of the shipment, would no longer be tolerated. The British considered this a violation of the Rule of 1756, which forbade belligerents to open to neutrals trade routes that were closed in peacetime. In other words, American ships loading goods in French West Indian ports destined for France could not claim the shipment was neutral by breaking the voyage with a stop in the United States.

The American government protested this, and Congress retaliated in April 1806 by passing the Nonimportation Act. This measure made illegal the importation of many goods that Americans obtained from Britain. The law was only a threat, however, and Jefferson chose not to exercise it for the time being.

Tensions increased as Britain announced a blockade of the European continent in May 1806. Orders in council, as they were called, authorized the seizure of any vessel that attempted to trade on the continent of Europe without having first secured British permission. The orders, which sought to cut France off from outside aid, were countered by Napoleon's Berlin (1806) and Milan (1807) Decrees proclaiming that British vessels and neutral ships first stopping at British ports would not be allowed to land their cargoes at any European port controlled by France or its allies.

Naturally, this British-French war of regulations greatly irritated the Americans. If American merchants bowed to the British they would offend the French, and vice versa. Quite simply, American merchants were bound to lose.

Still worse was the increased impressment of American seamen. Many British sailors deserted the Royal Navy with its harsh discipline, dangers, and bad food, for the good pay and lenient treatment of the American merchant marine. This incensed the British, many of whom believed the Americans actively encouraged British desertion, and Britain stepped up impressment.

In the summer of 1807, the British took their policy of impressment to a level hitherto unreached when they attacked the U.S.S *Chesapeake*. The *Chesapeake* was a Navy frigate not yet fully outfitted for combat. When it set sail from Norfolk, Virginia, allegedly with several deserters from the Royal Navy aboard, it was almost immediately intercepted by H.M.S *Leopard*. When the *Leopard's* captain demanded to board the *Chesapeake* to search for deserters, the American commander, Commodore James Barron, refused. The *Leopard* then opened fire on the ill-prepared American ship, killing three and wounding eighteen more. Having no other recourse but to surrender, Barron watched as a British search crew boarded his vessel and removed four Americans for impressment into the British Navy.

This was a more audacious attack upon the sovereignty of the United States than the British had ever before attempted. Many Americans now wanted and hoped for a war of revenge.

Jefferson could easily have complied. However, rather than use military or naval force he chose to attempt to bring England and France to terms through economic pressure. Hastily, the president drafted his response to the European powers , the Embargo Act, and Congress passed it, in December 1807. The Embargo Act simply prevented American ships from leaving this country for any port in the world.

The embargo sealed off the country from foreign trade on the theory that Europe needed America more than America needed Europe. Its effect, though, was to bring on a serious economic depression. In particular, the northeastern merchants, most of whom were Federalists, found the embargo to be devastating as they lost money every day their idle ships sat moored at the wharves. Once again the New England Federalists claimed, as they had with the Louisiana Purchase, that Jefferson had violated his constitutional powers.

By late 1808, the embargo was under such attack by the Federalists, and by a group of opposition Republicans led by John Randolph called the Quids, that the administration had to retreat. In March 1809, as one of his last official acts, Jefferson signed the Nonintercourse Act, repealing the embargo and reopening foreign trade except with Britain and France.

Though the third president had not managed to free the United States from the entanglements of the European conflict, he had avoided a showdown with the British for which America was militarily unprepared. Jefferson, not terribly proud of his presidency, retired to his home, Monticello, to live out the remainder of his life actively pursuing the arts and sciences.

Madison Becomes President

Jefferson's successor was his secretary of state, James Madison. Cofounder of the Republican Party and one of the chief architects of the Constitution, Madison had earned the right to be his party's choice. Though his nomination was contested by the dissident Republicans, the Quids, Madison was clearly the choice of most Republicans, and he went on in 1808 to defeat the Federalist candidate, Charles Pinckney.

Madison soon found that he had no more luck than Jefferson in getting Britain and France to respect American neutrality. In hopes of making some progress, Congress passed Macon's Bill No. 2 (1810). Under this bill, trade was reopened with both France and England. The bill also contained the proviso that the United States would restore trade sanctions against one of the two nations if the other repealed the measures which allowed seizure of American ships. In short, as an inducement to cease attacks on American trade, the United States promised to support against its enemy the first nation to call a halt to such attacks.

A Crisis in the West

Macon's Bill No. 2 brought no relief on the seas, and matters at home only worsened for the United States.

Though the British were innocent, many Americans blamed

them for inciting Indian riots in the West. Actually it was the land greed of many Americans and their cruel treatment of the Indians who refused to leave their own land that precipitated a crisis with the Indians.

In 1802, Jefferson had appointed William Henry Harrison governor of Indiana Territory. For years Harrison sought to carry out Jefferson's policies of Indian removal. In his efforts, he forced the Indians to give up their tribal lands and convert themselves into settled farmers or migrate west of the Mississippi River. By 1810–1811 Harrison had, by chicanery, cajolement, or force, obtained most of the Indians' land in his territory.

Unwilling to acknowledge their own errors and offenses against the Indians, westerners were certain that the English in Canada were responsible when western Indians sought to regain their illegally confiscated land in Indiana Territory. Led by Tecumseh, chief of the Shawnees, the Indians began to attack outlying settlements in the spring of 1810.

Tecumseh aimed to unite all the tribes of the Mississippi Valley and resist any further encroachments on Indian land. Assisting Tecumseh in his plans was his brother, a one-eyed epileptic medicine man known as the Prophet.

Harrison, though, was determined to thwart Tecumseh's plans, and when he saw his first opportunity, he provoked an attack by the Indians at the Battle of Tippecanoe (November 1811). Both sides sustained heavy losses, but Harrison went on to burn the Shawnee village of Prophetstown. Although the battle was considered a victory for Harrison and would make him famous as an Indian fighter, it could, in actuality, be regarded as a loss. Hatred for the American settlers in the West intensified, and the Indians fled to regroup.

While Harrison's "victory" at Tippecanoe temporarily quieted westerners' fears, it did not subdue their Anglophobia. They blamed the British for providing the guns and supplies that enabled the Indians to attack. To Harrison and other frontiersmen, the way to make the West safe for the white man was to remove the British from Canada. Only then, it was felt, would Indian problems permanently end.

The Rise of the War Hawks

Shortly before the Battle of Tippecanoe, a new Congress met in Washington for the 1811–1812 session. A large majority of the newly elected congressmen and senators from the West and South were fiercely nationalistic Republicans who eagerly wanted to even the score with Britain. News of the "victory" at Tippecanoe made them even more eager for war with England.

These "war hawks," as they were called, managed to get control of both the House and the Senate and succeeded in electing thirty-four-year-old Henry Clay of Kentucky as Speaker of the House. As Speaker, Clay held a position that was then second only to the president's in influence and power, and he quickly filled important committees with other war hawks. Clay appointed John C. Calhoun of South Carolina to the House Committee on Foreign Affairs and then launched a vigorous campaign to remove the British from Canada.

While Congress debated the issues, President Madison concluded that war with Britain was inevitable. Certainly, the economic policies of his administration and his predecessor's had brought little relief and had commanded no respect from the European powers. In May 1812, the war faction took the lead in the caucus of Republican congressmen who renominated Madison for president.

In June, Madison sent a war message to Congress. Madison maintained that Great Britain, by impressing American citizens, interfering with American trade, and inciting Indians along the frontier, was already waging war against the United States. He recommended that Congress declare war in return. Congress responded with a declaration of hostilities, but the vote in both houses, nineteen to thirteen in the Senate and seventy-nine to forty-nine in the House of Representatives, clearly showed how divided the American people were on the issue of war.

The division of public opinion that was evident in the congressional vote on the war declaration was again revealed in the election of 1812. Opposing Madison and the war, a peace faction of the Republicans nominated DeWitt Clinton of New York, and the Federalists supported him. Most of the electors in the Northeast voted for Clinton and peace. But all those in the South and West sustained Madison and the war, and Madison was reelected in a very close contest.

Divided numerically, Americans also were ill-prepared financially and militarily for the war with Britain. Congress had adjourned without increasing the size of the Army and Navy, voting war taxes or renewing the charter of the government's sole financial agency, the Bank of the United States, which had expired in 1811. Nonetheless, the war hawks and other nationalistic Americans in favor of war were not worried.

The War of 1812

The attempt to remove the British from Canada proved to be much more difficult than the Americans had anticipated. A three-pronged invasion of Canada failed in 1812. While the British dominated the seas, the American fleet gained control of the Great Lakes and made possible another invasion of Canada through Detroit. William Henry Harrison's troops won a victory in the Battle of the Thames (October 5, 1813), where they killed Tecumseh, whom the British had commissioned as a brigadier general. While Harrison's victory resulted in no lasting occupation of Canadian soil, it did demoralize the Indians of the Northwest, who had sided with the British.

To the south, another Indian fighter was defeating the Spanish-assisted Creek Indians. Andrew Jackson, Tennessee planter and militia general, pursued the Creeks and defeated them at the Battle of Horseshoe Bend in Alabama (March 27, 1814), where he sought revenge for a previous Creek victory at Fort Mims, just north of Florida. The retribution Jackson visited on the Indians was vicious; he slaughtered Indian women and children along with the warriors. After the battles of the Thames and Horseshoe Bend, the Indians were of little use to the British.

In 1814 the British prepared to invade the United States through three routes: the Chesapeake Bay, Lake Champlain, and the mouth of the Mississippi River. The British attempt at Lake Champlain was defeated when Commander Thomas Macdonough won an overwhelming victory.

On August 24, 1814, the British marched into Washington and deliberately set fire to public buildings, including the White House. Leaving Washington in partial ruin, they proceeded north up the Chesapeake Bay toward Baltimore. However, at Fort McHenry, guarding Baltimore, the Americans were ready. The British could only bombard the fort from a distance on September 12, 1814, and then were forced to withdraw. It was during the bombardment of Fort McHenry that Francis Scott Key, a young Baltimore lawyer, was inspired to write "The Star-Spangled Banner." Key could scarcely believe that the American flag was still flying after the intermittent twenty-five-hour shelling to which the fort had been subjected. The opening line of his four-stanza poem expressed his reaction: "Oh, say can you see by the dawn's early light." At the same time the British invading force in the North was defeated at the Battle of Plattsburg in upstate New York (September 11, 1814) and was forced to return to Canada.

In December 1814, the British attempted a major southern assault near New Orleans. Neither the British nor the Americans realized that their governments had just signed a peace treaty in distant Ghent, Belgium, and so the Americans under the command of General Andrew Jackson prepared to repel the British advance. The British were no match for Jackson's troops at the Battle of New Orleans (January 8, 1815), and the British retreated leaving behind seven hundred dead and fourteen hundred wounded, while Jackson's losses were eight dead, thirteen wounded.

The Hartford Convention

During most of the war, the northeastern portion of the United States refused to cooperate by offering men, supplies, and arms. Many New Englanders believed that Great Britain was not America's enemy, but rather the world's last hope against Napoleon, and that Madison had wrongly made the United States France's ally. Some of the Federalists in New England even celebrated British victories, sabotaged their own country's war effort, and plotted secession and a separate peace.

On December 15, 1814, after seeing their commerce virtually swept off the seas by the British Navy, antiwar Federalists forced the calling of a convention at Hartford, Connecticut. There they would discuss how to deal with the war and consider whether the disaffected states should secede from the Union.

The extremists at Hartford, however, were overruled by more moderate factions, and the convention took no action beyond endorsing state nullification of federal acts and proposing constitutional amendments limiting the power of the president and Congress over foreign relations. Yet this opposition to the war in almost one- fourth of the nation served as another hindrance to the American war effort.

The Treaty of Ghent

In the War of 1812, peace talks began even before the battles did. Reluctant from the outset, President Madison looked hopefully toward an early cessation of the hostilities. Soon after the declaration of war, the British government, wishing to liquidate a minor war and concentrate upon the major one against Napoleon, sent a negotiator to Washington with armistice proposals, but negotiations failed to develop because of Madison's continued insistence upon renunciation of impressment.

After repeated delays, the British and Americans met to discuss peace terms in Ghent, Belgium, in August 1814. Both sides initially made excessive demands. Soon they retreated and agreed to the *status quo ante bellum*, a return to things as they had been before the war began.

Each belligerent was to restore places and territory it had taken from the other in the war. The treaty said nothing about impressment, ignored neutral rights and Indian issues, and left the Canadian-United States boundary where it had been. A commission was set up to settle disputed or undetermined segments of the Canadian-United States boundary.

The Treaty of Ghent, though, was followed by other agreements that contributed to improving Anglo-American relations. A separate commercial treaty (1815) gave Americans the right to trade freely with England and the British Empire (except the West Indies). The Americans were allowed in 1818 to fish off the coasts of British North America, and the Rush-Bagot Agreement (1817) provided for the mutual disarmament of the Great Lakes. Gradually disarmament was extended to the land, and eventually, by 1872, the Canadian-United States border became the longest "unguarded frontier" in the world.

Though the British had not renounced impressment in principle, they ceased to apply it in practice after 1815.

Since the 1790s the Americans had been disrespected by the European powers. In particular, the British had interrupted, Americans' commerce on the high seas, impressed their sailors, and refused to recognize their policy of neutrality.

Certainly the War of 1812 was no overwhelming display of

military might on the part of the United States. Yet the war did reaffirm American self-pride and respect. Albert Gallatin, secretary of the treasury under both Jefferson and Madison, wrote: "The war has renewed and reinstated the national feelings and character which the Revolution had given and which were daily lessened. The people have now more general objects of attachments. . . . they are more American, they feel and act more as a nation."

President Madison's annual message to Congress in 1815 expressed the new feeling of self-confidence that had overtaken the nation. The same party that had attacked Hamilton and his plans for a national bank, protective tariffs for American commerce, and a federal program of internal improvements such as roads and canals was now asking Congress to appropriate funds for those very projects.

The war had made the Republicans nationalists. It also had ironically destroyed the Federalists, the party that had a virtual copyright on the nationalist label. Had the war ended on a negative note, the Federalists might have come out of it with enhanced prestige. As it was, their opposition now seemed unpatriotic and to some even treasonous. After 1815, Federalists would never again be a threat to Republicans on a national level.

With Napoleon's removal as an antagonist in Europe in 1814, the Continent settled down to a long period of relative international calm. For almost a century, the United States would be free from the clash of empires that had unsettled it for so long. With peace, the Americans could concentrate on internal and domestic affairs and take advantage of their bountiful resources to industrialize, urbanize, and mechanize. In so doing, they would emerge as one of the most powerful, affluent, and self-assured nations on the globe.

Recommended Reading

Thomas P. Abernathy, *The Burr Conspiracy* (1954)

James M. Banner, *To the Hartford Convention* (1970)

Irving Brant, *The Fourth President: A Life of James Madison* (1970)

Fawn Brodie, *Thomas Jefferson: An Intimate History* (1973)

James H. Broussard, *The Southern Federalists, 1810–1816* (1979)

Roger H. Brown, *The Republic in Peril: 1812* (1964)

Harry L. Coles, *The War of 1812* (1965)

Alexander De Conde, *This Affair of Louisiana* (1976)

Bernard De Voto, ed., *Journals of Lewis and Clark* (1953)

Richard Ellis, *The Jeffersonians and the Judiciary* (1971)

F. L. Engleman, *The Peace of Christmas Eve* (1962)

David Hackett Fischer, *The Revolution of American Conservatism: The Federalist Party in the Era of Jeffersonian Democracy* (1965)

Reginald Horsman, *The War of 1812* (1969)

Lawrence Kaplan, *Jefferson and France: An Essay on Politics and Political Ideas* (1967)

Linda Kerber, *Federalists in Dissent* (1970)

Ralph Ketcham, *James Madison* (1971)

Leonard Levy, *Thomas Jefferson and Civil Liberties: The Darker Side* (1963)

Shaw Livermore, Jr., *The Twilight of Federalism: The Disintegration of the Federalist Party* (1962)

Alan Lloyd, *The Torching of Washington: The War of 1812* (1975)

Milton Lomask, *Aaron Burr: The Years from Princeton to Vice President, 1756–1805* (1979)

Milton Lomask, *Aaron Burr: The Conspiracy and the Years of Exile, 1805–1836* (1982)

Forrest McDonald, *The Presidency of Thomas Jefferson* (1976)

Dumas Malone, *Jefferson and His Times*, 6 vols., (1948–1981)

Bernard Mayo, *Henry Clay: Spokesman of the New West* (1937)

Bradford Perkins, *Prologue to War: England and the United States, 1805–1812* (1961)

Merrill Peterson, *Thomas Jefferson and the New Nation: A Biography* (1973)

Julius Pratt, *Expansionists of 1812* (1925)

Robert Rutland, *Madison's Alternatives: The Jeffersonian Republicans and the Coming of War, 1805–1812* (1975)

Bernard Sheehan, *Seeds of Extinction: Jeffersonian Philanthropy and the American Indian* (1973)

Burton Spivak, *Jefferson's English Crisis: Commerce, the Embargo, and the Republican Revolution* (1979)

Gore Vidal, *Burr* (1973)

Raymond Walters, Jr., *Albert Gallatin: Jeffersonian Financier and Diplomat* (1957)

CHAPTER 9

Economic Growth and American Nationalism

Time Line

1792   The first toll road is constructed from Philadelphia to Lancaster, Pennsylvania

1793   Eli Whitney invents the cotton gin

1802   West Point is established

1807   Robert Fulton's and promoter Robert Livingston's steamboat, the *Clermont*, successfully travels up the Hudson River

1815	Boston merchant Francis Cabot Lowell uses waterpower to run power looms
1818	A National Road from Cumberland, Maryland, to Wheeling, Virginia, is opened
1824	Rensselaer Polytechnic Institute is founded
	The Erie Canal is completed and connects the Great Lakes with the Atlantic Ocean
1828	The Baltimore and Ohio Railroad is chartered
1830s	Obed Hussey and Cyrus McCormick invent machines to expedite the harvesting of crops
1834	The National Trades' Union is formed
1837	Horace Mann signs the momentous Education Bill of 1837 in Massachusetts
	Oberlin College in Ohio admits four women to become the first coeducational college
	Economic depression hits with the Panic of 1837
1840s	John Deere establishes a factory to produce more durable steel plows
1844	Samuel F. B. Morse transmits the first telegraph message from Washington to Baltimore
1848	The Associated Press is established to collect news by wire
1853	The Gadsden Purchase

1857   Economic depression hits with the Panic of
                       1857

---

*The Republicans ushered in a period of peace and prosperity. It
was also a time of exceptional growth and development in the
United States. Free from European entanglements for the first
time in its history, the United States pursued a course of
economic development that fostered a spirit of enterprise and
change.*

So different does the United States appear to be after the War
of 1812 that the year 1815 would seem to be a major watershed
in the history of the country. Upon closer examination, however,
the change to economic self-confidence and strength was not as
abrupt as it appeared to be. Wars tend to retard some tendencies
in a society and to accelerate others. In this case, latent economic
changes, already in place, were encouraged by the American effort during the war and appeared as if suddenly accomplished at
its end.

We must now turn our attention to how the War of 1812
resulted in an American economic boom and how, by the time
of the Civil War, America had become one of the world's
economic giants. What accounted for the massive growth?

America's Bountiful Resource Base

Certainly, the United States was richly endowed by nature.
Consisting in 1815 of over 1 billion acres, the nation had tremendous agricultural resources. No other nation possessed so much
usable, fertile land located within the earth's temperate zones,
where the growing season is long.

America's timber reserves were virtually unequaled. In this
regard, most nineteenth century Americans relied on wood and

wood by-products for virtually everything. Houses, fences, wagons, clocks, and machinery were all constructed out of the trees from America's vast forests. Wood was also a major source of fuel. During the antebellum period, steamboats, locomotives, and steam engines all burned logs, and most households, rural and urban alike, used wood for heating and cooking.

Minerals such as iron ore, copper, lead, petroleum, and coal were also found in abundance. After 1815, these resources were exploited as they had never been before. Indeed, by as early as 1820, coal slowly began to replace wood as an industrial fuel, particularly in the smelting of iron. Coal, in increasing amounts, was also beginning to replace the waterpower that had propelled most of the factory machinery in the Northeast. The production of coal, most of it mined in western Pennsylvania, increased from 50,000 tons in 1820 to 14 million tons by 1860.

Territorial Expansion

Learning to exploit their existing resources was only part of the Americans' economic boom. The country's resource base was greatly enhanced by the addition of new lands. Between the Louisiana Purchase in 1803 and the Gadsden Purchase fifty years later, the nation grew by 830 million acres. In these new areas, the United States obtained much more fertile land and natural resources. By the 1850s, the United States was able to exploit rich and fertile farmland in California, in Texas, and along the Gulf coast further east; had secured extensive deposits of silver, gold, copper, lead, and zinc in the Rocky Mountain regions; and had added to its already impressive timber reserves by acquiring the Pacific Northwest.

Immigration and the Growth of America's Labor Force

At the end of the war with Britain, the United States was a sparsely populated country. With 8.5 million people distributed over 1.7 million square miles, it had five inhabitants for every square mile. Today, the figure is approximately sixty per square mile.

Obviously, labor was scarce, but the country's potential for growth was high, since most Americans were young. In 1817, the median age in America was seventeen. An unusually high rate of natural increase helped ease the labor problem somewhat before 1830. Families were large—those with ten or twelve children were not all that uncommon. Many of the children, however, did not survive. There were major cholera epidemics in 1832 and 1849–1850 which killed thousands. Still, America was a healthier country than almost any other, and infant mortality was probably lower in America than in the rest of the Western world.

The labor shortage in the country also was offset by immigration. Between 1776 and 1815 no more than about ten thousand foreigners entered the country annually, but during the years 1815 to 1840 the average rose to thirty thousand a year.

In the 1840s came the first major wave of immigration of the nineteenth century. Economic woes in Germany and Scandinavia and the potato blight in Ireland brought misery to millions. These economic disruptions, combined with faster and more inexpensive trans-Atlantic passage and an increasing awareness of America's opportunities, brought unprecedented numbers of Europeans.

During the 1840s and 1850s, each year brought almost 200,000 new arrivals to the Atlantic and Gulf coast ports. During the 1840s alone, over 1.5 million Europeans moved to America. Of the 23 million people in the United States in 1850, almost 2.5 million were foreign-born; of these, 1 million were Irish and 500,000 were German. The decade of the 1850s brought in even more immigrants than the previous one. Approximately 2.5 million newcomers entered the country; they were also primarily from Ireland and Germany. Other ethnic groups entering during this period were the English, French, Italians, Poles, Scandinavians, and Dutch. Most of the immigrants settled in the urban centers of the northern states.

Many of these immigrants were young men and women in their most productive years, and they added their skills to the American labor force at virtually no cost to their adopted nation. By 1860, thanks in large part to a healthy natural increase and the arrival of the immigrants, the American labor force had swelled to over 11 million strong.

Most of the immigrants avoided the American South in the antebellum period. There were, however, significant pockets of Italians, Chinese, Germans, and Scotch-Irish in Mississippi, Texas, Louisiana, the Carolinas, and Missouri. New Orleans was the major urban area of immigrant life in the Old South. The climate, immigrants' opposition to slavery, fear of competition from slave labor, and the fact that most immigrants landed at northern ports and tended to remain close to their port of call were all major deterrents to a prominent foreign-born population in the South.

Improvements in Education and Skills

The increase in the labor pool, in and of itself, would not have been that significant had it not been matched by an accompanying improvement in the quality of labor. Inspired by such educational leaders as Horace Mann, many states, especially in the North, reformed their educational systems. Mann, a member of the Massachusetts legislature, pioneered in the establishment of public schools. As president of the state senate, he signed the momentous Education Bill of 1837. As secretary of the state board of education, he advocated nonsectarian instruction, established state teacher-training institutions, increased teacher salaries, founded fifty new high schools, improved curriculum, and provided a minimum school year of six months.

Thanks in large part to Mann's influence, other states soon followed suit. Throughout the North, in particular, school buildings were improved and repaired, new ones were built, high schools were opened, and minimum school requirements were established.

Teachers, many times ill-prepared themselves, relied almost exclusively on textbooks to educate their students. Noah Webster's spellers and grammar books were widely used. They were supplemented by the six *Eclectic Readers* (1835–1857), the first four of which were prepared by William Holmes McGuffey, who for many years was a professor at the University of Virginia. McGuffey's readers contained lessons of morality and patriotism, sentimental verse, and interesting facts. Eventually, these readers were adopted by some thirty- seven states.

In higher education, the coexistence of state and religious schools created conflicts over funding and curriculum. Denominational schools, beset by the need for funds, had to compete with tax-supported ones. In regard to curricula, a second Great Awakening had led many of the church schools to emphasize theology at the expense of arts and sciences. On the other hand, the United States' development necessitated broader education and programs geared to vocations. The University of Virginia, "Mr. Jefferson's university," founded in 1819, introduced seven years later a curriculum which reflected Jefferson's own view that education ought to combine pure knowledge with "all the branches of science useful to us, and at this day." The model influenced the other new state universities of the South and West.

Although great strides were being made in education, no institution of higher learning admitted women until 1837. In that year, Oberlin College in Ohio admitted four women to become the first coeducational college in American history. The first women's college to have a curriculum comparable to those of the men's schools was Mount Holyoke, in Massachusetts, founded in 1837.

The early standard curriculum in both state-supported and private colleges emphasized the traditional liberal arts. If a young man desired a professional career other than the ministry, he had few schools from which to choose. After 1812 this changed as American scientific and technical schools were established. Although many scientists, inventors, and engineers would continue to be self-educated or would acquire their training on the job, West Point (1802), Norwich University (1819), Rensselaer Polytechnic Institute (1824), and Lawrence Scientific School at Harvard (1847) were created for formal training of technicians and scientists.

By 1860, then, the United States had a highly skilled and literate labor force. This would make it possible for workers to read and implement the plans for the canals, bridges, and railroads that would soon bind the country together.

The Market Revolution

During the colonial period, the American economy was self-sufficient and staple-exporting; that is, people concentrated on producing tobacco, grain, and other staples for overseas markets. However, the War of 1812 and the surge of American nationalism that embraced it brought a market revolution in the United States.

The high demand for goods, both at home and abroad, and the growth of specialized labor brought on an unprecedented boom period. A staple-hungry Europe paid high prices for American goods. The American need for nonagricultural goods was met by the burgeoning industries in this country. More people had money to spend and invest and consequently were drawn, for the first time, into the market economy of the nation. With each passing decade, American industry expanded to meet growing demands. The American market economy, then, became far more diverse and nationwide than it had ever been.

The Farmer in the Period of Economic Growth

During the period of national economic growth following the successful war against Britain in 1812, the American farmer prospered. Literate, forward-looking, commercially oriented, the American farmer was quick to take advantage of every opportunity to improve methods, lower costs, enlarge crops, and increase profits.

In the South, cotton ultimately proved profitable. At first, the kind of cotton grown throughout most of the South was short-fiber cotton. However, this variety had burrlike green seeds that clung tightly to the fibers, and they were difficult and time-consuming to remove. As long as short-fiber cotton had to be processed manually, it simply was not economical to grow.

The high cost of the labor needed to do this prevented planters from taking advantage of the growing world market for cotton cloth. This was unfortunate, since the South's three major staples from colonial times—tobacco, rice, and indigo—had all experienced declining prices after 1776. Wheat and corn remained, but neither could produce the cash income of the major colonial crops. The South needed a new cash crop and it needed it soon if the region was to enter the nineteenth century on firm financial footing.

The South's problem was solved in 1793, when, on a visit to a southern plantation, New Englander Eli Whitney learned of the southern dilemma. To resolve the southerners' problem, Whitney constructed the cotton gin, a simple machine that would quickly and easily remove the sticky seeds from the short-fiber cotton. Thanks to Whitney, a single slave laborer could do the work of fifty in short order.

The cotton gin was an immediate success. In its wake, the

cotton culture quickly spread throughout the lower South—west Georgia, Florida, Alabama, Mississippi, Louisiana, Arkansas, and east Texas. Short-fiber-cotton production rose from 2 million pounds in 1793 to 80 million in 1811. By the Civil War, the United States had become one of the world's major suppliers of raw cotton.

A similar situation applied to the fertile wheat farms of the Midwest. At harvest time there simply had not been enough labor to gather in the crop quickly and efficiently. Here again, American technology prevailed.

In the 1830s Obed Hussey and Cyrus McCormick invented machines to expedite the harvesting and alleviate the farmers' problems. The McCormick and Hussey horse-drawn reapers replaced the sickle, cradle, and hand labor. The reaper enabled a crew of six or seven men to harvest in a day as much wheat as fifteen men could have harvested using the older methods. In the 1840s John Deere established a factory in Illinois to produce more durable steel plows.

The new machines added immensely to the productivity of harvest labor. By so doing, they lowered the costs involved and, of course, brought greater savings to the American farmer.

The Transportation Revolution

American technology improved the transportation systems in the country as well. American waterways were not ideal for navigation thanks to rapids, lack of lighthouses and port facilities, and difficulties in maneuvering against upstream currents.

In river travel especially, however, a new era began with the development of the steamboat. The high-pressure engine of Oliver Evans, lighter and more efficient than the earlier inventions of Britons Thomas Newcomen and James Watt, made steam power feasible for propelling boats as well as mill machinery and eventually even the locomotive. The perfecting of the steamboat as a mode of travel was the work of the inventor Robert Fulton and the promoter Robert R. Livingston. In 1807, their boat the *Clermont,* equipped with paddle wheels and a British-built engine, successfully traveled up the Hudson River. Even though it took thirty hours to travel some 150 miles, the *Clermont's* voyage clearly demonstrated the practicability of steam navigation. Soon, steamboats were operating on a regular schedule up and down the Hudson.

By 1855, there were 727 steamboats on western waters and many more on the Great Lakes and along the Gulf of Mexico and the Atlantic. The steamboat revolutionized the speed and cost of inland travel and transport. Before the invention of the steamboat, it had taken up to four months to pole a keelboat upstream from New Orleans to Louisville. By 1819, the steamboat had cut the time to seventeen days, and with further refinement, the time was under four and a half days by 1853.

As the amount of time needed for travel was reduced, so too was the cost to transport freight. Freight rates fell along the Mississippi River from an average of $5 per 100 pounds to under 15 cents.

To assist in this transportation revolution, state and federal governments spent considerable amounts to deepen channels and to build canals around river obstructions. The federal government also constructed lighthouses on the Great Lakes to facilitate travel.

Overland, the turnpike became the mode of travel. In 1792, the first toll road had been constructed from Philadelphia to Lancaster, Pennsylvania. For 60 miles travelers enjoyed an all-weather, hard-packed surface of crushed rock. This experiment was so successful that soon other turnpikes, named for the kind of tollgate often used, dotted the map. Initially, though, these roads were built and operated for private profit, so the construction costs had to be low enough and the prospective traffic high enough to ensure an early and sufficient return.

State and federal governments soon contributed funds and by 1818 a National Road had been constructed from Cumberland, Maryland, to Wheeling, Virginia. By 1850, this road reached Vandalia, Illinois—a distance of 700 miles, at a cost to federal taxpayers of $7 million.

Although turnpikes considerably lowered the cost and time of transporting people and goods, Americans, as they had in colonial times, still depended on water routes whenever possible. As steamboats grew in number and improved in efficiency, the larger rivers such as the Mississippi and the Ohio became increasingly useful. Where there were no navigable streams or lakes, the solution was to build canals.

After the War of 1812, a major increase occurred in the construction of artificial waterways. In 1817, for example, the New York State legislature appropriated funds for the digging of a considerable man-made waterway between the Hudson River and Lake Erie. The Erie Canal, completed in 1825, connected the Great Lakes with the Atlantic Ocean by a more direct route than the Mississippi River. When it opened it was considered an engineering marvel and brought worldwide acclaim.

New York's impressive canal system inspired other states to act. Ohio and Indiana established connections between Lake Erie and the Ohio River, and by so doing, they extended the New York system even further. Thanks to these new canal systems, it was now possible to travel or transport goods by ship all the way from New York to New Orleans on an inland route. It was also possible to go by way of the Great Lakes from New York to Chicago.

Canals and steamboats improved life for Americans in many ways. The significant decline in freight and passenger rates literally brought East and West together for the first time in history. Western farmers now found new outlets for their produce in the East, while eastern merchants discovered eager new markets for their goods in the West. By the 1850s, westerners were able to purchase manufactured goods and easterners were able to buy raw materials and foodstuffs, at all time low prices. The canals and steamboats had advanced the standard of living of the American people immeasurably by eliminating much of the high cost that distance had extracted.

The railroads also had a profound effect upon the life styles of the American people. In 1825, the Stockton and Darlington Railroad in England began to use steam power to carry coal from mines to the riverside. Its success was not lost on American entrepreneurs. The first to organize a railroad company was a group of New Yorkers who in 1826 obtained a charter for the Mohawk and Hudson Railroad Company and five years later began operating trains on the 16 miles between Schenectady and Albany. The first major American railroad was the Baltimore and Ohio, sponsored and financed by Baltimore merchants and chartered in 1828. Within two years the first 13 miles of track were in operation. In 1830, the Charleston and Hamburg Railroad ran trains over short distances in South Carolina. When this line was completed in 1833, it boasted 136 miles of track, the most in the world at that time.

By 1860, the United States had some 30,000 miles of track, and passengers and freight could travel by rail from the e coast as far west as St. Joseph, Missouri, and from Portland, Maine, to New Orleans. The railroads provided all-weather routes for passengers and freight. They served arid or mountainous regions where canals would be hard or impossible to construct and where streams were too shallow or too swift for navigation. Their speed was also a distinct advantage, making the railroads yet another major contributor to the tremendous American economic growth after 1815.

Accompanying the spread of the railroad was the appearance of one more technological marvel, the electromagnetic telegraph system. In concert with the railroads, the telegraph dramatically expedited the speed with which information traveled. The first message was transmitted by Samuel F. B. Morse in 1844 from Washington to Baltimore. Because of the relatively low cost of constructing wire systems, Morse's telegraph seemed to resolve the perennial problem of long-distance communication.

By the eve of the Civil War, more than 50,000 miles of wire connected most parts of the nation; by 1861, the Pacific telegraph, with almost 4,000 miles of wire, was open between San Francisco and New York. Independent wire companies initially operated particular parts of the telegraph network, but all of these companies soon were subsumed under one organization, the Western Union Telegraph Company.

The telegraph and the numerous refinements occurring in the newspaper industry made the gathering and disseminating of news much more efficient than they had ever been. In 1848, the Associated Press was established for the purpose of cooperative news collecting by wire, and no longer did journalists have to rely on other newspapers for out-of-town reports. Consequently, newspapers became more national in their coverage and were now able to report on the most current events of the day. Overall, this revolution in journalism was another unifying factor in American life, as it provided the quick information essential for a truly national economy.

The Emergence of the Factory System

The rise of the New England textile factories in this period of American history is an excellent example of the developing American economy. Under the leadership of Boston merchant Francis Cabot Lowell, Massachusetts cotton mills combined the best that American technology and economic progress had to offer. Using waterpower to run power looms, Lowell's mills processed cotton cloth at faster rates and for excellent prices.

This succeeding, Lowell saw that a bigger site was necessary and made plans for a complete textile community to be established along the powerful Merrimack River. He was joined by other merchants in this venture, and together they obtained a corporate charter for the Boston Manufacturing Company. To accomplish their objective, Lowell and his colleagues sold $600,000 in corporate shares to eager Boston investors.

Since mills in New England were previously small and employed whole families working together at the machines to ensure worker efficiency and contentment, Lowell encountered some new and unique problems. For instance, where would the labor force needed for his enterprise come from? How would he keep his workers satisfied, and where would they be housed to be certain that they were safe and healthy?

To resolve his logistical problems, Lowell decided to hire New England farm girls, a previously untapped labor resource. As a group these young women were quite anxious to earn some money to provide themselves with dowries or to send a brother to college or to pay off the family mortgage. And they came to Lowell's factory community for the good wages and for the cheap, yet pleasant dormitory housing built at the company's expense.

Concerned also about his workers' education and morality, Lowell constructed a lyceum, where the "Lowell girls" could hear educational lectures, and a church, with clergy, to minister to their religious needs. By the 1830s, Lowell, the factory community now named in honor of its deceased founder, was a town of eighteen thousand with a full complement of schools, libraries, paved streets, churches, and gymnasiums.

Foreign visitors to the United States regularly placed Lowell on their itinerary. Having observed the factory community, they invariably left impressed by the positive effects of industrialism. Soon, the Lowell community had established a glowing reputation on both sides of the Atlantic.

Vast Improvements in the Standard of Living

All of the economic and technological advances after 1815 profoundly affected the American standard of living. The factory system, as it was successfully employed at Lowell, was a highly profitable endeavor and did much to encourage the growth of the textile industry in New England. This, in turn, raised the standard of living for many in the area. In 1850, it was reported that in Boston alone there were eighteen millionaires.

Growth in the American economy benefited the urban middle class all over the land. Before the economic surge of this period the urban middle class had included shopkeepers, schoolteachers, and members of the traditional professions of law, medicine, and the ministry. As factories, mills, railroads, canals, and turnpikes appeared throughout the nation, new jobs were created. Not only were laborers needed for these jobs, but the industries hired engineers, clerks, bookkeepers, and office managers as well.

People in such office jobs formed an emerging new class of what would later be called "white-collar" workers. While they had less prestige than the traditional middle class, they nevertheless received higher salaries and had higher status than the "blue-collar" workers in the mines, mills, and railroads.

Ordinary wage earners still earned little, despite America's massive economic growth. "Lowell girls" received no more than $2 or $3 per week. In 1850, the domestic servants in the country, who were mostly women, were paid about $1 a week with their room and board. In the same year, the salary of the unskilled laborers who worked on the canals, turnpikes, or docks was 61 cents a day with board or 87 cents a day without.

For the small but growing class of skilled laborers, the situation was much better. During the 1850s, a blacksmith could earn about $1.10 a day while house painters could command about

$10.25 a week. A skilled iron founder could make as much as $30 a week.

Of course, these wages are not impressive today, but one must remember that before the Civil War prices were quite low. Meat sold for 10 cents a pound, a half bushel of potatoes for 50 cents, and a barrel of flour for $5. Conceivably, a single person or young couple could survive on an unskilled laborer's salary. For a family, it was estimated that $10 a week was necessary to survive in the 1850s.

Despite the low pay, American wage earners were much better off than their European counterparts. Across the Atlantic, workers endured peasantlike poverty and unsanitary, life-threatening conditions much more frequently than in the United States. This is not to say, though, that working conditions in the United States were not hard, for they certainly were. For six days a week, the "Lowell girls" worked in the mills about twelve hours a day. Workers on the expanding transportation systems in the country averaged around eleven hours a day. On-the-job accidents in most industries were all too common, and when workers were injured, their incomes and their jobs were threatened. During periods of economic depressions such as the panics of 1837 and 1857, unemployment rose drastically. When this occurred, the poor and unemployed had only soup kitchens or the "poor farm" upon which to rely.

Hard life notwithstanding, thousands of European immigrants annually made the arduous and dangerous trip across the Atlantic to America, where the standard of living and the wages were much higher than those to which they were accustomed. After 1840, Irish men and women, willing to accept lower wages than their American counterparts, began to replace them in unskilled jobs in the mills and mines. The result was dissension in the labor force and an accompanying deterioration of working conditions.

Attempts at Collective Action

Unskilled workers were not the first to organize and act collectively to improve their working conditions. That distinction belonged to the skilled workers, who created the first labor unions and called for the first strikes around 1800. The leaders in the incipient labor movement were the printers and the cordwainers (makers of shoes and boots). In major urban areas like Philadelphia, Boston, Baltimore, and New York, these skilled workers created mutual aid societies. In the 1820s and 1830s, the craft societies expanded to citywide dimensions, each now with central administrative organs known as trade unions. In 1834, these workers attempted to organize on a national level when delegates from six cities founded the National Trades' Union. Two years later, the printers and cordwainers established their own national craft unions.

Shortly thereafter, however, the young labor movement died. Failing to overcome hostility from the courts and in the laws, labor leaders found themselves frequently accused of conspiratorial behavior when they attempted collective bargaining. The Panic of 1837 and the ensuing depression sounded the death knell of the labor union movement. By the 1850s, a few national craft unions reemerged, but they were exclusively for such highly skilled workers as machinists, molders, hatters, printers, and stonecutters. As such, they only represented a very small minority of the American labor force and represented virtually no class awareness. The vast majority of American laborers remained unorganized.

Following the steady rise of American nationalism after the War of 1812, the economy matured in an unprecedented fashion. Many factors were responsible for this period of enormous growth. Skillful innovation and technological advancement had made tasks that were once tedious, time-consuming, and expen-

sive, quick, cost-effective, and profitable instead. Generous governmental support, bold entrepreneurial experimentation, and foreign investments provided the capital to subsidize the burgeoning businesses and industries. Increasing numbers of immigrants contributed to an already growing labor force. By 1860, then, the American people were well on their way to becoming the richest on earth.

Recommended Reading

Ray Billington, *The Protestant Crusade, 1800–1860* (1938)

Richard D. Brown, *Modernization: The Transformation of American Life, 1600–1865* (1976)

Elliott Brownlee, *Dynamics of Ascent: A History of the American Economy* (1979)

Stuart Bruchey, *The Roots of American Economic Growth, 1607–1861: An Essay in Social Causation* (1965)

Howard P. Chudacoff, *The Evolution of American Urban Society* (1981)

Thomas C. Cochran, *Frontiers of Change: Early Industrialism in America* (1981)

John R. Commons, *A History of Labour in the United States* (1918)

Alan Dawley, *Class and Community: The Industrial Revolution of Lynn* (1976)

Jay P. Dolan, *The Immigrant Church: New York's Irish and German Catholics, 1815–1865* (1975)

Elisha P. Douglass, *The Coming of American Business* (1971)

Albert Fishlow, *American Railroads and the Transformation of the American Economy* (1965)

Robert Fogel, *Railroads and American Economic Growth* (1964)

Carter Goodrich, *Government Promotion of Canals and Railroads, 1800–1890* (1960)

H. J. Habakkuk, *American and British Technology in the Nineteenth Century* (1962)

Erik Haites, James Mak, and Gary Walters, *Western Rivers Transportation: The Era of Early Internal Improvements* (1975)

Oscar Handlin, *The Uprooted* (1951)

Walter Havighurst, *Voices on the River: The Story of the Mississippi Water Ways* (1964)

Paul E. Johnson, *Shopkeepers' Millennium: Society and Revivals in Rochester, New York, 1815–1837* (1979)

Hannah Josephson, *Golden Threads: New England Mill Girls and Magnates* (1949)

John F. Kasson, *Civilizing the Machine: Technology and Republican Values in America, 1776–1900* (1977)

Dale Knobel, *Paddy and the Republic: Ethnicity and Nationality in Antebellum America* (1986)

Leo Marx, *The Machine in the Garden: Technology and the Pastoral Idea in America* (1964)

Kerby Miller, *Emigrants and Exiles: Ireland and the Irish Exodus to North America* (1985)

Douglas C. North, *The Economic Growth of the United States, 1790–1860* (1951)

Edward Pessen, *Most Uncommon Jacksonians: The Radical Leaders of the Early Labor Movement* (1967)

Joseph G. Rayback, *A History of American Labor* (1966)

Nathan Rosenberg, *Technology and American Economic Growth* (1972)

Ronald Shaw, *Erie Water West: A History of the Erie Canal, 1792–1854* (1966)

Jason H. Silverman, *Beyond the Melting Pot in Dixie: Immigration and Ethnicity in Southern History* (forthcoming)

Merritt Roe Smith, *Harper's Ferry Armory and the New Technology: The Challenge of Change* (1977)

John F. Stover, *Iron Road to the West: American Railroads in the 1850s* (1978)

George R. Taylor, *The Transportation Revolution, 1815–1860* (1951)

Phillip Taylor, *The Distant Magnet: European Emigration to the USA* (1971)

Anthony Wallace, *Rockdale: The Growth of an American Village in the Early Industrial Revolution* (1978)

Norman Ware, *The Industrial Worker, 1840–1860: The Reaction of American Industrial Society to the Advance of the Industrial Revolution* (1924)

Sam Bass Warner, *The Urban Wilderness* (1972)

Carl Wittke, *The Irish in America* (1956)

CHAPTER 10

From the "Era of Good Feelings" Through the Era of Jackson

Time Line

1810	*Fletcher v. Peck*
1816	James Monroe is elected president
	Dartmouth College v. Woodward
1818	Andrew Jackson invades Florida
1819	*McCulloch v. Maryland*
	The United States and Spain sign the

Adams-Onís Treaty, in which Spain surrenders Florida and its claims to Oregon

1820   Monroe is reelected to the presidency

The Missouri Compromise

1821   *Cohens v. Virginia*

1823   The Monroe Doctrine is announced

1824   *Gibbons v. Ogden*

Presidential contest between John Quincy Adams and Andrew Jackson is thrown into the House of Representatives for resolution; the House awards the victory to Adams, thereby precipitating charges from Jackson and his supporters of a "corrupt bargain"

1828   The "Tariff of Abominations" passes Congress

Vice President John C. Calhoun anonymously authors *The South Carolina Exposition and Protest*

Andrew Jackson is elected president

1830   Congress passes the Indian Removal Act

1831   *Cherokee Nation v. Georgia*

1832   Another high tariff passes Congress; South Carolina nullifies the tariffs of 1828 and 1832

Worcester v. Georgia

Jackson vetoes the bill renewing the charter of the Bank of the United States

	Jackson is reelected
1833	Congress passes a "force bill" to collect the tariff duties in South Carolina
	South Carolina agrees to a compromise tariff but nullifies the force bill
1834	Congress passes the Indian Intercourse Act
1836	Jackson issues his Specie Circular in his war against the Bank of the United States
	The Bank of the United States is dismantled
	Martin Van Buren is elected president
1837	The Panic of 1837 occurs and an economic depression ensues
1838	Cherokee Indians are forced off their lands and set out for Oklahoma on the "Trail of Tears"
1840	The Independent Treasury System is established by Van Buren
	William Henry Harrison is elected president

The War of 1812 made the Republicans the party of nationalists while all but destroying the Federalists. The political divisiveness so prominent during the first four presidential administrations was quelled with the Federalist demise, and politically the nation appeared as harmonious as it had ever been. Or did it? Upon closer examination, the quiet and calm characterizing the presidency of James Monroe belied some nascent but major differences among the American people. By the time Monroe's successors, John Quincy Adams and Andrew Jackson, assumed of-

fice, those differences were moving the country toward the second American political party system. In addition, sectionalism emerged as a compelling and dominating ideology serving, to the perceptive, as an ominous portent of things to come.

The Virginia Dynasty

After 1800 the presidency appeared to be the exclusive possession of Virginians. Following his eight years in office, Thomas Jefferson (who himself had been a secretary of state) named his secretary of state, James Madison, to succeed him. After being elected to two terms, Madison secured the nomination of his secretary of state, James Monroe. In fact, four of the first six presidents were from the state of Virginia.

This caused great consternation in the North, where people complained about this so-called Virginia Dynasty. Still, the Republicans had little difficulty in electing their candidate in the presidential election of 1816. Monroe received 183 of 217 electoral votes and easily defeated the Federalist Rufus King.

At the time of his election, Monroe was fifty-eight years old and at the end of a long and distinguished career as a Revolutionary War soldier, diplomat, and cabinet officer. Patient and cautious, Monroe was neither as innovative nor as imaginative as his predecessors Jefferson and Madison.

For his secretary of state Monroe chose Massachusetts native John Quincy Adams, son of the former president. Since the stepping stone to the presidency had become the State Department, Monroe, in essence, was announcing that after a second term, the Virginia Dynasty would end or at least be interrupted.

Shortly after his inauguration, Monroe did what no other president since Washington had done: he made a goodwill tour of the country, eastward to New England, westward as far as Detroit. In New England, so recently the scene of vehement

Federalist discontent, he was welcomed everywhere with enthusiastic demonstrations of support. Indeed, the *Columbian Centinel*, a Federalist newspaper in Boston, went so far as to cheer that with Monroe an "Era of Good Feelings" had arrived. The phrase spread quickly throughout the country and soon became synonymous with the presidency of Monroe.

The phrase was not entirely accurate, since political turbulence soon developed in the country. Nevertheless, Monroe was reelected in 1820 with the nearest thing to a unanimous vote in the electoral college since Washington. All but one of the electors cast their votes for Monroe, and the Federalists had not even bothered to put up an opposing candidate.

The Missouri Controversy

The "Era of Good Feelings" was interrupted in 1819, when Missouri applied for admission into the Union as a slave state. Congress was keenly aware of the potential controversy surrounding this, since every effort had been made in the past to balance the power between southern slave states and northern free ones. New states had more or less come into the Union in pairs, one from the North and one from the South. With the admission of Alabama in late 1819, the Union contained an equal number of slave and free states, eleven each.

Missouri's admission would tip the balance of power in favor of the South, and many northerners were particularly sensitive to that. Earlier, Representative James Tallmadge of New York had moved to prohibit the further introduction of slaves into Missouri and to provide for the gradual emancipation of those already there. By so doing, the Tallmadge amendment to a statehood bill sought to make abolition a condition for Missouri's statehood. Bitter and heated sectional debate ensued in Congress over this amendment for the next two years.

When Maine applied for admission into the Union, a solu-

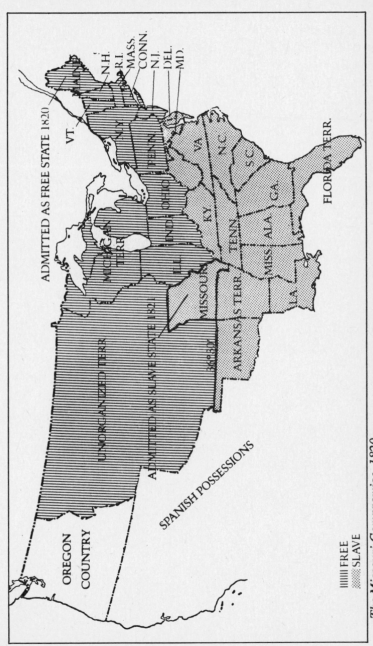

The Missouri Compromise, 1820

IIIIII FREE
SLAVE

tion seemed imminent. Yet many northern congressmen and antislavery advocates wanted to ensure that the remainder of the Louisiana territory, from which Missouri came, would not be dominated by the "slavocracy," as they called the South. Not necessarily motivated by a humanitarian concern for the slaves or even moral outrage, these northerners eagerly longed to check the growth and power of the South.

To resolve what appeared to be a sectional impasse in Congress, Senator Jesse B. Thomas of Illinois proposed an amendment that would prohibit slavery in the rest of Louisiana territory north of the southern boundary of Missouri at 36°30' latitude. The Senate approved this measure, and Speaker Henry Clay guided it through the House. Although it would take until 1821 to work out all the details, the Missouri Compromise (1820) did resolve the problems, albeit temporarily. Maine was admitted as a free state, Missouri a slave state, and slavery was prohibited north of 36°30' in the Louisiana territory.

But the Missouri Compromise was a sign of things to come. Thomas Jefferson, watching from his home in Virginia, perceptively noted that sectional jealousies in this "momentous question [the Missouri Compromise], like a firebell in the night, awakened and filled me with terror. I considered it at once as the knell of the Union."

Jefferson was right. The year 1820 marked the beginning of the long, tortuous road to civil war over slavery and sectional prerogatives. For the time being, the Missouri Compromise quieted things, but it solved nothing.

The Marshall Court

Such cannot be said about the man who dominated the Supreme Court from 1801 to 1835. Chief Justice John Marshall successfully exerted his will over the Court and shaped the country's judicial policies despite appointees by Republican presidents Jefferson, Madison, and Monroe to vacancies on the Court.

The net effect of the hundreds of opinions delivered by the Marshall court was to strengthen the judicial branch at the expense of the other two branches of government, increase the powers of the federal government while decreasing those of the states themselves, and advance the interests of the propertied classes, especially those engaged in commerce.

In 1810, in *Fletcher v. Peck*, Marshall struck down a state law as unconstitutional, the first time the Court had done so, on the grounds that it violated a private contract. The Court declared that an act of the Georgia legislature had violated the Constitution by impairing a contract. The case arose out of fraudulent land grants to stockholders of the Yazoo Company, a southern land company, in 1795 and the subsequent cancellation of these land grants by the legislature in 1796. Marshall held that a grant of land, even though made under circumstances of the most scandalous corruption, was a contract within the meaning of the constitutional provision and could not be rescinded after the land in question had passed into the hands of innocent buyers.

In 1816, in the Dartmouth College Case, he again used his authority to uphold the sanctity of a contract when he forbade the state of New Hampshire to amend the royal charter of Dartmouth College. In 1769, Dartmouth College had been granted a charter by King George III which was later acknowledged by the legislature. In 1816, the state of New Hampshire passed a law entirely reorganizing the government of the college. The trustees of the college brought an action questioning the constitutionality of this statute. Marshall's decision in this case was that a corporate charter was a contract that could not be impaired by legislative enactment. This decision assured those who invested money in corporate enterprises that corporations would be free from legislative interference and encouraged the expansion of private enterprise in such areas as railroad construction, insurance, commerce, and industry.

In 1819, Marshall expanded the power of the federal government over the states when the state of Maryland attacked the second Bank of the United States (rechartered in 1816) by taxing its paper-money issues. Marshall declared the Maryland tax law void. The issue, he announced in *McCulloch v. Maryland*, was twofold. First, did Congress have the power to charter a federal bank? Maryland had said no, since the Constitution did not specifically give the government that right. Second, could the states tax federal property?

Marshall upheld the constitutionality of the Bank of the United States even though there was no provision for such a bank in the Constitution. Congress could charter a bank, he said, since it was implied in the Constitution that the federal government could do so under its powers to tax, borrow money, and regulate commerce. This supported the doctrine of implied powers so readily used today.

As for state taxation of federal agencies, Marshall said the "power to tax involves the power to destroy." No state could destroy a legal creation of Congress, and hence the Maryland law was unconstitutional. If states were permitted to nullify acts of Congress by attacking its agencies, they could, according to Marshall, "defeat and render useless the power to create."

Two years later, in 1821 in *Cohens v. Virginia*, Marshall asserted that state court decisions were subject to Supreme Court review in cases involving federal laws. Marshall upheld the Virginia State Court of Appeals conviction of the Cohens, who had been found guilty of selling lottery tickets in violation of a state law. The Cohens had based their appeal on the ground that the Constitution had been violated. Virginia, for its part, contended that the Supreme Court had no jurisdiction in the case. While upholding the conviction, on the larger issue, Marshall affirmed the Court's right to review the judgment of a state court in accordance with the doctrine of national supremacy.

In 1824 in *Gibbons v. Ogden,* Marshall voided an act of the New York legislature which granted exclusive steamboat navigation on the Hudson River to Robert Fulton's and Robert Livingston's operating company. Speaking for the Court, which struck down the New York licensing act, Marshall held that it violated Congress's right to regulate interstate commerce, which he broadened to include navigation inside the limits of the individual states. Aaron Ogden, licensed by Fulton and Livingston to operate a ferry between New York and New Jersey, had successfully obtained a New York court order restraining Thomas Gibbons from competing with him. Gibbons had operated his ferry under a federal coasting license. Marshall's decision struck down the state-granted monopoly and once again established the supremacy of the federal government in clashes with the states.

An Aggressive Foreign Policy under Monroe

The first major problem confronting Monroe's secretary of state, John Quincy Adams, was that of Florida. The United States had already annexed West Florida, and America now eyed the remainder of Florida to round out the southeastern corner of the nation and to settle the perpetual problems of slaves escaping across the border in one direction and the marauding of Indians crossing it in the other. In 1817, then, Adams began negotiations for the purchase of all of Florida with the Spanish minister to the United States, Don Luis de Onís.

After all, the time seemed right, since Spain was seriously enfeebled by over twenty years of European conflicts. Spain, however, would not relinquish the territory.

Sent to patrol the Georgia-Florida border was General Andrew Jackson, in command of the troops along the Florida frontier. Jackson was instructed by Secretary of War John C. Calhoun to "adopt the necessary measures" to end the troubles along the borders. In 1818, Jackson, tired of Spain's inability to control the Seminole Indians and renegade slaves, invaded Florida, seized the Spanish forts at St. Marks and Pensacola, executed two British subjects for allegedly helping the Indians, and deposed the Spanish governor.

Americans applauded Jackson's action, while Spain protested vehemently. Clearly, Jackson's raid had demonstrated how incapable the Spanish were of maintaining their North American empire. Seeing his opportunity, Adams, instead of apologizing for Jackson's action, charged Spain with failure to protect its own possessions.

Unable to obtain British support in fighting back, the Spanish had no recourse but to come to terms with the United States. The Adams-Onís Treaty (1819) included Spain's surrendering Florida and its claims to Oregon. In return, the United States assumed the claims of its citizens against the Spanish government in the amount of $5 million. The southwestern boundary of Louisiana was fixed to exclude the Mexican province of Texas.

Spain's weakness not only provided opportunities for the United States, it also made them vulnerable. By 1820, thanks in large part to this weakness, all of Spanish America except the Caribbean islands had gained its independence. But Spain naively hoped to regain its lost colonies in Latin America and was encouraged by Prussia, Austria, and Russia, whose monarchs in 1815 had created the Holy Alliance to withstand liberalism and democracy wherever they existed.

Fearful of losing influence in the Western Hemisphere should Spain and its allies regain dominance, British foreign secretary George Canning suggested to the United States that the two countries work together to prevent Spain from regaining control of its former colonies. The Americans, disturbed at the prospect of Spanish restoration, were also alarmed by the

Russians' recent expansion from their Alaskan settlements down the west coast of North America.

Secretary of State Adams, though, refused any joint venture with the British. Then, on his recommendation, President Monroe included in his December 1823 message to Congress a statement of independent American principles regarding Latin America that has since become known as the Monroe Doctrine.

The president stated four principles that would guide the United States in its relations with Europe and the rest of the Western Hemisphere. First, the American continents were not open to any further colonization. Second, the United States would oppose any attempt to extend European political systems to the Americas. Third, the United States would not interfere with existing colonies in the Americas. Fourth, the United States would not meddle in the internal affairs of any European country but would oppose any transfer of existing colonies in the Americas from one European country to another.

European reaction to this policy was predictable; the Monroe Doctrine was regarded contemptuously. Most believed it was arrogant, belligerent, and hostile. Many also believed that the United States would not be able to back up its words when, in time, it was tested, as of course it would be.

Nonetheless, the United States, barely over forty-five years old and with a population of scarcely 10 million people, challenged the European powers with a clear statement in defense of international freedom and liberal institutions.

Popular Changes in American Politics

By the end of Monroe's second term in 1824, politicians were searching for his successor. Had these been normal times, Adams, as secretary of state, would have succeeded Monroe without trouble. But 1824 was not a year for politics as usual.

Between 1796 and 1820 candidates had been nominated by

party caucuses. By the end of Monroe's second term, however, Americans, growing in numbers, self-pride, and confidence, were refusing to have decisions made for them anymore. As a result of this, a quiet political revolution occurred.

States did away with the last vestiges of property qualifications for voting and the caucus system of nominating a candidate. The convention system replaced the caucus as a method for nominating candidates for office. Americans now demanded and received more of a say in the choosing of their political candidates than ever before. By 1832, all the states in the Union except South Carolina had removed their legislatures' power to select presidential electors; there, the people had no opportunity to vote in presidential elections until after the Civil War. The national trend was toward political democratization. Many states changed appointive positions into elective ones and, by so doing, gave many more people access to the political process.

The Election of 1824 and the "Corrupt Bargain"

Due in part to his heroic military exploits, Andrew Jackson was the only genuinely popular candidate in the election of 1824. President Adams was a man of great ability, but the voters found his aloofness and association with the Virginia Dynasty somewhat disconcerting. William Crawford of Georgia had the support of the lower South and of the dying "King Caucus" system in Congress, yet outside the South he was not a strong candidate. Henry Clay and Secretary of War John C. Calhoun were endorsed by local groups in Kentucky and South Carolina respectively, but despite their impressive records as national leaders, neither yet had extensive enough national support, and Calhoun soon dropped out of the race.

Interestingly, in 1824, thanks to the "Era of Good Feelings" and the concurrent demise of the Federalist Party, there was no opposition party. Except for a small group of Anti-Masons, everyone considered himself to be a Republican. The campaign, then, turned out to be a popularity contest.

When the smoke cleared, Jackson had finished first in both popular votes and electoral votes but did not have a majority of electoral votes. Adams was second and Crawford and Clay placed a distant third and fourth, respectively, in electoral votes. Clay actually had a higher popular vote than Crawford.

In accordance with the Twelfth Amendment to the Constitution, when no candidate received an electoral vote majority, the selection of the president would reside with the House of Representatives, where each state would cast a single vote for one of the top three candidates. The Constitution did not require that individual representatives vote for the man with the largest electoral or popular vote, for if it had there would be no point to the procedure.

Nevertheless, Jackson's supporters believed the House to have a moral obligation to award the presidency to their man, as he was the most popular candidate. When the votes were counted in the House, thirteen state delegations (more than 50 percent) gave Adams a majority. The Jackson people immediately denounced the process as a flagrant and impudent denial of the will of the American people.

Speaker Henry Clay, Jackson's supporters charged, had used his influence in the House to throw the election to Adams. When Adams appointed Clay his secretary of state, in essence making him his heir apparent, Jackson's men said the two had struck a "corrupt bargain." The Jackson people conveniently ignored the fact that Adams and Clay were ideologically compatible; very likely, while there had been some sort of understanding between the two men, nothing improper had occurred. Still, as soon as Adams was inaugurated, Jackson resigned his Senate position and returned to Tennessee to begin a four-year campaign for the presidency.

The Adams Administration

Despite all of the controversy, then, John Quincy Adams became the sixth president of the United States. His administration, however, was dominated for four years by the "corrupt bargain" charge and the opposition of Jackson's growing camp. The country had not seen such political divisiveness since the Federalists attacked the Republicans' policy in their conduct of the War of 1812 in the previous decade.

Because of this, almost nothing in Adams's domestic program passed Congress. Even in foreign affairs, where his knowledge and expertise should have made him very successful, he accomplished little. The best Adams could do was to obtain a few million dollars from Congress to improve rivers and harbors and to extend the National Road westward from Wheeling, Virginia.

As if Adams did not have enough problems, conflict arose in 1828 over a tariff measure debated in Congress. Northerners favored a strong tariff to protect them from foreign competition, while southerners saw the tariff as an instrument for increasing northern profits at their own expense. When the tariff, with its high duties on woolens, flax, hemp, iron, lead, molasses, and raw wool, finally cleared Congress, southerners were outraged and called it the "Tariff of Abominations."

Southerners now feared that everything they bought would cost more. This anxiety was exacerbated by the fact that a sharp decline in world cotton prices had just occurred.

Vice President Calhoun defended his section's interests in an anonymously published constitutional defense entitled *The South Carolina Exposition and Protest* (1828). In it, Calhoun denied that Congress had the right to levy a tariff so high that it would exclude certain imports. The Founding Fathers, he maintained, wished to impose only moderate duties on imported goods to raise revenue. The 1828 law was obviously discriminatory, for it favored the manufacturing states of the North and hurt sections of the country like the South that relied on imports and had little industry to protect. Yet Calhoun took the familiar low-tariff argument even further when he insisted that if Congress continued on such an unconstitutional course, it was the right of any state to call a convention and declare such a measure as the 1828 tariff null and void. The publication of *Exposition and Protest* clearly demonstrated that Calhoun, once a confirmed nationalist, was well on his way to becoming the South's great sectional champion.

The Election of 1828 and the Ascendancy of the Common Man

In the election of 1828 Jackson and Calhoun were selected by the Tennessee legislature and then placed on the ballot by their supporters in the various states. Adams and Richard Rush of Pennsylvania were nominated by the National Republican Convention at Harrisburg, the first major party presidential convention.

The campaign was a mudslinging, personality-ridden contest. Jackson's supporters were still brooding over their 1824 defeat and revived the charges of a "corrupt bargain." Adams and his people resorted to scandal-mongering about Jackson and his wife, who they claimed had not been officially divorced when she married the general. Few issues were discussed in the campaign.

In larger numbers than ever before, voters came out to cast their ballots. Jackson won an emphatic electoral victory—178 votes to Adams's 83—but a large minority (44 percent) of the popular vote was for Adams, who received all but one of the electoral votes from New England.

The Era of Andrew Jackson

While the new president was no democratic philosopher in the Jeffersonian mold, he maintained that government should offer "equal protection and equal benefits" to all the people. His opponents would insist that Jackson never really championed the people's cause, but they could not deny that he became a living symbol of the democratic spirit. Whether true or not, Jackson, far more than any of his predecessors, gave the appearance that the common man figured prominently in his administration.

As president, Jackson promptly set about reforming the personnel procedures of the federal government. For over a generation, ever since the demise of the Federalist Party, there had been no complete party turnover in Washington. As a result, government workers remained in their positions for many years, regardless of who was president, growing old (and often corrupt) in office.

To Jackson, these offices belonged to the people, not to entrenched officeholders, and the president went about initiating the "spoils system," appointing those people to office who were loyal to him and his policies. In this regard, Jackson appointed ordinary people as well as those from the upper class.

Jackson also initiated the doctrine of rotation in office. Since ordinary men presumably could be easily placed in office and serve satisfactorily and since loyal party members deserved government jobs, no one person should occupy a particular position for too long; rather, these political "plums" should be frequently rotated among the deserving applicants.

Although he made no wholesale change of government workers, in eight years about 20 percent of the positions changed hands, and Jackson thereby fixed the spoils system firmly upon national politics. Jackson also relied heavily upon an unofficial circle of political cronies known as the Kitchen Cabinet. These were fiercely loyal political advisers who exerted much influence over the president. Chief among these friends of the president was Martin Van Buren of New York.

The Nullification Crisis

As Jackson surrounded himself with his loyal friends, his relationship with Vice President John C. Calhoun steadily deteriorated. Indeed, the two men soon found themselves on a collision course over the issue of tariffs.

When Congress passed another tariff in 1832 which provided no real relief to southerners, some South Carolinians were ready for revolt. Carolina cotton planters justifiably argued that high duty increased the prices of things they had to buy, whether they were domestic or imported, while the high tariff lowered the prices they received for their exported cotton. In their opposition to the tariff they looked to Calhoun for leadership. Having ceased to be Jackson's friend and prospective successor, Calhoun courageously came out openly for nullification.

Following Calhoun's lead, South Carolina responded with a state convention that adopted an ordinance of nullification that declared null and void the tariffs of 1828 and 1832 and forbade the collection of duties within the state. The state legislature then passed laws to enforce the ordinance and prepare for a military defense. Needing a strong voice in Congress, Calhoun resigned the vice presidency and quickly returned to Congress as a senator from South Carolina.

Livid, the president unofficially threatened to hang Calhoun personally the next time that he saw him. Officially, he proclaimed that nullification was treason and the nullifiers were traitors. Jackson then made military preparations to ensure that the law would be obeyed. A "force bill" allowing him to use the Army and Navy if necessary to enforce congressional law was proposed in Congress.

This, of course, antagonized South Carolina even more, and

violence seemed imminent in 1833. Only a compromise tariff, proposed by Henry Clay and designed to reduce gradually the tariff duties, averted armed conflict between South Carolina and the federal government.

Jackson was satisfied, and finding no other southern support, South Carolina adopted the measure as well. In another state convention, South Carolina rescinded its ordinance of nullification. But as a final gesture of defiance, it nullified the force bill to reinforce the impression that Calhoun's program was a success and was still a force with which to be reckoned.

Calhoun and his forces quickly claimed victory for nullification when the tariff was lowered. Yet the system had not worked exactly the way Calhoun had intended. No other southern state had come to South Carolina's aid, and the message was not lost on Calhoun. One state, acting alone, could not hope to assert and maintain its rights against the federal government. For the remainder of his life, Calhoun would continue to talk of states' rights and nullification as he concurrently sought to create a sense of southern solidarity. Should another conflict emerge, Calhoun hoped the entire region would be prepared to act as one in resisting federal authority. He would not live to see it, but his hopes would be realized.

Jackson and the Indians

During the nullification controversy with South Carolina Jackson refused to allow the supremacy of the federal government to be threatened. Had he been consistent in this regard, it would have been much easier to predict the president's behavior. However, Jackson was perfectly willing to see the federal government's power disregarded or even overruled when it came to Indians, the victims of one of his deep-rooted prejudices.

The president eagerly sought to continue the old Jeffersonian policy of relocating all eastern tribes west of the Mississippi

River. By the Indian Removal Act (1830) Congress attempted to exchange the Indian lands in the East for what many assumed was the "Great American Desert" in the West. Four years later, Congress approved the Indian Intercourse Act, which in essence cordoned the Indians off from the white settlers in the West by a string of military installations. In the meantime, Jackson oversaw the signing of treaties with the Indians which often resulted in their removal at bayonet point.

In Georgia, the Cherokee Indians were a peaceful, highly literate, agricultural people with a sophisticated political and social system. When the Georgia legislature put pressure on the Cherokees to sell their lands and move west, the tribal leaders sued in federal court and were upheld in two Supreme Court cases by Chief Justice John Marshall.

In *Cherokee Nation v. Georgia* (1831) Marshall stated that the Indians had a right to the land they occupied. In *Worcester v. Georgia* (1832) Marshall stated that the Cherokees were a definite and separate political community, owning land over which the laws of Georgia had no force and into which Georgians could not enter without permission.

Vigorously supporting the Georgia legislature's position, Jackson did nothing to assist the Indians or to see that the rulings of the Supreme Court were enforced. Indicative of his attitude was the president's flippant remark, "John Marshall has made his decision; now let him enforce it."

As a result of this, the Cherokees were forced off their land by United States troops sent by the federal government in 1838. When they finally set out on the "Trail of Tears" for Oklahoma, their remaining property was quickly confiscated by corrupt state officials, speculators, and white settlers eager to get bargains.

Some four thousand men, women, and children out of an Indian population of fifteen thousand died of sickness, exposure, exhaustion, and malnutrition on their forced march west. While some humane Americans protested the Indian removal policy, it nevertheless continued unabated for many years to come.

Jackson and the Bank War

The only thing Jackson hated more than Indians was banks, having almost been ruined in 1819 by the financial policies of the Bank of the United States. The second Bank of the United States had grown enormously under its third president, Nicholas Biddle. With headquarters in Philadelphia, branches in twenty-nine other cities, and $35 million in capital, it was by far the nation's largest corporation. Its size was, in itself, frightening and also gave it potential power over the entire economy.

Thanks to Biddle's leadership, the Bank played a major role in overseeing the economy by lending money to merchants, expediting foreign trade, issuing paper money backed by gold, and providing credit. Given all this, along with the influence the Bank exerted on politicians (for example, Daniel Webster and Henry Clay were on the Bank's payroll in several capacities), it seemed obvious to Jackson that the Bank must be destroyed before it destroyed the country.

The Bank's application for renewal of its charter, which was due to expire in 1836, was prepared by Biddle in 1832 to ensure continuity. The measure to renew the charter passed Congress, but when it reached Jackson, the president vetoed it. In his veto message, Jackson sharply attacked the Bank in old Jeffersonian terms, calling it unconstitutional, undemocratic, and un-American. He denounced the Bank as a private monopoly controlled by foreign investors and warned that the Bank would wield its great powers to punish its enemies if it became firmly established. To the president, the Bank was a dangerous institution in a nation composed of many small economic units.

The bank veto was sustained, but it unleashed a storm of protest and immediately became the chief party issue in the presidential election of 1832. Jackson's supporters treated it as an attack on monopoly and privilege; his detractors condemned it as another example of Jackson's tyrannical behavior.

In the election of 1832, Jackson's party called themselves the Democratic Party; they were a hodgepodge group whose programs and principles differed from one part of the country to another. They claimed to be the party of the common man, and there was some truth to this. Generally speaking, they favored low tariffs, were antimonopoly, and had a laissez-faire attitude toward the nation's economy. They proposed the elimination of government favors to private enterprise, the dismantling of government-granted monopolies, and the reduction of other corporate privileges.

To many of the Jacksonians, once these programs were enacted, the American people would be able through free and fair competition to fend for themselves, prospering according to their own labor and skill. When the government ceased supporting the rich and hindering the poor, poverty and social inequality, now so prevalent in the country, would be significantly reduced. Most Democrats, of course, did not advocate social revolution, but the more radical of them, called the Locofocos, did suggest that revolutionary violence might occur if the economic inequities in the country were not soon rectified.

Jackson's opponents were beginning to coalesce in the form of the Whigs, an aggregation of dissimilar groups such as old Republicans, Federalists, and those who had switched from Jackson's camp. The Whigs were named for the traditional English party that stood to limit the powers of the king. The American version of the Whig Party sought to restrict the activities of "King Andrew," as they called him.

The Whigs recommended a system of protective tariffs, federal support for internal improvements, and a strong national bank—an "American System" first announced by Henry Clay in 1824. This system called for a paternalistic national government that would encourage and subsidize business, protect industrial workers from inexpensive foreign competition, and establish a stable home market for American farmers in the growing cities.

In 1832 though, the Whigs were not fully organized, and Jackson's opponent was Henry Clay, nominated by the National Republican Convention. The chief issue in the campaign was the Bank of the United States and Jackson's veto of its charter. Personalities still played a major role, however, and the president remained a great national hero to many Americans. It was because of this that Jackson was decisively reelected.

Jackson interpreted his reelection as a mandate for further action against the Bank. Although the Bank had only four more years of life based on its charter, Jackson, ignoring the advice of two successive secretaries of the treasury, ordered the immediate removal of government deposits from the Bank. He then placed these funds in twenty-three state-chartered banks favored by the Democrats, which the Whigs snidely called "pet banks."

What followed was a virtual bank war, with Biddle fighting back by limiting credit, calling in loans, and raising the Bank interest rates, all of which did severe damage in the business community. Biddle believed that perhaps if he could bring on a slight depression, the pressure from the corporate sector would force Jackson to recharter the Bank.

Jackson in turn fought back with the Specie Circular (1836), issued to curb land speculation caused by the paper money printed by state banks without adequate specie backing. This piece of legislation required that all purchases of public lands be paid for in specie (gold or silver). The result of this was to stop the wild land speculation, and the sale of public lands did indeed decline sharply. The Panic of 1837 soon followed. Outmanned and seeing the absolute determination of Jackson to defeat him, Biddle relented and surrendered to Jackson.

The bank war was over, and Jackson had won. But with the

passing of the Bank of the United States in 1836, the country lost an indispensable financial institution, and ominous economic clouds lay on the horizon.

The Election of Martin Van Buren

The presidential election of 1836 was a confused affair. In lieu of a single candidate, the Whigs selected several regional candidates including Daniel Webster of Massachusetts, William Henry Harrison, former governor of Indiana Territory, and Hugh Lawson White of Tennessee. This strategy, masterminded by Nicholas Biddle, was to force the election into the House of Representatives if no one candidate in the election received the requisite majority. The Democrats nominated Vice President Van Buren, who pledged to remain loyal to Jackson's policies. On this basis he won a comfortable victory and became the eighth president of the United States.

Scarcely had Van Buren taken the oath of office when the full force of the destruction of the national bank hit. The Panic of 1837 and the ensuing depression were the worst economic troubles the country had experienced up to that time. While they plagued the nation, Van Buren proposed little more than ending government connections with banks, central and pet alike. In a classic laissez-faire statement Van Buren suggested that the government end its involvement with business and the economy, concluding, "The less government interferes with private pursuits the better for general prosperity."

For four years the severe depression dogged Van Buren's administration. Politicians remained preoccupied with the economy and economic legislation. Out of this came perhaps Van Buren's greatest contribution: banking and economic reform. After much wrangling, Van Buren was able to establish the Independent Treasury System (1840). This "divorce of banks and state" required that government specie (gold and silver) be removed from private banks and placed in subtreasuries along with tariff revenues and receipts from land sales. While this plan protected government funds and discouraged specula- tion, it removed large sums of specie from banks, which used specie to expand the credit needed for carrying on business. By the end of 1837 more than six hundred banks had failed.

The Log Cabin Campaign

By the presidential election of 1840, Van Buren, despite four years of economic woes, still had the endorsement of the Democratic Party. For the Whigs, the most likely candidate would have been Henry Clay. But the Whigs were wary of selecting a man too scarred from the political battles of the past. Instead they went for a man without strong political commit- ments, sixty-seven-year-old famed Indian fighter William Henry Harrison.

A southerner by birth, Harrison could be counted upon, the Whigs hoped, to receive many votes that otherwise would go to the Democrats. He was also a military hero from the War of 1812, and after Jackson, the Whigs had good reason to recognize what an advantage this could provide. Most important of all, he indeed had no known political views, and having lost with their prominent leaders, the Whigs viewed this as an asset.

Throughout the campaign the eager Whigs assumed the of- fensive. To counter their own aristocratic image, they portrayed themselves as not only the party of the people but one that could rescue the nation from depression as well. They criticized Van Buren for his aristocratic habits of using cologne and drinking champagne, and they claimed he engaged in many other "un- democratic and un-American practices."

In response, a Democratic newspaper scornfully suggested that Harrison was a simple soul who would be content to retire to a log cabin if provided with a pension and plenty of hard cider.

This was a major political blunder. In a nation where many people lived or had lived in log cabins, this was virtually handing the election over to the Whigs. Freely acknowledging that their candidate was a man of the common people, the Whigs boasted that Harrison loved log cabins and cider. In truth, however, Harrison was quite affluent and resided in a rather large and stylish house.

That fact notwithstanding, the log cabin became the established symbol at every Whig meeting, and hard cider became the preferred beverage. It became fashionable for Whig politicians either to brag about being born in a log cabin or apologize for not. Against such an onslaught and with the effects of the depression lingering on, the Democrats could not survive.

When Americans cast their ballots for president in 1840, Harrison won a sweeping electoral vote, 234 to Van Buren's 60. The Whigs had succeeded in the formidable task of turning out of office an incumbent president. Once again, the nation had a dynamic and healthy political party system.

Thanks in large part to the presence of Andrew Jackson, by 1840 two new major political parties dotted the American political landscape. After a considerable hiatus that saw government become merely the private domain of public-spirited gentlemen, the American people once more insisted on being heard.

Neither new party was as tied to a single class as the parties' predecessors, the Republicans and Federalists, had been. In all likelihood, the Democrats garnered more support among the independent yeoman farmers than did the Whigs; since small farmers constituted a majority of Americans this made the Democrats in one sense the party of the common people.

Though they differed on banks, tariffs, and internal improvements, the two parties were more accommodating and practical than the Federalists and Republicans had been in the time of the first party system. The emergence of the second party system represented an attempt by both parties to avoid extreme ideological positions and remain as close to the political center as they possibly could.

In 1829, Jackson and his followers had firmly implanted political democracy upon the national government. Refusing to accept the aristocratic practices of the Virginia Dynasty, they had rejuvenated American political life by fostering a healthy opposition. The result was that after the election of 1828, the country never again would be without a two-party system.

Recommended Reading

Harry Ammon, *James Monroe: The Quest for a National Identity* (1971)

Leonard Baker, *John Marshall: A Life at Law* (1974)

Samuel F. Bemis, *John Quincy Adams and the Union* (1956)

Lee Benson, *The Concept of Jacksonian Democracy: New York as a Test Case* (1961)

Richard N. Current, *John C. Calhoun* (1963)

James C. Curtis, *Andrew Jackson and the Search for Vindication* (1976)

James C. Curtis, *The Fox at the Bay* (1970)

George Dangerfield, *The Awakening of American Nationalism, 1815–1828* (1965)

George Dangerfield, *The Era of Good Feelings* (1952)

Donald Dewey, *Marshall vs. Jefferson: The Background of Marbury v. Madison* (1970)

Clement Eaton, *Henry Clay and the Art of American Politics* (1957)

Richard E. Ellis, *The Union at Risk: Jacksonian Democracy, States' Rights and the Nullification Crisis* (1987)

Robert K. Faulkner, *The Jurisprudence of John Marshall* (1968)

Michael Feldberg, *The Turbulent Era: Riot and Disorder in Jacksonian America* (1980)

Grant Foreman, *Indian Removal: The Emigration of the Five Civilized Tribes of Indians* (1932)

Ronald Formisano, *The Birth of Mass Political Parties: Michigan, 1827–1861* (1971)

Allison G. Freehling, *Drift toward Dissolution: The Virginia Slavery Debate of 1831–1832* (1982)

William W. Freehling, *Prelude to Civil War: The Nullification Controversy in South Carolina, 1816–1836* (1966)

Thomas Govan, *Nicholas Biddle, Nationalist and Public Banker* (1959)

Robert G. Gundersen, *The Log Cabin Campaign* (1957)

Richard Hofstadter, *The American Political Tradition and the Men Who Made It* (1948)

Richard Hofstadter, *The Idea of a Party System* (1969)

Daniel Walker Howe, *The Political Culture of the American Whigs* (1979)

Richard P. McCormick, *The Second American Party System: Party Formation in the Jacksonian Era* (1966)

Ernest May, *The Making of the Monroe Doctrine* (1975)

John Mayfield, *The New Nation, 1800–1845* (1981)

Marvin Meyers, *The Jacksonian Persuasion: Politics and Belief* (1957)

Chase C. Mooney, *William H. Crawford, 1772–1834* (1974)

Sydney Nathans, *Daniel Webster and Jacksonian Democracy* (1973)

Dexter Perkins, *A History of the Monroe Doctrine* (1963)

Edward Pessen, *Jacksonian America: Society, Personality, and Politics* (1978)

Robert Remini, *Andrew Jackson* (1966)

Robert Remini, *Andrew Jackson and the Bank War* (1967)

Robert Remini, *Andrew Jackson and the Course of American Empire, 1767–1821* (1977)

Robert Remini, *Andrew Jackson and the Course of American Freedom, 1822–1832* (1981)

Robert Remini, *The Election of Andrew Jackson* (1963)

Robert Remini, *Martin Van Buren and the Making of the Democratic Party* (1959)

Michael P. Rogin, *Fathers and Children: Andrew Jackson and the Subjugation of the American Indian* (1975)

Ronald N. Satz, *American Indian Policy in the Jacksonian Era* (1975)

Arthur M. Schlesinger, Jr., *The Age of Jackson* (1945)

James Roger Sharp, *The Jacksonians versus the Banks: Politics in the States after the Panic of 1837* (1970)

Peter Temin, *The Jacksonian Economy* (1969)

Glyndon Van Deusen, *The Jacksonian Era, 1828–1848* (1959)

Glyndon Van Deusen, *The Life of Henry Clay* (1931)

John William Ward, *Andrew Jackson: Symbol for an Age* (1955)

Charles M. Wiltse, *John C. Calhoun,* 3 vols, (1944–1951)

CHAPTER 11

Antebellum Culture and Reform

Time Line

1775	The Quakers found the first antislavery society in America
1787	Richard Allen organizes the Free African Society
1794	Allen founds the African Methodist Episcopal Church
1800–1817	Paul Cuffe tries to establish a back-to-Africa movement to relocate his people to their ancestral homeland

1800–1820	The second Great Awakening
1820–1860	Many utopian communities are established in the United States
1820	Washington Irving publishes *The Sketch Book*
1823	*The Pioneers*, the first of the Leatherstocking Tales by James Fenimore Cooper, is published
1826	The American Society for the Promotion of Temperance is founded
1829	David Walker authors *Walker's Appeal. . .to the Colored Citizens*
1831	The first issue of William Lloyd Garrison's *The Liberator* appears
	Nat Turner's slave insurrection in Virginia
1832	The New England Anti-Slavery Society is founded under the leadership of William Lloyd Garrison
1833	Oberlin College, later the first to admit women, is opened
	The American Anti-Slavery Society is founded
1835	Alexis de Tocqueville writes *Democracy in America*
1836	The House of Representatives adopts the "gag rule," cutting off debates on antislavery petitions

1837	Abolitionist Elijah Lovejoy is killed by a mob in Alton, Illinois
1839	Theodore Dwight Weld and his wife Angelina Grimké publish *American Slavery as It Is*
1841	Catherine Beecher pens *Treatise on Domestic Economy*
1845	Edgar Allen Poe wins fame for *The Raven and Other Poems*
1847	The independent black Republic of Liberia on the west coast of Africa is established
1848	Lucretia Mott and Elizabeth Cady Stanton organize the first women's rights convention at Seneca Falls, New York
	John Humphreys Noyes's utopian community, Oneida, is founded in New York
1850s	Immigration reaches 2.3 million
1850	Nathaniel Hawthorne publishes *The Scarlet Letter*
1851	Herman Melville writes *Moby Dick*
	Maine passes first statewide prohibition law
1854	Henry David Thoreau, practitioner of transcendentalism, publishes *Walden*
1855	Walt Whitman publishes the first edition of *Leaves of Grass*
1860	Dorothea Dix finally persuades many states

to provide humane asylums for the mentally ill

1865   Vassar College opens, the first all-women's institution of higher education

---

No sooner had the nation developed another two-party political system for representing the majority's will while moderating conflict than innumerable social problems emerged. This era of enterprise and egalitarianism had brought Americans to unprecedented levels of confidence and optimism about the future of their society. Yet it was also a reforming age, one characterized by attempts, real or visionary, to eradicate all signs of injustice and inhumane treatment from American society. Some reformers advocated utopian schemes calling for the perfection of the whole of society. Some advocated the abolition of slavery, the most glaring affront to the principles of the Declaration of Independence. Whatever their cause or purpose, beginning in the 1840s, Americans experienced a heightened sense of awareness about their unique society and its continuing ills.

The Frontier

During the antebellum era, the West was the most rapidly growing part of the nation. Between 1815 and 1860, this region of the country became home for 15 million Americans. By the eve of the Civil War, some eleven years after the gold rush, distant California had a population of 380,000. America, in 1860, was a nation of 31 million inhabitants, half of whom lived in states and territories where settled communities had not existed at the time of Washington's presidency.

Restlessness or flight from law or from creditors prompted this massive westward movement. To many single women the West was a land of opportunity where they could find a husband.

Most settlers, though, moved west for economic reasons, finding commodities cheap and soil fertile.

During the forty-five years after 1815 the American center of population shifted sharply westward. In 1790, the geographic center of American population was only 23 miles east of Baltimore. By 1860, it had reached southeastern Ohio, having moved over 300 miles in little more than four decades.

In many ways most Americans resembled the frontiersmen of the West. Foreigners were appalled by the habits of the ordinary American. "I have rarely seen so many people drunk," wrote one foreign visitor in the 1830s. Chewing tobacco and the accompanying spitting were almost universal.

Violence was commonplace as well. In New York and other major cities it was not unusual for gang wars to occur—between one another or with the police. City immigrant districts were often quite violence-prone, a fact that encouraged many Americans erroneously to conclude that the foreign-born were a threat to society.

During the antebellum era, Americans seemed to have a penchant for rioting. For example, in 1837, Boston volunteer firemen and Irish mourners clashed violently at a funeral procession, and the state militia had to be called out to restore order. A dozen years later, the appearance of a British actor at the Astor Place Theater in New York set off a riot that left twenty-two people dead. The cause of this mayhem? A British actor had snubbed an American actor while on tour!

Discrimination and Prejudice

Besides violence, antebellum American society was plagued by prejudice and discrimination. Obviously, slavery contradicted the American ideal of egalitarianism as epitomized in the Declaration of Independence: "All men are created equal." Critics of the United States eagerly pointed to the glaring discrepancy between the concept of American equality and the presence of black slaves. In the next chapter, the institution of slavery will be discussed at length. But discrimination was apparent in other areas of American society as well, affecting immigrants, free blacks, and women.

The Foreign-Born

Immigration had been light between 1776 and 1826. The number of new arrivals in the 1830s was 600,000. In the next decade the number was 1.7 million. In the 1850s, a staggering 2.3 million people arrived.

These immigrants came mostly from the British Isles, especially the south of Ireland, and from Germany, but they also came from almost every other European country. Most found America a mixed blessing. There were jobs and some land, and no one starved. They could even send their children to school. Indeed, the more fortunate and enterprising could rise from unskilled laborer to small businessman, often providing services or Old World goods for their fellow countrymen.

Nevertheless, a sizable number of Americans were offended by immigrants and treated them with scorn or disdain. Because of the previously light flow of immigrants, Americans were unprepared for, and overwhelmed by, the flood of newcomers after 1830. To many native-born Americans, these foreigners did not appear to be desirable citizens, as they broke the law and drank too much. The Europeans were clannish and refused to accept the customs and practices of their adopted country. Above all, the immigrants were poor.

Confusing causes with consequences, many Americans held the immigrants responsible for their squalid housing, their shabbiness, their ill health, and the unsanitary conditions in which they lived.

Thousands of the new arrivals, including virtually all the

Irish and many Germans, were Catholic, and this incurred the wrath of Protestant Americans, who had a long tradition of anti-Catholicism. Between 1830 and 1860 many violent confrontations occurred between immigrant Catholics and militant native Protestants.

More common, however, was the day-to-day discrimination that immigrants experienced. Foreigners, especially the Irish, were considered undesirable neighbors, and landlords would often not rent to them. When they had any choice, many employers refused to hire Irish laborers or servants. During the 1850s, the classified sections of city newspapers frequently carried the warning "No Irish Need Apply."

Out of the tension and prejudice emerged a number of secret societies designed to combat the "alien menace." Originating in the East but later spreading to the South and West, groups such as the Sons of '76, the Sons of America, the Druids, and the Order of United Americans joined together in 1850 to form the Supreme Order of the Star-Spangled Banner. Quickly, this group became dedicated to preventing Catholics or aliens from holding public office, and to the strengthening of naturalization laws and literacy tests for voting. When members of this secret society were asked what they stood for, they were admonished by their leaders to reply, "I know nothing." Hence they came to be known as the Know-Nothings.

The leaders of the Know-Nothings had political ambitions. Soon they founded the American Party and scored impressive victories in the 1854 elections. In Pennsylvania and New York, the Know-Nothings commanded a large following, and in Massachusetts they gained control of the state government. Opposing immigration and resenting German and Irish Catholics for their religion, the American Party advocated a twenty-one year residence requirement for citizenship. The party's considerable growth soon would be interrupted by the rise of a larger issue in America: slavery.

Free Blacks

The issue of race strained American ideals about equality to an even greater extent than nationality. By 1850, there were about 250,000 free blacks, largely the descendants of slaves freed after the American Revolution, living in the northern and western states. They were concentrated mainly in the cities with about 22,000 residing in Philadelphia and about 12,000 in New York.

Some of the most fashionable restaurants, barbershops, and catering companies in northern cities were run by blacks. The larger cities also had black ministers and journalists. The great majority of northern free blacks, however, were unskilled laborers at the bottom of the social structure.

Bigotry permeated every aspect of the free blacks' lives. They had little or no political influence and could vote only in New England (excluding Connecticut) and in New York—and in these places only if they owned a substantial amount of property, a stipulation not required of white voters. Virtually everywhere they were denied access to the public schools that white children attended. In most northern states they were denied citizenship. Free blacks lived in constant fear of being attacked by white mobs or kidnapped by slave traders who would sell or resell them into slavery. At best, many could hope only for a low-paying job as a domestic servant or unskilled worker.

In the Northwest, various state "black laws" excluded free blacks from residential areas, and Jim Crow laws (so named for a popular blackface minstrel character) imposed separate public facilities for blacks and whites.

Their exclusion from many aspects of white society inspired some free blacks to take matters into their own hands. Richard Allen, for example, organized the Free African Society in 1787, when white officials of the St. George Methodist Church in Philadelphia segregated black parishioners. Seven years later,

Allen founded the African Methodist Episcopal Church, which eventually claimed thousands of black communicants throughout the North and South.

Early in the nineteenth century, a Massachusetts free black, Paul Cuffe, attempted to establish a back-to-Africa movement to relocate his people to their ancestral homeland. Although unsuccessful in his endeavor, Cuffe had spent $4,000 of his own money for this project by the time he died in 1817. In that same year, a group of prominent white Virginians created the American Colonization Society to purchase the freedom of slaves and colonize them in Africa. Northern blacks opposed this scheme as a veiled attempt to get rid of blacks, and led by James Forten, a prosperous black businessman, they rejected the society's plans. With private contributions and appropriations from Congress and the Virginia and Maryland state legislatures, the American Colonization Society did succeed in founding and governing the colony of Liberia for freed southern slaves, on the west coast of Africa, which it converted into an independent black republic in 1847.

Thanks to David Walker, a free black born in North Carolina, a new level of black militancy was reached. Walker left the South and settled in Boston, where he made his living selling secondhand clothing. While there, Walker authored a pamphlet entitled *Walker's Appeal . . . to the Colored Citizens* (1829), an eloquent indictment of slavery. In it, Walker implored all black people to rise in violent insurrection, if necessary, against their oppressors and their oppression. "Kill, or be killed!" Walker warned.

Other free blacks became prominent opponents of slavery. None was more accomplished than Frederick Douglass, who was born a slave in Maryland but escaped as a young man. Having purchased his own freedom after becoming a renowned anti-slavery lecturer, Douglass founded the most respected black newspaper of the antebellum era, the *North Star*, in Rochester, New York.

Despite the emergence of such leaders as Frederick Douglass, things continually got worse for the free black community instead of better. Before the 1830s there had been a place, albeit an inferior one, for blacks in the northern economy. With the arrival of immigrants, the economic situation for blacks deteriorated. While employers, of course, preferred employees born in the United States, they would hire newly arrived Germans and Irish before free blacks.

The immigrants themselves, especially the Irish, were hostile to blacks, perceiving them as an economic threat. And occasionally the immigrants made blacks scapegoats for their own trials and tribulations. Tensions between blacks and Irish sometimes erupted into riots in which numerous people were injured and thousands of dollars worth of property destroyed.

The American Woman

As antebellum society was male dominated, discrimination plagued women as much as it affected immigrants and free blacks. Within the family women were inferior and in their legal status they were humiliated. Unless they were widows, women were required to seek the protection of a man, whether father, husband, or brother. When married, their earnings and property normally reverted to the husband. Women could not sign legal papers, and except in the most unusual of circumstances, their husbands could beat them without legal interference. In a divorce action they lost all claims to their children even if the husband was the guilty party.

Not surprisingly, in these circumstances, females also could not vote or hold office, and their education was often badly neglected. Higher education and professional training were out of the question. Nowhere in 1815 did an American college or university admit women. Oberlin College opened in 1833 and, as noted earlier, became the first to admit women. In 1865, Vassar College, the first all-women's institution of higher learning, was opened.

Urban middle-class women were taught the "3 Rs," sewing, music, and dancing, but subjects like science, Latin, and math were considered too great a strain for their minds. Farm girls and daughters of urban workingmen and craftsmen were taught to read and write, but their educations ended there. Poor parents might sacrifice to send a talented son to secondary school, but they seldom saw the value of educating even the most brilliant daughter.

The need for education for women caused many women to seek careers as teachers. During the 1840s and 1850s thousands of middle-class women assumed positions as teachers. Their mentor was Catherine Beecher, who had established academies for young women in Hartford and Cincinnati.

Led by Beecher, some female reformers sought to improve the quality of family life. Toward this end, they penned books and articles on "domestic economy," encouraging Christians to infuse their households with love. Through magazines and manuals, *Godey's Lady's Book* for example, women were instructed on how to make their homes more efficient and more moral. Beecher's own *Treatise on Domestic Economy* (1841) became the standard text on housekeeping and child rearing.

Yet some women were not content to sacrifice job equality for more control over family life and more access to an education. Because women met discrimination in the job market, they were commonly paid lower wages than men. This fact angered a growing number of women, who demanded more than just domestic equality.

Representative of the more assertive women reformers were Angelina and Sarah Grimké, daughters of a prominent South Carolina planter. In challenging Catherine Beecher, Angelina

Grimké maintained that "it is a woman's right to have a voice in all the laws and regulations by which she is governed, whether in Church or State." By 1840, the Grimkés were calling the traditional familial roles of husband and wife the "domestic slavery" of women to men.

During the late 1840s, various elements of the women's movement, many of whose members did not share the militancy of the Grimké sisters, came together to discover a pragmatic course upon which they could embark to advance women's rights within the existing sociopolitical structure. They did not seek to threaten the traditional division of labor within the family. Their goal was to strengthen the legal position of women in American society.

The opening salvo in this crusade was fired at a women's rights convention in 1848 at Seneca Falls, New York. Led by abolitionists Elizabeth Cady Stanton and Lucretia Mott, the Seneca Falls Convention proposed, for the first time, a systematic and coherent means by which women could achieve equality. The 250 women who met there issued a manifesto of female independence modeled after the Declaration of Independence. The document demanded that women be given control of their own earnings, guardianship of their own children, equal education, and the right to an easier divorce.

"The history of mankind," wrote the women at Seneca Falls, "is a history of repeated injuries and usurpations on the part of man toward woman, having in direct object the establishment of an absolute tyranny over her." They asserted "that all men and women are created equal" and that it was time this fact was recognized.

Seneca Falls was only the beginning. During the 1850s, feminist leaders met in annual national conventions as well as numerous local and regional meetings. They tried, sometimes successfully, to get legislators to liberalize their laws concerning women. They also established newspapers, printed pamphlets, and delivered speeches. Though they met with much scorn and hostility, they kept on insisting that women deserved the rights to sue and bear witness, that the concepts of female inferiority found in accepted religious theology should be revised, and that women should be given the right to vote. In the case of the latter demand, very little headway was made before the Civil War, though suffrage became the ideological and organizational cornerstone of the women's movement.

Equality, then, was a highly conditional element of antebellum America. Even if we disregard slavery, equality was limited and was enjoyed primarily by native, white, adult, propertied males. This evaluation must be kept in perspective, however. Although no one can condone the racism, religious bigotry, and sexism which pervaded antebellum America, it must be remembered that equality was an even rarer commodity in the rest of the world.

The Culture of Antebellum America

During the nineteenth century, American cultural expressions began to become less imitative and assume more of an original nature. By the eve of the Civil War, American literature, architecture, and painting would compare favorably with the best that other areas of the world could offer.

The Emergence of an American Literature

Throughout their history Americans have been readers. During the colonial era they read, among other works, practical manuals, almanacs, and religious works. In the latter part of the eighteenth century, American literary talent found its expression in newspapers, pamphlets, and politically oriented books.

But Americans lacked a true literary culture until after 1815 when the works of two New Yorkers, Washington Irving and James Fenimore Cooper, appeared in print.

With classics such as *The Sketch Book* (1820)—including his well-known tales "The Legend of Sleepy Hollow" and "Rip Van Winkle" (which introduced Ichabod Crane, the gawky school master who became one of the best-known characters in all American literature)—Irving assured his reputation as the first major American author. Born in New York City, Irving first practiced law for a short time but soon became the first American man of letters to win international reputation and to write full time for a living. He was the moving spirit in the publication of *Salmagundi* (1807–1808), a series of whimsical essays in which the name Gotham was first applied to New York City. His genially satirical *History of New York . . . by Diedrich Knicker-bocker* (one of his pseudonyms) popularized the name Knicker-bocker as a word for people and things Dutch in New York.

The novels of James Fenimore Cooper were even more American. Cooper was born in Burlington, New Jersey. His novel *The Spy*, 1821, became the best-selling American book up to that time. Best known for his Leatherstocking Tales of the American frontier, he created a picture of the wilderness which he later found did not necessarily exist. The first of the Leatherstocking Tales, *The Pioneers* (1823), introduced the the adventures of Natty Bumppo, the "typical" American fron-tiersman.

Most of Cooper's novels expressed his contempt for the commercial eastern civilization and attested to the individualis-tic nature of the frontiersman. The five Leatherstocking Tales, which culminated in *The Last of the Mohicans* (1826), concerned the struggle of the proud individual against powerful human and physical forces.

Besides Washington Irving and James Fenimore Cooper, the nation had Edgar Allan Poe, with his mysterious, macabre, and violent stories. A major lyrical poet, he first won fame with *The Raven and Other Poems* (1845). His reviews, poems, and stories boosted the circulation of the *Southern Literary Messenger*

(Richmond, Virginia, 1835–1837). Commonly considered the originator of the detective story, he published "The Gold Bug," "The Murders in the Rue Morgue," "The Pit and the Pendulum," and "The Fall of the House of Usher." Near the end of his short life, troubled by illness and alcoholism, he wrote some of his best-known poems, such as "The Bells," "Annabel Lee," and "El Dorado."

Much antebellum literature flowed from Boston and was characterized by the philosophy of transcendentalism. This philosophy was optimistic inasmuch as it emphasized that people were perfectible and God was forgiving. It was also individualistic, stating that each person must follow his or her own desires. And it was democratic, asserting that all men and women possessed within themselves part of the divine spark.

The transcendental spirit was best exemplified in the works of Ralph Waldo Emerson, who emphasized American freedom and self-reliance, and deplored excessive concern with materialism. His reputation was international, and he was at the center of a group that included such luminaries as Henry Wadsworth Longfellow, Nathaniel Hawthorne, Henry David Thoreau, Louis Agassiz, and Oliver Wendell Holmes. Emerson drew for his lectures and essays from his *Journal* (begun in 1820). Among his most famous works are his first book, *Nature* (1836), and *Essays* (1841, 1844). His *Poems and May-Day and Other Poems* place him in the first rank of American poets.

If Emerson was the theorist of transcendentalism, Henry David Thoreau was its practitioner. Born in Concord, Massachusetts, Thoreau loved nature and disdained material values. He went off to live in the woods at Walden Pond. There he discovered a simplicity in life that caused him to conclude that human beings required very little to achieve happiness. A courageous individualist, Thoreau defied the authorities during the Mexican War by refusing to pay his taxes to support a war that he considered unjust. His essay "Civil Disobedience"

(1849) grew out of that experience. A classic of individualism, the essay inspired believers in passive resistance. His greatest achievement was *Walden* (1854) in which he recorded his life at the pond.

Nathaniel Hawthorne's work reflected the dour, pessimistic mood of early Puritanism. Hawthorne was sardonic, skeptical, and believed the human being had a strong capacity for evil. This attitude he incorporated in such novels as *The Scarlet Letter* (1850), in which he criticized the hypocrisy, insensitivity, and inhumanity of the colonial New England Puritans. His fictional exposure of their cruelty to a woman who had committed adultery mocked the reformers and scientists who wrote and spoke of progress. Other major works by Hawthorne are *The House of Seven Gables* (1851), *Twice-Told Tales* (1837, 1842), and *The Blithedale Romance* (1852).

Herman Melville and Walt Whitman were two more major American literary figures of the antebellum period. In 1851 Melville wrote *Moby Dick,* on the surface a sea adventure but actually much more profound. In the novel's examination of the protagonist, Captain Ahab, and his absolute determination to destroy the white whale, Melville created a powerful allegory of human obsession. The first major author to write of life in the South Sea Islands, Melville penned four novels on Polynesia between 1847 and 1850. His last novel, *Billy Budd,* was written in 1891 but not published until 1924.

Whitman's poetry spoke for American individualism and democracy. He was a sensualist, and few Americans of the antebellum generation so openly stated their lustiness, admiration of personal beauty, and enjoyment of physical love as he did. American readers were surprised by the arrogance and sexual explicitness of his volume of poetry *Leaves of Grass (1855— 1892).* In his prose work, *Democratic Vistas* (1871), he discussed the weaknesses of American democracy.

American Painting

In painting as well, Americans flourished in the antebellum era. Thomas Cole, Asher B. Durand, and other artists of the Hudson River school celebrated the American scene through their works. Emphasizing the American countryside, these artists captured the beauty particularly of the Northeast on their canvases. Their works, however, were more idyllic and romantic than realistic.

More popular were the later works of William Sidney Mount and George Caleb Bingham, who depicted bucolic scenes of rural America. George Catlin and John Audubon brilliantly and unsentimentally captured the spirit of the American Indian and scenes from nature, respectively.

Antebellum Reform

No people in the world exhibited such zeal as the antebellum Americans did for destroying old institutions and replacing them with new ones or such willingness to attack existing social practices and customs. Alexis de Tocqueville, the famed French nobleman who visited the United States in 1831 and 1832 and wrote a two-volume study entitled *Democracy in America* (1835) astutely observed that "in no country in the world has the principle of association been more successfully used, or more unsparingly applied to a multitude of different objects than in America. Societies are formed to resist enemies which are exclusively of a moral nature, and to diminish the vice of intemperance: in the United States associations are established to promote public order, commerce, industry, morality, and religion..."

This, then, was a time of intense social dissent.

Much of the antebellum reform drew its energy and substance from a new religious spirit that swept the nation. In 1800, American religion had not been flourishing. Between 1800 and

1820, however, there occurred a second Great Awakening led by traveling bands of Methodist, Baptist, and Presbyterian evangelists. These evangelists induced thousands of Americans to consider their sins, contemplate a new life, affirm or reaffirm their faith, and join the church.

During these years vast outdoor revivals called camp meetings attracted impressive numbers of rural citizens to preaching sessions, where eloquent evangelists like Charles Grandison Finney, Francis Asbury, and Peter Cartwright exhorted sinners to abandon their evil ways and seek salvation in God's everlasting love and grace. Emphasizing that individual salvation was attainable through good deeds as well as through faith, and maintaining that revivals were needed to preserve the spirit of American democracy, Finney asserted that "the church must take the right ground on the subject of Temperance, and Moral Reform, and all the subjects of practical morality which come up for decision from time to time."

The most memorable of all camp meetings occurred in 1801 at Cane Ridge, Kentucky, where for almost a week, between twenty thousand and forty thousand participants listened to the admonitions of some forty preachers. Hundreds of repentant sinners would lie exhausted on the ground after intense exhortation, agitation, and frenzy. Hearing the fire-and-brimstone sermons, men and women alike would have fits, roll in the dust, and writhe with the "holy jerks."

The zeal to uplift and improve touched almost every institution and every form of behavior. Prison reform was directed at the unsanitary conditions, bad food, and indiscriminate mixing of first offenders and hardened criminals present in the nation's penitentiaries. The unduly harsh sentences and the ambivalence toward rehabilitating those incarcerated also attracted the attention of critics of America's penal system.

Some advocated solitary confinement, hard physical labor, and substantial time for felons to contemplate and repent their sins. Reformers such as Louis Dwight and Elam Lynds, however, achieved the separation of first offenders from perpetual criminals and insisted upon better sanitary conditions, creating more privacy for the prisoners.

With the work of Boston schoolmistress Dorothea Dix, progress was made in caring for the insane. Prior to her reform movement there were few mental hospitals, and the insane were most likely to be confined or abandoned in almshouses, where they were often treated like animals.

With continued and persistent lobbying, Dix had, by 1860, persuaded many states to provide humane asylums for the mentally ill and the insane. In her quest for proper treatment for mental patients, Dix received the timely and influential support of Samuel Gridley Howe, Horace Mann, and Luther Bell.

In searching for the reasons behind insanity, crime, and pauperism, many reformers concluded that these evils could be clearly traced to strong drink. Temperance, then, became a major concern of social activists, who insisted that drunkenness went with lewdness. These reformers erroneously believed that alcoholism was especially prevalent among the lower classes and immigrants. In truth, all classes had their share of excessive drinkers.

In 1826, the American Society for the Promotion of Temperance appeared. Later, as it developed, the temperance movement split into two factions. On one side were the moderates, who wished to educate society on the evils of alcohol in order to minimize the amount of drinking. On the other side were the "total abstainers," who condemned drinking as a sin and insisted that state legislatures prohibit the production, transportation, and consumption of alcoholic beverages.

The conflict between these two factions hindered the progress of this movement until the 1850s, when the total abstainers, under the leadership of Neal Dow, emerged victorious. Maine passed the first statewide prohibition law in

1851. Twelve other states, northern and western, followed with similar laws.

Certainly, the most controversial and momentous of the reform movements was the antislavery crusade. The American Revolution had, of course, undermined slavery in the North. In the succeeding decades, the Quakers, who had founded the first antislavery society in America in 1775, continued to oppose slavery, but they avoided strong attacks on the slaveholders themselves.

By the end of the 1820s, when slavery seemed more firmly entrenched in the South than ever, the antislavery crusade had assumed a more assertive and immediate tone. The most active opponent of slavery during this decade was the New Jersey Quaker Benjamin Lundy, who published the most significant antislavery newspaper until that time, the *Genius of Universal Emancipation*, in Baltimore.

Sounding a much more strident note was Lundy's former assistant, a young Massachusetts printer, William Lloyd Garrison. In 1828, Garrison became editor of the *National Philanthropist*, the first temperance newspaper, and quickly turned it into a journal of general moral reform.

Soon Garrison, caught up in the emotion of the reform movements, developed a strong determination to drive slavery from the land. Toward this goal, Garrison advocated the concept of "immediatism." To him, the gentle, persuasive tone and gradual approach of the Quakers were wrong. Now was the time to demand immediate abolition, he felt, and, if necessary, in a loud, hostile voice.

On January 1, 1831, the first issue of Garrison's own vehement antislavery journal, *The Liberator*, appeared. For the next thirty-five years it would harangue and provoke the South. Garrison's *Liberator* rang with fervor for liberty and righteous determination to end slavery. "I will be as harsh as truth, and as uncompromising as justice," he wrote. "On this subject, I do not wish to think, to speak, or write with moderation. . . . I will not retreat a single inch—AND I WILL BE HEARD."

Despite its urgent tone, at first *The Liberator* attracted little attention. Then, in August 1831, Nat Turner, a visionary slave preacher, led a slave uprising in the Virginia countryside in which 57 whites and at least 120 slaves lost their lives. In the aftermath, a wave of horror gripped the South, and even though Garrison had nothing to do with the slave insurrection, southerners were certain he had instigated it.

In response, the southerners insisted that Garrison and his fellow abolitionists be silenced. Garrison, though, refused to cease publication, and with each passing year he became more intransigent and uncompromising.

Under Garrison's leadership, the New England Anti-Slavery Society was founded in 1832 and the American Anti-Slavery Society the next year. To Garrison, the United States had become wicked by its condoning of slavery. But he alienated many friends of the movement by the extremes to which he went. For example, in 1843, he wrote that the Constitution of the United States was a "Covenant with Death and an Agreement with Hell . . . and should be immediately annulled."

Garrison's rhetoric and principles outraged many, and he was frequently physically attacked where he spoke. Other abolitionists were denounced, heckled, mobbed, and censored. At least one antislavery leader, Elijah Lovejoy, was murdered in 1837 by an antiabolitionist mob in Alton, Illinois.

Antiabolitionist sentiment penetrated to the highest levels of public life. President Jackson attacked abolitionists as fanatics intent on instigating slave insurrections. The president directed his postmaster general, Amos Kendall, to deny the abolitionists the use of the mails to distribute their newspapers, books, and pamphlets. In 1836, the House of Representatives adopted the "gag rule," which successfully cut off debate on the antislavery petitions which were inundating Congress by directing that they be completely ignored.

Yet the abolitionists persevered. Theodore Weld, converted to reform by the preachings of Charles G. Finney, worked against slavery within the Presbyterian and Congregational churches. Weld and his wife, the prominent reformer Angelina Grimké, accumulated an overwhelming amount of information about slavery and published it in a stinging indictment of the institution entitled *American Slavery as It Is: Testimony of a Thousand Witnesses* (1839).

By 1840, there were nearly two thousand local antislavery societies in the country with a membership in excess of two hundred thousand. Such female leaders as Angelina and Sarah Grimké proved to be most effective spokespersons for the antislavery crusade. Free blacks tried to assist the cause as well. However, they were hampered by the prejudice of many abolitionists who defended human equality in theory but could not overcome their actual bigotry toward black people in practice.

In spite of the opposition against them, such prominent blacks as Frederick Douglass, the brilliant editor of the antislavery newspaper, the *North Star,* and Sojourner Truth, an illiterate former slave who spoke with effective simplicity for the cause of freedom, performed important services in the antislavery movement.

Each of the movements discussed thus far—women's rights, prison reform, improved treatment of the insane, temperance, and the abolition of slavery—was an attempt to cure a specific ill of American society. Antebellum America also saw groups of people who rejected wholesale all of American society and chose to withdraw from it completely rather than reform it.

America seemed to be spacious enough to allow models of a perfect society to exist, separate from the influence or contamination of competing life styles or ideologies. Success would lead to imitation, these reformers believed, and soon the country would be replete with communities free of poverty, crime, or sin. Reformers of this sort went off to the woods to found societies based on their idealistic economic, social, or religious philosophies.

During the nineteenth century, it was estimated that more than one hundred utopian communities, with over one hundred thousand members, developed in the United States, most of them during the antebellum years 1820 to 1860.

Utopian communities came in all shapes and forms. Several, including the one created by John Humphrey Noyes, a Yale-educated minister, were inspired by the desire to revise the traditional relationship between the sexes. Noyes's Oneida Community in upstate New York implemented his unorthodox sexual theories: Older men mated with younger women and vice versa, all changing partners at his direction. Men were considered married to all the women. Women had the same rights as men, and the whole community took care of the children.

Most utopian groups, however, sought to replace the deficiencies of capitalism by pooling work, property, and profit in some form of socialism. Scottish mill owner Robert Owen's New Harmony community, founded in Indiana, lasted but two years before internal dissent resulted in the demise of the socialist experiment. Brook Farm, an association of intellectuals established near Boston by George Ripley, also survived only a few years and closed its doors for good when the enterprise continually lost money.

Other groups, such as the Mormons and the Shakers, formed their communities out of religious motivations. All utopians sought relief and escape, however, from a society they considered unjust, imperfect, or without salvation.

All in all, antebellum America was riddled with inconsistencies. People were reform-minded, but there was still racism and prejudice. People were humane-minded, but there were still great signs of violence. People were pragmatic, but there were many unorthodox idealistic experiments in society. Americans were very definitely, as one historian has perceptively labeled them, a "people of paradox."

Interestingly, antebellum reforms and attempts at reform for the most part occurred north of the Mason-Dixon Line. Southerners were becoming a nation within a nation. They closed ranks over the issue of slavery and successfully resisted all the major contemporary reform movements that overtook the rest of the country.

This was ominous. Slowly, but consistently, the South was getting onto a collision course with everyone else over the major issues of the day. To understand how and why this was happening, we must, in the next chapter, stop to look closely at this region.

Recommended Reading

Robert Abzug, *Passionate Liberator: Theodore Dwight Weld and the Dilemma of Reform* (1980)

Sydney E. Ahlstrom, *A Religious History of the American People* (1972)

Gay Wilson Allen, *Ralph Waldo Emerson: A Biography* (1981)

Ira Berlin, *Slaves without Masters* (1975)

Ray Allen Billington, *America's Frontier Heritage* (1966)

Ray Allen Billington, *The Protestant Crusade, 1800–1860: A Study of the Origins of American Nativism* (1938)

Carl Bode, *The Anatomy of American Popular Culture in America, 1840–1861* (1959)

John B. Boles, *The Great Revival* (1972)

Roger Brown, *Modernization: The Transformation of American Life, 1600–1865* (1976)

Frank L. Byrnes, *Prophet of Prohibition: Neal Dow and his Crusade* (1961)

Marin L. Carden, *Oneida* (1969)

Nancy Cott, *The Bonds of Womenhood: "Women's Sphere" in New England, 1780–1835* (1977)

Whitney R. Cross, *The Burned Over District* (1950)

David Brion Davis, *The Problem of Slavery in Western Culture* (1966)

Carl Degler, *At Odds: Women and Family in America from the Revolution to the Present* (1980)

Henri Desroche, *The American Shakers from Neo-Christianity to Pre-Socialism* (1971)

Merton L. Dillon, *The Abolitionists: The Growth of a Dissenting Minority* (1974)

Ellen C. DuBois, *Feminism and Suffrage: The Emergence of an Independent Women's Movement in America, 1848–1869* (1979)

Michael Fellman, *The Unbounded Fame: Freedom and Community in Nineteenth Century Utopianism* (1973)

Louis Filler, *The Crusade against Slavery* (1960)

Linda Gordon, *Woman's Body, Woman's Right: A Social History of Birth Control in America* (1976)

Gerald Grob, *Mental Institutions in America* (1973)

Oscar Handlin, *Boston's Immigrants, 1790–1880* (1968)

Oscar Handlin, ed., *This Was America* (1949)

Klaus Hansen, *Mormonism and the American Experience* (1981)

J. F. C. Harrison, *Quest for the New Moral World: Robert Owen and the Owenites in Britain and America* (1969)

Mark Holloway, *Heavens on Earth* (1951)

Justin Kaplan, *Walt Whitman: A Life* (1980)

Richard LeBeaux, *Young Man Thoreau* (1977)

Gerda Lerner, *The Grimké Sisters from South Carolina: Rebels Against Slavery* (1967)

Gerda Lerner, *The Woman in American History* (1970)

Richard W. B. Lewis, *The American Adam: Innocence, Tragedy, and Tradition in the Nineteenth Century* (1955)

Leon Litwack, *North of Slavery: The Negro in the Free States, 1790–1860* (1961)

John R. McKivigan, *The War against Proslavery Religion: Abolitionism and the Northern Churches, 1830–1865* (1984)

William G. McLoughlin, *Modern Revivalism: Charles Grandison Finney to Billy Graham* (1959)

Helen D. Marshall, *Dorothea Dix: Forgotten Samaritan* (1937)

Waldo Martin, *The Mind of Frederick Douglass* (1984)

Donald G. Mathews, *Religion in the Old South* (1977)

Keith Melder, *The Beginnings of Sisterhood* (1977)

Walter M. Merrill, *Against Wind and Tide: A Biography of William Lloyd Garrison* (1963)

Perry Miller, *The Life of the Mind in America: From the Revolution to the Civil War* (1966)

Perry Miller, ed., *The Transcendentalists* (1950)

Barbara Novak, *Nature and Culture: American Landscape and Painting, 1825–1875* (1980)

Russel B. Nye, *Society and Culture in America, 1830–1860* (1974)

William L. O'Neill, *Everyone Was Brave: The Rise and Fall of Feminism in America* (1970)

Benjamin Quarles, *Black Abolitionists* (1969)

Leonard L. Richards, *"Gentleman of Property and Standing": Anti-Abolition Mobs in Jacksonian America* (1970)

W. G. Rorabaugh, *The Alcoholic Republic: An American Tradition* (1979)

David Rothman, *The Discovery of the Asylum: Social Order and Disorder in the New Republic* (1971)

Mary P. Ryan, *Womanhood in America* (1975)

Henry Nash Smith, *Virgin Land: The American West as Symbol and Myth* (1950)

James Brewer Stewart, *Holy Warriors: The Abolitionists and American Slavery* (1976)

Lamont D. Thomas, *Rise to Be a People: A Biography of Paul Cuffe* (1986)

Alice Felt Tyler, *Freedom's Ferment: Phases of American Social History to 1860* (1944)

Richard Wade, *The Urban Frontier: The Rise of the Western Cities, 1790–1830* (1959)

Ronald Walters, *American Reformers* (1978)

Ronald Walters, *The Anti-Slavery Appeal* (1976)

CHAPTER 12

The Old South and the "Peculiar Institution"

Time Line

1739	The Stono Slave Conspiracy occurs near Charleston, South Carolina
1800	Gabriel's Insurrection, led by Gabriel Prosser, occurs in Henrico County, Virginia, the first of the three great southern slave insurrections of the nineteenth century
1822	Denmark Vesey, a Charleston free black, organizes an ill-fated slave insurrection
by 1830	Every southern state has established strict

	legal codes which govern the institution of slavery in detail
1831	Nat Turner leads a slave rebellion in Southampton County, Virginia
1832	In the aftermath of Turner's Rebellion, the Virginia legislature debates the possibility of abolishing slavery in the state—the last serious discussion of abolition in the South
1836	The House of Representatives adopts the "gag rule" on antislavery petitions
1849	John C. Calhoun devises his theory of "concurrent majority" to protect his section's minority interests
1854	George Fitzhugh publishes *Sociology for the South*
1858	Senator James Hammond of South Carolina delivers his "mud sill" speech
1860	The slave population in the south is about 4 million; the free black population is 250,000, about the same number as in the North

Most of our comments concerning antebellum society have pertained to the North and West. The South, in many ways, was becoming a separate entity altogether as the nineteenth century progressed. At the heart of its differences was its reliance upon slavery, a genuinely "peculiar institution," in the Old South.

Diversity

The South possessed climate and topography as diverse as the remainder of the nation and in this sense was not completely distinct. Nor was southern agriculture monolithic. Cotton, of course, was one of the major crops of the region in the nineteenth century. It was the South's greatest cash crop, being exported to Europe and other regions of the nation. Corn was quite significant as well, comprising a very important element in the southern diet. Cotton may have paid the bills, but corn fed the people and cattle.

The South was not an economically backward region. It did develop its manufacturing potential at a slower pace than the Northeast and the more industrially advanced European nations such as Great Britain, France, and Belgium, but it was by no means devoid of industry. There were lumber and turpentine industries in the Carolinas; extensive mining in Virginia, Kentucky, and Missouri; the Tredegar Iron Works in Richmond, Virginia; cotton mills in South Carolina, Florida, and Alabama; and tobacco factories and gristmills scattered throughout the South.

Since agricultural investment brought such high returns in the Old South, there really was no demand for massive industrializing. Indeed, if one were to consider the South on the eve of the Civil War as a separate country, its per capita income then would rank fourth in the world, behind those of Australia, the remainder of the United States, and Great Britain.

White society in the Old south was complex. In 1860, there were about 383,000 slaveholding families, but few southerners owned one hundred or more slaves. The following chart graphically demonstrates to just what extent the large plantation-owning slaveholders were in a distinct minority:

SOUTHERN WHITE SOCIETY 1860

Nonslaveholders	76.1%
Slaveholders	23.9%
owning:	
1–9 slaves	17.2%
10–99 slaves	6.6%
100+ slaves	0.1%

Clearly, the large plantation of the "Gone with the Wind" kind was rare. Most slaveowners belonged to the middle class and had fewer than ten slaves. This class was made up of planters of modest means who lived in small houses, ate plain food, and, while aspiring to be like the planter elite in wealth and gentility, still had a considerable distance to go.

More common in the Old South, however, was the non-slaveholding yeomanry. These white farmers worked their acres themselves and could hope for assistance only from their grown sons or daughters, or perhaps occasional hired labor. Yet the yeomen were a substantial group, "sturdy, independent, and democratic," as one historian has described them, and they wielded some power. The franchise for adult, white males in the Old South was considerable, and southern politicians had to be responsive to the wishes and needs of the yeoman class if they intended to remain in office.

That fact notwithstanding, the South, much more than the North, was still a land where wealth was concentrated in the hands of a very few. Southern yeomen, however numerous, were economically worse off than their northern counterparts. Travelers throughout the antebellum South frequently commented on the rather impoverished life style of the yeoman farmer. In fact, in some rural areas of the Old South where poor soils and broken topography made farming difficult, white yeoman farmers barely survived.

Too, although the yeoman class had to be politically heeded, its political power could be effectively blunted. The lion's share of political clout in the Old South belonged to the small class of the planter elite, who exercised power and influence far beyond their actual means. This aristocracy personified the aspirations and ideals of many of the nonslaveholding whites. Thus, the nonslaveholding whites, who revered the planters, deferred to them, and could be intimidated by them.

Prominent southerners like Jefferson Davis, John C. Calhoun, and Andrew Jackson, not born into wealth and status, achieved political power by marrying into wealth or after becoming prosperous planters following years of work.

The South's "Peculiar Institution"

Of course, at the heart of southern life was slavery, and that too was an institution characterized by diversity. Like most white southerners, most blacks were employed in agriculture. By 1860, only a very small proportion of the southern population was urban. Of that urban population, about 17 percent was black.

Most southern blacks were of course slaves. But by 1860 about 250,000, the same number as in the North, were free blacks. Free blacks lived primarily in the upper southern states of Maryland, Kentucky, Delaware, Missouri, and Virginia. They also lived in such urban areas as Baltimore, whose free black population outnumbered its slave population ten to one on the eve of the Civil War, and Washington, D.C., whose 1860 census revealed that its population contained 9,000 free blacks and only about 1,800 slaves.

Discounting the few free blacks who became successful in business, trade, or agriculture, most in the South, as in the North, were unskilled laborers who resided in the slums of southern towns, worked at menial tasks, incurred the hostility of whites, and lived without civil rights. Law or custom closed many occupations to them, forbade them to assemble without white supervision, and placed innumerable other restrictions upon them. In truth, they were only quasi-free, yet they had all the responsibilities of freedom including the paying of taxes.

As difficult as it may have been for the free blacks, most slaves would have certainly traded their shackles for the hardships of freedom. Many slaves sought escape to the North and then on to Canada with help from friendly blacks along the Underground Railroad. For fugitives from the deep South, though, the hazards of distance and geographic confusion, of white slave patrols and bloodhounds, were virtually insurmountable. Then, too, for the fortunate blacks who made it to the antebellum North or into Canada, there was the shock and realization that they had entered a hostile world not terribly unlike the one from which they had fled. For, with the exception that slavery was outlawed, the North and British Canada exercised no great liberality where the issue of race was involved. Discrimination, prejudice, hostility, and violence all abounded in these areas which the propagandists portrayed as havens and sanctuaries for the fleeing slave.

By 1860, the South had a slave population of about 4 million, or sixteen times the number of free blacks. Most were on farms or plantations. In contrast to the white farmers, who more commonly lived on their small farm units, almost 75 percent of the South's slaves were found on relatively large plantations, as the chart on the following page demonstrates.

This concentration made a considerable difference in their lives. Where there were many slaves, some could serve exclusively as house servants or skilled craft workers. On large plantations, slave women worked as seamstresses, cooks, or maids in the master's house. By no means were these female house servants free, but their jobs kept them out of the fields and brought them into the world of the "big house," where they tended to be treated better than the field servants were.

SOUTHERN BLACK SOCIETY 1860

Free	6.0%
Slave	94.0%
in groups of:	
1–9 slaves	24.1%
10–99 slaves	60.5%
100+ slaves	9.4%

Skilled male slaves on large plantations also enjoyed advantages. There they worked as drivers, mechanics, craftsmen, butlers, coachmen or valets. A slave with a labor skill was in an unusually strong position. Because skilled workers were often needed in the urban areas, a slave with a benevolent master, and who could fill the need was sometimes even allowed to negotiate his own terms of hire. To be able to do this was in itself an extraordinary freedom for a slave.

Even the field hands on larger plantations were better off than their counterparts on smaller farms. It is certainly true that the life of a slave was a difficult one, but it has been shown that force was not necessarily helpful when it came to producing hard work. Most intelligent and efficient plantation owners realized this and treated their slaves more generously for the sake of productivity. Large plantation owners alone, though, could provide the medical services, weather-tight cabins, and varied diet that were required to approach the maximum efficiency of slave labor.

On the smaller plantations or farms, the slaves lived in much closer contact with the white owner and his family. They often ate at the same table and, because economically the owner had no other recourse, slept in the same cabin. However, such was no advantage for the slaves. A slave who labored under these conditions, in such close quarters with his owner, was constantly subjected to the scrutiny of his master and so forever reminded of his subjugation and inferior status.

It was far more probable that a small farm would face a major economic crisis than a large plantation. What this meant for the slave who lived on a modest farm was the constant fear of being sold to resolve a financial problem. Thus the prospect that their families might be destroyed always accompanied the slaves on a smaller farm unit.

Also, on the small farm the slave was often prevented from establishing the cultural identity and expression that existed in the slave community as a whole.

In this regard, we now know that slavery did not prevent the emergence of an Afro-American culture. Quite the contrary, in fact. The merging of African oral traditions with the American environment flourished, resulting in a particularly rich black music and oral literature.

Songs and stories about God and salvation, about their work, and about their daily lives allowed the slaves to develop a form of group consciousness. These oral expressions often obliquely expressed the slaves' true feelings about their condition, by directly or indirectly calling for freedom.

Music and oral literature, then, comforted the slaves and helped to create an identity for black people. Religion played much the same role, as it was an integral part of the slaves' lives. Travelers throughout the Old South always commented on the deep religious commitment of the black men and women whom they observed. Indeed, many shrewd white planters even employed white ministers to preach to their slaves on the plantations.

The slaves, however, preferred religious autonomy and throughout the Old South black preachers, many of them self-taught and unordained, administered to the spiritual needs of their own race, sometimes in secret. These black religious leaders were much more than mere ministers to their congregations. Frequently the black clergy were the social and political leaders in the slave community as well.

White slaveholders naively hoped that blacks would learn from Christianity the message of submission, would accept their condition, and learn obedience. But black religion had quite different consequences. In the same way that black music and literature helped to engender a sense of black independence, the slaves found in their own version of Christianity a message of hope and freedom. Slaves identified with the Children of Israel and eagerly anticipated their escape from bondage, as evidenced in the popular spirituals of the day.

Intelligent and efficient slaveowners might accommodate the religious needs of their slaves and provide them with medical attention, adequate food, and adequate housing. They might also choose to control slaves' behavior and encourage their efforts by instituting a system of rewards such as allowing the slaves to cultivate their own garden plots, visit friends and relatives, hold parties, or hire their labor skills out to a third party. Yet slavery still remained a system predicated upon coercion.

When slaves needed to be punished, they usually had their privileges withdrawn or additional and arduous work assigned. In addition, the fear of the lash was always present in the lives of the slaves. They could be whipped for stealing, disobeying orders, running away, fighting or drinking. Young males were more likely to be lashed than other slaves, but no group was free from the fear of physical punishment, and this served as a strong force intimidating the members of the slave community.

By 1830, every southern state had strict legal slave codes which governed in detail the institution of slavery. Slaves could not hold property, leave their master's premises without permission, be out after dark, congregate with other slaves except at church, carry firearms or strike a white man even in self-defense. The codes prohibited teaching a slave to read or write, and denied the right of a slave to testify in court against a white person. They contained no provisions to legalize slave marriages or divorces, and the threat of separating families by sale always provided a powerful weapon of social discipline. Modern historians, though, believe that the slave family not only existed, but formed bonds that survived the degradation of slavery.

Physical cruelty may not have been the common experience of the average slave, but it is undeniable that slavery abolished black individual freedom. Ultimately, the slaves' lives were not their own. They could not withhold their labor and could hardly ever benefit from it directly, nor could they express them- selves fully.

However kind masters might be, slavery provided no assurances against cruelty, and when it occurred, the slave had no legal recourse. Black families were preserved when possible, but when it conflicted with the master's interests, they were not. Though some slaves learned to read and write, most did not, and the high rate of illiteracy limited their access to many areas of knowledge and experience.

In the end, of course, slavery reinforced racism. It was a mark of inferiority that stigmatized all black people throughout their lives in the nineteenth century. Its very existence served to encourage the racist theories of black inferiority that were so prevalent in the South and in America as a whole at this time.

The Slave's Response

For the vast majority of the slaves, there was no way out of their bondage. Occasionally slaves were allowed to keep whatever money they had earned and hence were able to purchase their own and their families' freedom. A fortunate few received their freedom at the deathbed of their master, like the four hundred slaves belonging to the early-nineteenth-century political figure John Randolph of Roanoke. Beginning in the

1830s, however, southern states made it difficult, if not impossible, for owners to manumit, or liberate, their slaves. Where permitted, the laws usually called for the removal from the state of the recently manumitted slave. Clearly, the slaveowners opposed the very presence of free blacks, who, by their existence, set a disturbing example for the slaves and who could also provide shelter for any fugitive slave.

The slave system, then, adversely affected white society, as it was forever beset by fear. Although most southerners refused to acknowledge that slavery was an exploitive and cruel system, many realized that the slaves resented their bondage and would end it if they could.

Discontented slaves could express their feelings through individual acts of resistance. They could be intentionally careless with their master's property, destroying or losing tools, setting fire to sheds, barns or farmhouses. They could feign illness or fatigue. Most common of all was the day-to-day resistance of ignoring directions, engaging in slowdowns, and running away. Rarely would a slave attack his master or overseer.

The most feared form of slave resistance was the slave revolt. In actuality, there were very few full-scale slave insurrections in the south. The Stono Slave Conspiracy occurred in 1739 near Charleston, South Carolina. It was the most violent in the predominantly black colony's history. Despite rumors of slave unrest and planned revolts, the timing of the outbreak was a surprise, catching white planters at weekend church services. It began at St. Paul's Parish near the Stono River, within 20 miles of Charleston, and its suppression cost the lives of some twenty whites and a much larger number of slaves.

The first of the three great southern slave insurrections of the nineteenth century occurred in 1800, in Henrico County, Virginia. Led by Gabriel Prosser, Gabriel's Insurrection had an elaborate plan and a large, though uncertain, number of slave conspirators. It attempted to end slavery in the region by capturing Richmond and then killing slaveowners of the area. The insurrection's success was prevented by a sudden torrential downpour, betrayal by two of the conspirators, and Governor James Monroe's quick military intervention. Although he escaped, Prosser was later captured and executed along with thirty-five of his fellow slaves. This insurrection resulted in the tightening of the laws governing slaves and free blacks, gave rise to thoughts of colonizing free blacks, often considered to be agitators, back to Africa, and helped kill whatever antislavery sentiment existed in the south.

In 1822, Denmark Vesey, a free black from Charleston, organized a slave insurrection that was once again betrayed by one of the conspirators. Vesey was a successful carpenter in the city, and his earnings had enabled him to purchase his freedom. His craftsman status afforded him ample opportunity to travel outside Charleston and contact potential conspirators on the plantations. Profoundly influenced by the successful and bloody 1791 slave revolt in Santo Domingo that resulted in the creation of the black republic of Haiti some twelve years later, he offered it as an example to his followers. With advance warning, though, the Charleston authorities had taken precautionary steps, and Vesey's attempted insurrection collapsed. Some observers feared that Vesey had amassed an army of approximately nine thousand slaves, but most likely that was an overstatement. In any event, Vesey and thirty-five of the other participants were hanged and another forty-five were expelled from the state. One of the immediate repercussions of the plot was the swift and harsh repression of Charleston's blacks.

Most successful of all the revolts in southern history was Nat Turner's in Southampton County, Virginia, in 1831. Turner, a field hand and preacher, claimed to have religious visions in which an angry Jehovah appointed him an instrument of divine vengeance, both to free the slaves and to punish a guilty white world. Unlike his predecessors Gabriel Prosser and Denmark

Vesey, Turner concealed his exact plans until the very eve of the rebellion, intending it to happen spontaneously as he went from farm to farm. Along with seventy other slaves, Turner marched through the Virginia countryside killing and burning. Before the rebellion was suppressed by state and federal troops thirty-one hours after it began, some fifty-seven whites had been brutally killed and more than fifteen homesteads ransacked.

In retaliation, white volunteers and militiamen savagely murdered at least 120 innocent blacks. Most of Turner's party was either caught or killed in skirmishes with the soldiers but it took two months to capture Turner, who was tried, convicted, and hanged along with twenty-one others. In the aftermath of Turner's Rebellion, southern states expanded their militia systems, enacted new and strengthened existing slave codes, and closed ranks for good behind proslavery propagandists.

Slave revolts occurred far less frequently in the American South than in other New World slave societies. But whatever psychological or spiritual composure American slaves were able to obtain under the "peculiar institution," an insurrection revealed the genuine feelings of blacks in a particularly chilling fashion. And the revolts never failed to send a tremendous wave of fear throughout the white South.

Slaveowners became obsessed with the fear of slave revolts, and that fear fed on itself, so that for each instance of actual slave unrest in the antebellum South there were hundreds of rumors of slave plots. The result was a population of slaveholders who, by day, convinced themselves that theirs was a paternalistic and benign institution and, by night, feared for their very lives.

Southerners Close Ranks

At times, southern fears and paranoia led to a sincere form of introspective soul-searching. Indeed, even as late as 1832 slavery had not yet become sacred and untouchable. Soon after the suppression of Nat Turner's Rebellion, the Virginia legislature conducted what many considered to be a frightening debate on the possibilities of abolishing slavery in the state.

The debate ended with little accomplished. Slavery in Virginia, as elsewhere in the South, was closely intertwined with the culture and economy of the community, and abolition seemed an evil far worse than the southern fears engendered by the institution. The Virginia debate was the last serious discussion of abolition in the south. Thereafter, the response to slave unrest was simply repression.

Laws requiring slaves to carry passes when they were away from their masters were tightened following slave unrest or rumors of slave unrest. In scores of southern communities, innocent slaves were jailed or even executed in paranoid reaction to anticipated or imagined slave uprisings.

These fears unfortunately cast a pall over the political and intellectual life of the Old South. Many southerners convinced themselves that slave unrest was directly attributable to such outside agitators as free blacks or northern abolitionists. To counteract this, southern legislatures passed laws that made the manumission of slaves virtually impossible as well as laws severely restricting the rights and movements of free blacks. Several states even considered removing free blacks from their midst by expelling them through back-to-Africa colonizing schemes.

The most concerted attack was on the abolitionists, whom southern slaveowners perceived as the greatest threat to the peace, tranquility, and safety of the South. Mails were censored to prevent the distribution and reading of abolitionist literature in the South.

Intellectual censorship occurred as well. Almost everywhere in the slave states after 1830 toleration for social and intellectual dissent weakened. After the Virginia debates of 1832, the subject of abolition was considered closed. When white southern abolitionists like James G. Birney of Alabama, Angelina and Sarah Grimké of South Carolina, and Cassius M. Clay of Kentucky continued to speak out against the South's coveted "peculiar institution," they were denounced, threatened, and ultimately driven from the South.

Whenever possible, southern leaders also sought to prevent abolitionist activity elsewhere in the country. For instance, as we have already noted, in 1836, southerners in Congress, frustrated by the number of petitions seeking the abolition of slavery in the District of Columbia, convinced the House of Representatives to adopt a rule automatically laying such petitions "on the table" without action. This "gag rule" survived until 1844 despite the continued outrage of antislavery leaders and civil liberties champions, who considered it a denial of free speech and a violation of the constitutional right of free petition.

The Proslavery Argument

Not content to be merely on the defensive, white southerners also launched a counteroffensive against their critics. Until approximately 1830, southerners seldom relied upon a spirited defense of slavery; in fact, they spent an inordinate amount of their time apologizing for it. They acknowledged that their agricultural and economic interests depended upon the "peculiar institution," but when pressed they admitted that slavery was indeed a violation of human rights.

Slavery before 1830, then, was a "necessary evil." The South simply could not survive without its black labor force. And because to most white southerners blacks could not be anything but social and economic subordinates, slavery was right for their black population and vice versa. However wrong slavery might be, southerners concluded, it was an economic necessity.

After 1830, though, southerners rarely questioned the institution and began to defend it vigorously. According to the proslavery doctrine, southern plantation life was beneficial for the slaves because they were inferior beings who could survive in society only with the guidance and care of the white master class. Furthermore, the whites claimed that the slaves were treated in a much better fashion than industrial workers in the north or the peasant class of Europe. They also were better fed, clothed, and housed, and more secure than free workers anywhere, the argument went.

Slavery had thus become a "positive good," for it benefited white society as well. To most white southerners, it was the only way for the two races to live together harmoniously. They also maintained that slavery was good for the entire nation because all of the southern economy depended upon it, and, of course, the economic well-being of the nation depended on the prosperity of the South.

The proslavery argument also contended that the Bible and the Christian faith sanctioned slavery. In the Old Testament God made Ham, the second son of Noah, a servant of his two brothers. Ham's descendants, the dark-skinned races, must therefore serve the lighter-skinned offspring of Shem and Japheth. On the other hand, the slaveowners insisted, did not the New Testament apostle Paul advise, "Servants, obey your masters?" By the 1830s, the Bible had become a compelling weapon used by southern slaveholders to justify their institution.

Beyond religion, southerners relied on "science" to explain and defend black bondage. Biologically, blacks were said to be inferior to whites because they had smaller cranial capacities and a more limited intelligence. Thus, these characteristics constituted the specific reasons they could not survive on their own, the argument went.

Southerners such as George Fitzhugh used sociology to champion slavery. Northern freedom had been a failure, according to Fitzhugh. It had not brought prosperity or security to the white population; rather, it had resulted in slums, social instability, and "wage" slavery. The South had avoided all of the pitfalls of a competitive society such as the North by rejecting egalitarianism and individualism and accepting the idea of social hierarchy. Slaves, unlike white free laborers, were not discarded after they ceased being useful to their employers. Instead, they were cared for from cradle to grave by their "betters" in a genteel, civilized society built upon slavery.

In his classic work *Sociology for the South; or, The Failures of a Free Society* (1854), Fitzhugh wrote, "In the whole South, there is not one Socialist, not one man rich or poor, proposing to subvert and reconstruct society." In this boast the South stood in direct contrast to the North, with its numerous reformers and reform groups active at the same time, as discussed in the previous chapter.

Fitzhugh's critique of northern society and its democracy quickly became a cornerstone of the proslavery argument. John C. Calhoun echoed it on the floor of the United States Senate. It appeared throughout Dixie in the pages of newspapers, books, and pamphlets and was frequently heard from the pulpits.

Senator James Hammond of South Carolina gave Fitzhugh's ideas a classic form when he declared in an 1858 speech that there had to be a "mud sill" upon which to erect a civilized, cultured society. This "mud sill" was a class "to do the menial duties, to perform the drudgery of life . . . a class requiring but a low order of intellect and but little skill." Hammond archly concluded that it was far better that these people be black as in the South, than white, as in the North.

Southern Pride

Southern apologists insisted not only that slave society was kinder and more stable than free society, but also that it was more cultivated and creative. In the North, communities were materialistic and money-grubbing, while white southerners were true gentlemen descended from English aristocracy.

With this in mind, many southerners began to demand that the South free itself from northern commercial domination. These southerners argued that the North controlled their commerce, regulated their agriculture, and administered their finances because of its superiority in industry, banking, and trade, and by its continued domination over the federal government.

By 1837, the drive to "liberate" the South economically from the North had commenced. It was proclaimed by such southerners as J. D. B. De Bow, William Gregg, and Edmund Ruffin that the South should do its own importing and exporting as well as its own banking. Though, in the end, this drive did not accomplish its purpose, it did nevertheless contribute to the rapidly growing antinorthern attitudes already present in the South. By 1860, when sectional antagonisms had reached their zenith, southerners were on record against books, schools, magazines, teachers, and everything else northern.

As the imbalance between population and wealth in the North and South increased, southerners began to worry if they would be adequately represented in the Union. Their anxiety was justified, since throughout the antebellum era the South increasingly fell behind the North in wealth, population, and then representation in the House of Representatives.

Until the 1850s, sectional equity was maintained in the Senate by simultaneously admitting into the Union one slave state and one free one. Southerners feared this maneuver could not be employed indefinitely and inevitably more free states would be carved out of the western territories. When this occurred, the South would lose its fragile political balance with the North.

Agonizing over this problem, the South's premier spokesman, John C. Calhoun, devised a formula to protect his section's minority interests. His previous doctrine of nullification no longer seemed adequate—indeed, hadn't since the tariff crisis of 1833— and to prevent the North from eventually dominating the South completely, Calhoun devised his theory of "concurrent majority." Before enacting any law that significantly affected the interests of either section, let it be ratified by both the North and the South. This arrangement would be ensured by a dual presidency, with one president being selected from each region.

Both presidents would have to approve any important measure passed by Congress before it became law. In this way, the South could exercise a veto over an increasingly powerful North and negate the normal tendency of a majority to ignore the rights of a minority.

Calhoun died before the 1850s proved to be the final road to civil war. While his theory of concurrent majority was certainly not practical, Calhoun had not wanted to see the Union destroyed. Indeed, he had desperately sought to preserve it by finding an acceptable accommodation within which the South could live.

By the 1830s, because of their respective courses of development, the North and the South were becoming dangerously antagonistic. Many people in the North, seeing the increased insistence of the South about slavery, began to ally with the abolitionists. Though not necessarily in favor of black equality, these northerners feared that left unchecked, a "slave power conspiracy" would destroy the civil liberties of the entire nation.

Northerners began to wonder aloud whether it was still feasible for the nation to continue to be half slave and half free. Thus, the majority of northerners, though not due to any affection for the black, came to sympathize in varying degrees with the antislavery cause. For the most part, southerners became even more united in defense of their "peculiar institution."

While the Old South was not the cruel, sadistic, exploitive society of the abolitionist propaganda, it was not the "moonlight and magnolias" world that the white planters had envisioned. Rather, it was somewhere between the two extremes. Certainly, there was exploitation aplenty. But there was also a degree of psychological and spiritual autonomy in the slave community, albeit brought on by economic expediency. The white planters' ever-present paternalism was necessary to preserve and maintain the well-being of their slaves—their greatest resource. The southern white planter was a businessman, of sorts; and the bottom line for him was the profit motive.

As they became more convinced that theirs was an ideal world, the planters also became obsessed with the expansion of slavery into the western territories. Certain that slavery must expand for their world to survive, southerners began to view decisions of the federal government as life-threatening. Determined to check the growth of the "slavocracy," northerners became increasingly uncompromising.

The results of these developments were ominous. As we shall soon see, events that ultimately would tear the nation apart began occurring in rapid succession. At the heart of them all would be the controversy over slavery. In this regard, the South was truly a society that contained the seeds of its own destruction.

Recommended Reading

Herbert Aptheker, *American Negro Slave Revolts* (1943)

John W. Blassingame, *The Slave Community: Plantation Life in the Ante-Bellum South,* rev. ed. (1979)

John W. Blassingame, ed., *Slave Testimony* (1977)

John Boles, *Black Southerners, 1619–1869* (1983)

Benjamin A. Botkin, ed., *Lay My Burden Down: A Folk History of Slavery* (1945)

Dickson D. Bruce, Jr., *Violence and Culture in the Antebellum South* (1979)

Wilbur J. Cash, *The Mind of the South* (1940)

Catherine Clinton, *The Plantation Mistress: Woman's World in the Old South* (1982)

William J. Cooper, *The South and the Politics of Slavery, 1828–1856* (1978)

Avery O. Craven, *The Growth of Southern Nationalism, 1848–1860* (1953)

Carl Degler, *The Other South: Southern Dissenters in the Nineteenth Century South (1974)*

Robert Durden, *The Self-Inflicted Wound: Southern Politics in the Nineteenth Century* (1985)

Clement Eaton, *Freedom of Thought in the Old South* (1940)

Clement Eaton, *The Growth of Southern Civilization, 1790–1860* (1961)

Clement Eaton, *The Mind of the Old South* (1967)

Stanley Elkins, *Slavery: A Problem in American Intellectual Life* (1963)

Drew Gilpin Faust, *James Henry Hammond and the Old South* (1982)

Drew Gilpin Faust, *A Sacred Circle: The Dilemma of the Intellectual in the Old South, 1840–1860* (1977)

Robert W. Fogel and Stanley L. Engerman, *Time on the Cross: The Economics of Negro Slavery* (1974)

George Fredrickson, *The Black Image in the White Mind* (1971)

Eugene Genovese, *From Rebellion to Revolution: Afro-American Slave Revolts in the Making of the Modern World* (1979)

Eugene Genovese, *The Political Economy of Slavery* (1962)

Eugene Genovese, *Roll, Jordan, Roll: The World the Slaves Made* (1974)

Eugene Genovese, *The World the Slaveholders Made* (1969)

Claudia Goldin, *Urban Slavery in the South, 1820–1860* (1976)

Lewis C. Gray, *History of Agriculture in the Southern States to 1860,* vol. 2 (1933)

Herbert Gutman: *The Black Family in Slavery and Freedom, 1750–1925* (1976)

Herbert Gutman, *Slavery and the Numbers Game* (1975)

Nathan I. Huggins, *Black Odyssey* (1977)

Ernest Lander, *Antebellum Textiles in South Carolina* (1969)

Lawrence W. Levine, *Black Culture and Black Consciousness: Afro-American Folk Thought from Slavery to Freedom* (1977)

Donald Mathews, *Methodism and Slavery* (1965)

Broadus Mitchell, *William Gregg* (1928)

James Oakes, *The Ruling Race: A History of American Slaveholders* (1982)

Stephen Oates, *The Fires of Jubilee: Nat Turner's Fierce Rebellion (1975)*

Frederick Law Olmsted, *The Cotton Kingdom* (1861, 1953)

Leslie H. Owens, *This Species of Property* (1976)

Frank Owsley, *Plain Folk of the Old South* (1949)

Ulrich B. Phillips, *American Negro Slavery* (1919)

Ulrich B. Phillips, *Life and Labor in the Old South* (1929)

Albert Raboteau, *Slave Religion: The "Invisible Institution" in the Antebellum South* (1978)

George Rawick, *From Sundown to Sunup* (1972)

Ann F. Scott, *The Southern Lady from Pedestal to Politics, 1830–1930* (1970)

Jason H. Silverman, *Beyond the Melting Pot in Dixie: Immigration and Ethnicity in Southern History* (forthcoming)

Jason H. Silverman, *Unwelcome Guests: Canada West's Response to American Fugitive Slaves, 1800–1865* (1985)

H. Shelton Smith, *In His Image, but . . .: Racism in Southern Religion, 1780–1910* (1972)

Kenneth Stampp, *The Peculiar Institution* (1956)

Robert Starobin, *Industrial Slavery in the Old South* (1970)

Sterling Stuckey, *Slave Culture: Nationalist Theory and the Foundations of Black America* (1987)

William Styron, *Confessions of Nat Turner* (1967)

Charles S. Sydnor, *The Development of Southern Sectionalism, 1819–1848* (1948)

William R. Taylor, *Cavalier and Yankee: The Old South and American National Character* (1961)

Richard C. Wade, *Slavery in the Cities* (1976)

Thomas Weiss and Fred Bateman, *A Deplorable Scarcity* (1981)

Deborah White, *Ar'n't I A Woman: Female Slaves in the Plantation South* (1985)

Joel Williamson, *New People: Miscegenation and Mulattoes in the United States* (1982)

Harvey Wish, *George Fitzhugh* (1943)

Harold Woodman, *Slavery and the Southern Economy* (1966)

Gavin Wright, *The Political Economy of the Cotton South* (1978)

Bertram Wyatt-Brown, *Honor and Violence in the Old South* (1986)

CHAPTER 13

Manifest Destiny and the 1840s

Time Line

1818	The United States and Great Britain agree to a joint occupation arrangement in Oregon
1820s	The Mexican government starts to encourage American immigration by offering generous land grants
1821	The Hudson Bay Company, a British fur-trading business, establishes a post at Fort Vancouver in Oregon
by 1835	Some thirty-five thousand Americans are living in Mexico

1836   Texas proclaims its independence from Mexico

                The Mexican Army defeats the Texans at the Battle of the Alamo

                Led by Sam Houston, the Texans defeat the Mexicans at the Battle of San Jacinto, capturing Mexican dictator Santa Anna in the process

                Santa Anna signs treaties recognizing the independence of Texas

1841   Vice President John Tyler becomes president upon the death of William Henry Harrison; he is the first vice president to accede to the presidency in such fashion

1842   The Independent Treasury System is abolished

                The Webster-Ashburton Treaty is signed, resolving some boundary and other differences between the United States and Great Britain

1844   James K. Polk is elected president

1845   Texas enters the Union as a slave state and the Mexican government immediately breaks off diplomatic relations with the United States

                The Slidell mission to Mexico fails to resolve the problems over Texas and the Southwest

                President Polk dispatches General Zachary

	Taylor and his troops to north of the Rio Grande to occupy the disputed Texas border region and protect the Texans against possible attack
1846	The United States and Britain agree to the 49th parallel as a boundary for Oregon
	Mexico declares a "defensive war" against the United States
	The United States responds by declaring war against Mexico
	The Bear Flag Revolt occurs in California
1847	Under the leadership of General Winfield Scott, the Americans defeat the Mexicans at Veracruz and Mexico City, thereby ending the war
1848	The Treaty of Guadalupe Hidalgo gives the United States the provinces of California and New Mexico and confirms the Rio Grande as the southern boundary of Texas

The decade of the 1840s saw many Americans moving west. Whether they sought fame or fortune, wealth or adventure, the call beckoned thousands of Americans to the Northwest and to the Southwest, lands hitherto sparsely populated.

In Oregon, California, New Mexico, and Texas, the American presence signaled potential conflict with the European nations that held dominance there. Out of the Americans' migrations, however, an expansionist spirit arose, a spirit reinforced by American nationalism. As we shall soon see, this burst of nationalism was to intensify sectional hostility. In the end, ter-

*ritorial expansion would open up a Pandora's box over the issue
of slavery in the territories.*

The Oregon Issue

Fur trading had initially opened the West, but in the 1840s
"Oregon fever" struck and many settlers went to the Pacific
Northwest in search of cheap land. A vast territory extending
from the northern boundary of California to the southern boundary of Russian America (Alaska) at 54°40' north latitude, Oregon
was the home of many diverse Indian tribes. The Tlingits, Haida,
Kwakiutl, and Salish—salmon-fishing, wood-working tribes—
were located along the coast. To the interior, the Flatheads and
the Nez Percés lived. Although some of these tribes cooperated
with the white invaders, others resisted. As was the case on other
frontiers, all eventually would be pushed aside by land-hungry,
aggressive whites.

By 1845, there were over five thousand Americans living in
Oregon and they were demanding that their government lay
claim to the area. The ownership of Oregon, though, had long
been held in dispute. At various times in the past, Spain, Russia, France, England, and the United States had all claimed
Oregon country. During the second decade of the nineteenth
century, only Britain and the United States remained in contention. Both countries had equally valid, or invalid, claims, as each
could lay title to the area on the basis of the activities of its ex-
plorers, maritime merchants, and fur traders. Nevertheless, the
British had one indisputable advantage: they were in actual possession of the area with a controlling military presence.

At times, the British suggested that the Columbia River
would be an appropriate boundary between their settlements and
those of the Americans. But the Americans refused, insisting at
least on the 49th parallel, further north. In 1818, failure to reach
any accord had resulted in the two nations' agreeing that the

citizens of each should have equal access to the area for a period of ten years. This arrangement, called joint occupation, was renewed in 1827 for an indefinite period, with either nation allowed to terminate it on a year's prior notice.

By the 1840s, the British in Oregon were watching the steady influx of Americans with growing apprehension. The incoming settlers were clearly reinforcing American claims to Oregon country, and the British simply could not match them in numbers.

The southern portion of Oregon, where most Americans had established themselves, did not interest British officials since it no longer had much value as fur-trapping country. The region to the north, what is now Washington State, was, however, still valuable. The effort to preserve this area proved futile as well to the British, and consequently they moved their base of operations further north into what is now British Columbia. By doing this, the British virtually conceded to the Americans complete control of the Pacific Northwest.

The American Presence in the Southwest

Before Oregon aroused their attention, a few Americans were drawn to the southwest, where Mexico, a former Spanish colony, loosely administered a million square miles of territory. Generally an arid region, these Mexican borderlands from Texas to California did possess some excellent tracts of farmland that looked quite enticing to some American farmers.

These lands once were the northern provinces of Mexico— Texas, New Mexico, and Upper California—in Spain's colonial empire in North America, but after 1822 were provinces in the independent Republic of Mexico. Under Spanish rule the provinces had received little attention from the government of the viceroyalty in Mexico, and only a few thousand whites had settled in them. A similar situation existed under the Republic of Mexico, which lacked the power, the population, and the economic incentive to settle such distant areas.

At one time the United States had made overtures toward Texas claiming that it was part of the Louisiana Purchase. In 1819, however, the United States renounced that claim. Twice thereafter, during the presidencies of John Quincy Adams and Andrew Jackson, the United States offered to buy Texas, only to meet with strong Mexican objections and refusal.

For a while, Mexican borderlands remained sparsely populated, with about half of its inhabitants being Indians. In Texas, the Comanche, Apache, Kiowa, and other nomadic tribes hunted buffalo on foot with bow and arrow as their ancestors had done for centuries. During the late seventeenth century they had acquired horses, and then rifles, from Spanish Mexico. These acquisitions enhanced their hunting skills but more importantly made them formidable opponents of neighboring Indians and the Spaniards who migrated up from Mexico after 1700.

To the west, in what are now New Mexico and Arizona, were the Zunis, Acomas, Hopis, and other tribes grouped under the name Pueblos. Predominantly farmers, these Indians lived in densely populated communities with mud-brick (adobe) structures, called pueblos, that resembled apartment houses. Generally peaceful, these Indians seldom waged offensive war against their neighbors.

Along the Pacific Ocean, in what is now California, existed many diverse Indian tribes. When the whites arrived in the eighteenth century, as many as 350,000 Indians lived there in harmony with their environment.

Into these Mexican borderlands Americans slowly began to migrate. They came to California attracted by its climate and prosperity. They came to Arizona and New Mexico to trade manufactured goods for a hefty profit. But the American presence in the Mexican provinces of New Mexico and California was minor compared with the American impact in Texas, a broad region between Louisiana and the northern desert of Mexico.

The Annexation of Texas

Beginning in the early 1820s, the Mexican government encouraged American immigration by offering land grants in Texas to men like Stephen Austin who promised to colonize the land, swear loyalty to Mexico, and abandon Protestantism. Thousands of Americans attracted by reports of rich soil in Texas availed themselves of Mexico's generous offer. Indeed, by 1835, some thirty-five thousand Americans were living in Texas, a total that was ten times the number of Mexicans living there.

Yet friction immediately arose between the American settlers and the Mexican officials. The Americans were overwhelmingly Protestant and resented Mexican efforts to make them Catholics and prevent Protestant worship. Most were southerners who wanted to grow cotton using slave labor and thus objected to Mexico's attempts to forbid slavery.

The Americans also failed to appreciate the existence of Spanish culture. In condescending fashion, the Americans blamed the illiteracy of the Mexican peasants on their racial inferiority and believed that, in every way, Anglo-Americans were superior to the Mexicans. Convinced that they must bring progress to a backward society, by the 1830s the Americans had become increasingly assertive over the native Mexican population.

The Mexican government, recognizing that its authority over Texas was being challenged by the arrogant settlers, moved to regain control. One new law reduced many of the powers of the settlers, and the government threatened to prohibit slavery after 1842. Stephen Austin protested the changes in policy and found himself thrown in jail.

In protest and defiance, the Texans responded in 1836 by

proclaiming their independence from Mexico. Some fifty-nine Texan delegates met in the little village of Washington, adopted a declaration of independence, established a provisional government, and selected Sam Houston, a former United States Army officer and governor of Tennessee, as commander in chief of the Texas army.

To chastise the rebellious Texans, the Mexican dictator, Antonio Lopez de Santa Anna, advanced into Texas with a large army. Even with the assistance of volunteers, money, and supplies from private groups in the United States, the Texans experienced great difficulty in organizing their resistance.

The American garrison at the Alamo, an abandoned mission in San Antonio, was defeated. The 187 Texans there for a time courageously defended themselves against a Mexican army of 4,000. In the end, however, every Texan, including the frontier heroes William B. Travis, Jim Bowie, and Davy Crockett, died. Shortly after this victory, the Mexicans attacked a Texan force of 300 at the town of Goliad. Significantly outnumbered again, the Texans surrendered, only to be shot down in cold blood on Santa Anna's orders.

Although things looked hopeless for the Texans, Sam Houston, emerging as the national hero of Texas, was able to keep together a small army of 800. At the Battle of San Jacinto in April 1836 (near present-day Houston), he defeated the Mexican Army, killing 600 and capturing 730 prisoners, including Santa Anna himself.

This battle brought independence to Texas. Houston forced Santa Anna to sign treaties ending the war and recognizing independence. Quickly the new republic sought to join the United States. Through its president, Sam Houston, the Lone Star Republic, as it was called, asked for recognition to be followed by annexation.

Although the Mexican government refused to recognize Santa Anna's promises to withdraw Mexican authority from

Texas, it made no further attempt to subdue the province. Texas had won its independence and uneasily settled down to a brief existence as an independent nation.

The Tyler Administration

The controversies over Oregon, the Mexican borderlands, and indeed virtually all the boundaries of the United States fell upon the shoulders of President John Tyler. A stern and rigid Virginian, Tyler acceded to the presidency in April 1841 when William Henry Harrison contracted pneumonia and died a month after his inauguration.

As this was the first time a president had died in office, confusion reigned over whether "His Accidency," as his opponents called Tyler, could exercise the full powers of a duly elected chief executive. In fact, many Whigs, sensitive to the fact that Tyler was a Democrat prior to being named Harrison's running mate in 1840 to win southern and Democratic votes, were reluctant to accord him the respect a president deserved. Tyler, however, refused to accept an inferior status, and firmly asserted his full prerogatives.

In domestic matters Tyler accomplished little. With Harrison in office the Whigs had eagerly anticipated rechartering the national bank, raising the tariff, and implementing other nationalistic measures. Congress, under Whig control, did pass a bank bill, but Tyler, loyal to his Jeffersonian states' rights principles, immediately vetoed it. In protest, Tyler's entire cabinet, with the single exception of Secretary of State Daniel Webster, who had many important diplomatic negotiations to complete, resigned.

From this point on, Tyler found himself in constant conflict with Congress. Thanks to mediation by Henry Clay, however, the Whigs were able to enact part of their program with Tyler's reluctant approval. The Independent Treasury System was abolished, and the tariff of 1842 was passed, raising the tariff rates to approximately the same levels as 1832.

In foreign affairs, Tyler was far more effective. As a southerner, he sought more lands for slavery to expand and flourish. Toward this goal, the president eyed Texas as a warm-climate region where slave-grown crops could prosper. But before he could act on Texas, Tyler's attention was diverted to boundary problems with the British that had intensified shortly before he became president.

In 1837, some American partisans had attempted to assist Canadian insurgents in overthrowing the "tyrants of Britain." Their activities, though, led to the burning of the *Caroline,* a small American steamer that had been ferrying them supplies across the Niagara River. The ship had been moored on the American side of the river, and in the conflict with Canadian regulars who had come across the river, one American was killed on American soil.

Before the controversy over the *Caroline* affair could subside, a bloodless war between Canada and Maine arose over the uncertain boundary that had existed between the two since the Treaty of Paris in 1783. When Canadian lumberjacks began operations to build a road along the Aroostook River, American lumbermen moved in to stop them. Maine called out its militia, as did New Brunswick, in the Aroostook War in 1839. Serious fighting was avoided when the two militias were ordered to desist temporarily as a compromise was attempted.

Such was the strained situation between the United States and Britain when Tyler became president. To resolve the problems, Tyler instructed Secretary of State Daniel Webster to negotiate with British minister Lord Ashburton. With both sides wanting to avoid increased hostilities, many recurring differences were compromised in the Webster-Ashburton Treaty (1842). By its terms, the United States and Great Britain agreed on a Canadian-American boundary from the Atlantic to the Rocky

Mountains. In the matter of Britain's practice of searching vessels suspected of engaging in the slave trade, it was agreed that each nation would keep a squadron off the African coast and enforce its own laws on those merchantmen flying its flag. In supplemental notes, Ashburton apologized for the *Caroline* incident.

Although the Webster-Ashburton Treaty was criticized on both sides of the Atlantic as "capitulation," it had the effect of easing the long existing tensions. The treaty also facilitated peaceful settlement of other controversies that would soon arise between the United States and Great Britain.

The Oregon boundary dispute, however, remained unsettled. Many Americans claimed that the United States owned all of Oregon country from the northern boundary of California at 42° north latitude to the southern boundary of Russian America at 54° 40′ north latitude. Tyler informed the British that he would compromise at the 49th parallel, but the British were not predisposed toward his offer. Consequently, nothing was resolved in the Pacific Northwest.

Tyler's greatest diplomatic success came in Texas. No sooner had the Texans declared their independence from Mexico than they sought admission into the Union. Their request, though, was not met with universal approval. The Whigs, eager to centralize national power within the existing boundaries of the United States, feared that the annexation of Texas would spread that power over too large a domain. Many northerners opposed Texas on the grounds that it would surely enter the Union as one or more slave states and thus disrupt the delicate balance by giving the slave states too much power. Others were certain that since the Mexican government refused to recognize the independence of Texas, annexation would precipitate war with Mexico.

With so many Americans opposed to slavery, skeptical of territorial expansion, or frightened at the prospects of war, the annexation of Texas seemed like a political time bomb, and for a while, American politicians gingerly avoided it.

Yet the issue could not be sidestepped for very long. Soon, a number of factors prompted the Americans into action. Discouraged by American indifference, the Texans began to consider negotiations with France and England for recognition and loans, which disturbed many Americans. Proannexation sentiment was further reinforced by an influential group of American businessmen who owned Texas bonds and lands and who believed that annexation would guarantee the safety and profit of these investments.

An annexation treaty was submitted to the Senate in 1844, but a strong element of that body, certain that Texas would unbalance the relations between free and slave states, caused its defeat to avoid that. Then, as the presidential contest of 1844 approached, the annexation of Texas and definition of the Oregon boundary became the main issues.

The Election of 1844

Because of his four years of opposing the Whigs, Tyler had completely lost the support of his nominal party and was not seriously considered for renomination. Instead, the Whigs again turned to Henry Clay, who opposed annexation on the grounds that it would mean war with Mexico. Rather than contradict their candidate's stated principles, the Whigs avoided any mention of Oregon or Texas in their platform in order to maintain party harmony.

The Democrats found themselves deadlocked over a presidential candidate. Martin Van Buren, defeated four years earlier by William Henry Harrison, would have seemed to be the front-runner, but he opposed annexation, which ran counter to the majority of the party.

Finally, after days of political wrangling and on the ninth

ballot, the Democrats were able to agree on a candidate. James K. Polk of Tennessee, former Speaker of the House of Representatives, became his party's choice.

The Democratic platform called for "the reoccupation of Oregon and the reannexation of Texas at the earliest practicable period." This wording clearly implied that the United States was merely exerting preexisting rights in these regions. That this belief represented accurate history was dubious at best; that it adequately expressed the convictions of the enthusiastic expansionists was not.

Winning by just a few popular votes, Polk emerged victorious, and consequently the annexationist cause received much impetus. Although Polk's election was not a strong mandate for expansion, many formerly undecided citizens, now concluding that annexation was inevitable, threw their support to it.

Indeed, even Tyler, as lame-duck president, viewed the election returns as a mandate for annexation. With this in mind, he shrewdly proposed that Congress adopt a joint annexation resolution that would require only a simple majority in both houses. Tyler knew that this device would avoid the cumbersome necessity of obtaining a two-thirds majority in the Senate for ratification of a treaty with the Lone Star Republic.

Tyler's ploy worked and Congress passed the resolution. In the closing hours of his administration, Tyler signed the joint resolution. By the end of 1845, Texas entered the Union as a slave state.

The Influence of Manifest Destiny

The annexation of Texas reawakened old boundary disputes with Mexico, and immediately, the Mexican government broke off diplomatic relations with the United States. The Mexican minister to Washington eagerly returned to Mexico City to tell his superiors that the Americans were weak and divided and would avoid war at all costs.

But the minister had vastly underestimated the new American president, James K. Polk. A remarkably strong-willed man, Polk resembled his hero and mentor, Andrew Jackson, in aggressiveness and determination. Soon Polk had mastered the details of government and set out to accomplish his campaign goal of territorial expansion.

Like many Americans of his generation, Polk was influenced by the doctrine of Manifest Destiny. First given a name in 1845 by newspaper editor John L. O'Sullivan in his paper, *Democratic Review*, this doctrine prophesied "the fulfillment of our manifest destiny to overspread the continent allotted by Providence for the free development of our yearly multiplying millions." In other words, the United States had a divine mission to subdue the whole of North America, by force if necessary, not stopping until it reached the oceans, its natural boundaries. Thus room would be made for the rapidly growing American people, who would carry the blessings of democracy to less fortunate people who just happened to occupy attractive lands nearby.

Manifest Destiny was certainly not a new doctrine. It had been with Americans from their earliest history. However, the tremendous national energies that had been unleashed by independence and the aggressive economic opportunism and confidence that accompanied antebellum economic growth brought it to a peak in the 1840s.

It did serve, at times, to justify selfish national interest. All too often, it sanctioned brutal disregard of the rights of others because it contained a large degree of cultural and racial arrogance. Its implicit theme that American civilization and "Anglo-American stock" were superior revealed a contempt for the nonwhite and Hispanic peoples and cultures of North America.

Yet the doctrine also paradoxically presupposed the extending of civil and political equality to all those, except tribal Indians and blacks, incorporated into the Union. The result was not to be an empire of subjected peoples, but a nation of equal, self-governing states in which the laws and a democratic political system would apply to all regardless of national origins, religion, or language. Only Americans, though, were divinely chosen.

Polk and his cabinet fully endorsed the principles of Manifest Destiny. The president believed American claims in Oregon and California were superior to all others. Enthusiastically Polk echoed the battle cry of the expansionists, "Fifty-four forty or fight," in regard to the northern border of Oregon country. He also supported the Texans' claims that their territory extended south to the Rio Grande. The Mexican government insisted instead that Texas stopped at the Nueces River, many miles to the northeast of the Rio Grande. Polk never questioned the Texans' claims and stood ready to use force to defend them.

Opposition to Manifest Destiny and expansion largely came from New England antislavery advocates, who feared that any territorial growth, and particularly Texas, would only enhance an already dangerous "slavocracy." Primary support came from the northeastern and northwestern commercial and industrial communities, which looked forward to continental markets and the access to the Far East that Pacific ports might provide. Of course, southerners were eager to expand their "peculiar institution" into Texas, but they were largely indifferent about Oregon.

Politically speaking, antislavery Whigs saw expansion as favoring slavery and thus opposed territorial growth on moral and ethical grounds. On the other hand, the Democrats generally favored expansion and regarded slavery as either a tangential issue or, if they lived in the South, welcomed it.

Through a variety of negotiations, the Oregon boundary was soon settled. With both the British and Americans wanting to avoid war, a compromise was enacted in June 1846. In this agreement, the existing Canadian-American boundary, the 49th parallel, was extended all the way to the Pacific. This boundary had been established in the Rush-Bagot Agreement back in 1817. Named for acting Secretary of State Richard Rush and British minister Charles Bagot, the agreement had initially applied only to the Great Lakes region. Now, with the exception of Vancouver Island, which was to be reserved entirely for Britain, the Rush-Bagot line was extended to the west coast making an unarmed frontier line of some 3,000 miles, the longest such boundary in the world.

Despite some chest pounding by bellicose expansionists, the Senate ratified the treaty, embodying the agreement by an almost three-to-one margin. The Oregon question, which had dragged on since 1819 when Spain renounced to the United States the territory north of California, had finally been settled by common sense and conciliation on both sides.

The Road to War with Mexico

The treaty with Britain was concluded not a minute too soon for the United States, since war with Mexico seemed imminent. In the fall of 1845, Polk had sent John Slidell, a Louisiana politician, to Mexico in hopes of negotiating for what the United States wanted. If Mexico would acknowledge the Rio Grande boundary for Texas, the United States would assume damage claims, amounting to several million dollars, which Americans held against Mexico. If Mexico would cede New Mexico, the United States would pay $5 million. For California, the United States would pay up to $25 million. Perhaps naively, Polk did not expect these negotiations to fail despite many Mexican officials' openly calling for war against the United States.

The Slidell mission was a failure from the start. The incumbent Mexican government of José Herrera, initially inclined to negotiate, backed down under public pressure and then was overthrown by a more militant government. The new government under Mariano Paredes immediately began to negotiate with Britain for support against the United States should war come.

Disgusted with what he considered Mexican treachery, Polk dispatched General Zachary Taylor and his troops to the north bank of the Rio Grande to occupy the disputed Texas border region and protect Texas against possible attack. In retaliation, Mexico expelled Slidell, and with his dismissal any hope for a negotiated settlement faded.

By spring 1846, Polk concluded war was unavoidable. On April 23, Paredes announced that Mexico was declaring a "defensive war" on the United States, and word soon reached Washington that the Mexicans were preparing to attack Taylor's army.

Polk and his entire cabinet, with the lone exception of Secretary of the Navy George Bancroft, agreed that a declaration of war was justified. But before Secretary of State James Buchanan could present a needed preliminary formal declaration of grievances against Mexico, news reached Washington that the Mexicans had crossed the Rio Grande into the disputed region and attacked Taylor's army.

Within forty-eight hours, the president was reading his war message to Congress. "Mexico has passed the boundary of the United States," Polk said, "and shed blood upon American soil." By a vote of 40 to 2 in the Senate and 174 to 14 in the House, Congress heeded the president's request and declared war on Mexico.

Although Congress had approved the war with near unanimity, there was much more opposition than appeared on the surface, and it intensified as the costs and casualties of the war came home to the American people. While the Whigs in Congress supported the military appropriations bills, they became increasing-

ly strident in denouncing "Mr. Polk's War" as aggressive in
origin and objectives.

The Mexican War

From the outset, President Polk assumed the responsibility
of formulating a grand strategy, and he continued this practice
for virtually the duration of the war. Quite simply, it was his intention to capture key areas along the Mexican frontier early in
the war and then force the Mexicans to negotiate on American
terms. Toward this goal, he ordered Taylor to cross the Rio
Grande into northeastern Mexico and take the city of Monterrey.
Old Rough and Ready, as Taylor was called, accomplished this
in September 1846.

Two more offensives were aimed at New Mexico and
California. General Stephen W. Kearny took the town of Santa
Fe, the key to control of New Mexico, in the summer of 1846,
encountering almost no opposition along the way. From there
he marched on to take California, but when he arrived, he found
a revolt being staged by the settlers. The fear of Americans in
California that they might be forced to leave by a hostile Mexican
government gave rise to this Bear Flag Revolt (1846) against
Mexican rule. It received its name from the design of their flag
of the "Republic of California," which displayed a grizzly bear
facing a red star. John C. Frémont, who had ostensibly been ex-
ploring the area for the American government, joined the settlers
in their revolt and was eventually joined by American naval forces when they arrived off the coast of California.

Nevertheless, it took Kearny several months to bring all the
disparate factions in California under his command. By the fall
of 1846, Kearny had completed his conquest of California.

With California, New Mexico, and northeastern Mexico
under American command, the United States now had possession of more than what it had gone to war to obtain. But even

with America's war objectives achieved, the Mexican government would not agree to a peace and cede the desired territory. Frustrated by this, Polk turned to the commanding general of the Army and a much-decorated and revered soldier, Winfield Scott, for assistance.

Polk and Scott then devised a plan that would force the Mexicans into peace. From Veracruz, on the Gulf coast, Scott would march westward along the National Highway to Mexico City. As Scott was organizing his army off the coast, General Santa Anna, again in power as Mexican dictator, attempted to take advantage of the temporary division of American forces. Santa Anna hoped to march northward, crush Taylor's army, and then return to deal with Scott.

With a much larger army than Taylor's, Santa Anna attacked the Americans at Buena Vista in February 1847. But he could not defeat Taylor and instead was forced to return to Mexico City to defend the capital. In the meantime, Scott had taken Veracruz and had commenced moving inland. Without losing a battle, Scott marched an army whose numbers never exceeded fourteen thousand well into enemy territory. In April 1847, he encountered Santa Anna at Cerro Gordo and routed the Mexicans. Resuming his advance on Mexico City, Scott again defeated Santa Anna at Contreras and Churubusco.

After capturing the fortress at Chapultepec, Scott and the Americans captured the Mexican capital. On September 13, 1847, the American flag was raised by a battalion of U.S. Marines over the "halls of Montezuma." The war was over.

Making the Peace

The war lasted two years and cost thirteen thousand American lives and $100 million. As wars go, the Mexican conflict was brief. The peace negotiations, however, dragged on for some five months. Although they were clearly beaten by any military measure, the Mexicans refused to accept the consequences of defeat.

Negotiations begun by Nicholas Trist well before the fall of Mexico City and Santa Anna's defeat broke down innumerable times when the Mexicans refused to surrender any of their country's territory. For their part, the Americans' indecision about how much territory they should demand also prevented a rapid settlement. At the beginning of the war, the ambitions of most Americans were modest: California and New Mexico. With each victory the demands became greater until "All Mexico" became a popular slogan and movement.

For a time, the "All Mexico" movement seemed too compelling to stop. Besides its appeal as the logical outcome of Manifest Destiny, it was attractive to America's commercial interests. The apprehensions of a majority of Americans over assuming the responsibility of governing an alien, non-English-speaking people with different institutions and traditions, however, ultimately put an end to the "All Mexico" issue.

In the meantime, negotiations went agonizingly slowly. In October 1847, the president recalled Trist, but the stubborn diplomat refused to leave and instead continued his talks with the Mexicans. Faced with the alternative of continued fighting, the Mexicans finally concluded they must make peace.

On February 2, 1848, they signed an agreement with Trist. The Treaty of Guadalupe Hidalgo gave the United States the provinces of California and New Mexico and confirmed the Rio Grande as the southern boundary of Texas. From the Mexican cession came the present states of California, Nevada, and Utah—the province of California—and parts of Arizona, New Mexico, Wyoming, and Colorado—the province of New Mexico. In return, the United States agreed to pay Mexico $15 million and assume $3.5 million of American claims against the Mexican government.

These terms differed only slightly from those Slidell had

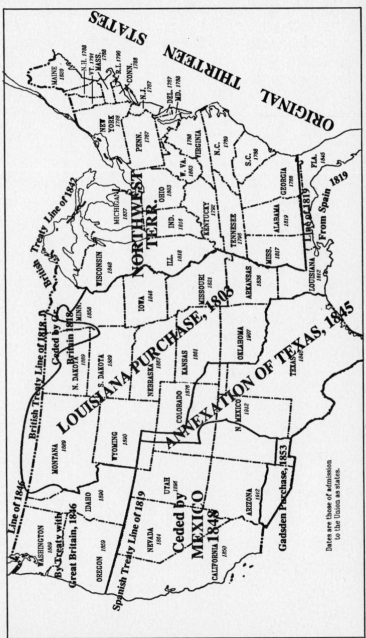

Territorial Growth of the United States

been authorized to propose before the war, and some Americans were opposed to them. Why, they asked with much indignation, after engaging in a costly but completely victorious military campaign, take only what you had asked for in the first place?

Most Americans, however, were inclined to accept the terms, and the treaty was ratified in the Senate by a vote of thirty-eight to fourteen.

The Mexican War was part of an expansion movement that had excited most Americans. In seeking territorial gain, Americans appeared to be unified. Indeed, their zeal for Manifest Destiny would indicate that westward migration was a phenomenon over which most Americans—and their government, for that matter—had little control. Greed, or acquisitiveness, and aggressiveness were integral parts of nineteenth-century Americans' character, and in all likelihood no exhortation—moral, legal or otherwise—would have deterred them. In this sense, perhaps the Mexican War was inevitable.

Most Americans welcomed the fruits of their victory with Mexico by basking in the glow of nationalism and ethnocentrism. But as we shall shortly see, the Mexican War, with the vast territory it yielded, ironically led to the most serious threat of disunion yet to confront the United States. The many sectional issues that the cession of all these lands would raise would not be settled until the culmination of a bitter and destructive civil war some seventeen years hence.

Recommended Reading

Eugene C. Barker, *Mexico and Texas, 1821–1835* (1928)

K. Jack Bauer, *The Mexican War, 1846–1848* (1974)

Ray Allen Billington, *The Far Western Frontier, 1830–1860* (1956)

Ray Allen Billington, *Westward Expansion* (1974)

William C. Binkley, *The Expansionist Movement in Texas, 1836–1950* (1925)

William C. Binkley, *The Texas Revolution* (1952)

Gene M. Brack, *Mexico Views Manifest Destiny, 1821–1846* (1975)

Edward M. Burns, *The American Idea of Mission: Concepts of a National Purpose and Destiny* (1957)

Albert B. Corey, *The Crisis of 1830–1842 in Canadian-American Relations* (1941)

Bernard De Voto, *Across the Wide Missouri* (1947)

Bernard De Voto, *Year of Decision!* (1942)

Robert L. Duffus, *The Santa Fe Trail* (1930)

Charles W. Elliott, *Winfield Scott* (1937)

William H. Goetzmann, *Army Exploration in the American West, 1803–1863* (1959)

Norman A. Graebner, *Empire on the Pacific: A Study in American Continental Expansion* (1955)

Holman Hamilton, *Zachary Taylor: Soldier of the Republic* (1941)

Julie Roy Jeffrey, *Frontier Women: The Trans-Mississippi West, 1840–1880* (1979)

Robert W. Johannsen, *To the Halls of the Montezumas: The Mexican War in the American Imagination* (1985)

Frederick Merk, *Manifest Destiny and Mission in American History* (1963)

Frederick Merk, *The Monroe Doctrine and American Expansion, 1843–1849* (1966)

Frederick Merk, *Slavery and the Annexation of Texas* (1972)

Robert J. Morgan, *A Whig Embattled* (1954)

Francis Parkman, *The Oregon Trail* (1849, 1964)

Leonard Pitts, *The Decline of the Californias* (1970)

David M. Pletcher, *The Diplomacy of Annexation: Texas, Oregon, and the Mexican War* (1973)

O. B. Raulk, *North America Divided, 1846–1848* (1971)

John H. Schroeder, *Mr. Polk's War* (1973)

Robert Seager, *And Tyler Too* (1963)

Charles G. Sellers, *James K. Polk: Continentalist, 1843–1849* (1966)

Otis Singletary, *The Mexican War* (1960)

Henry Nash Smith, *Virgin Land: The American West as Symbol and Myth* (1950)

Kevin Starr, *America and the California Dream, 1850–1915* (1973)

John David Unruh, *The Plains Across: The Overland Emigrants and the Trans-Mississippi West, 1840–1860* (1978)

Albert K. Weinberg, *Manifest Destiny* (1936)

CHAPTER 14

The Bonds of Union Loosen

Time Line

1780	Pennsylvania is the first state to abolish slavery
1787	The Northwest Ordinance excludes slavery from the territory west of Pennsylvania and north of the Ohio River
1820	The Missouri Compromise excludes slavery north of 36°30′ in the Louisiana Purchase territory
1839	The Liberty Party is founded to stop the "slave power"

1846	David Wilmot proposes his Proviso to exclude slavery from every part of the Mexican cession
1848	The Free-Soil Party is formed and endorses Martin Van Buren as its presidential candidate
	Zachary Taylor is elected president
1849	The California gold rush draws thousands to the West
1850	Zachary Taylor dies and Vice President Millard Fillmore becomes president
	The Compromise of 1850 is passed, including a new federal Fugitive Slave Law
	John C. Calhoun dies
1852	Daniel Webster and Henry Clay die
	Harriet Beecher Stowe publishes *Uncle Tom's Cabin*
	Franklin Pierce is elected president
1854	The Gadsden Purchase—America's purchase of the southern part of Arizona and New Mexico—is ratified by the Senate
	The Kansas-Nebraska Act is passed
	Southerner William Walker establishes himself as dictator of Nicaragua
	The Ostend Manifesto is issued
	The Republican Party is formed

1856	John Brown and his followers murder proslavery settlers at Pottawatomie Creek in "Bleeding Kansas"
	The Brooks-Sumner affair brings violence to the U.S. Capitol
	James Buchanan is elected president
1857	The Dred Scott decision states that Congress has no authority to prohibit slavery from the territories
1858	The English Bill passes Congress
	The Lincoln-Douglas debates focus national attention on the Illinois senatorial contest
1859	John Brown leads a raid on the federal arsenal at Harpers Ferry
1860	The Democratic Party splits over the nominating of a presidential candidate; northern Democrats nominate Stephen A. Douglas and southern Democrats nominate John C. Breckinridge
	The Constitutional Union Party is formed and nominates John Bell as its presidential candidate
	Republican Abraham Lincoln is elected president
	South Carolina secedes from the Union and is soon followed by six more lower southern states

1861   The Confederate States of America is
                formed; Jefferson Davis is named president

                Confederate troops under the command of
                General Pierre G. T. Beauregard attack
                federal-held Fort Sumter in Charleston
                harbor

                Four upper southern states—Virginia, North
                Carolina, Arkansas, and Tennessee—secede
                from the Union to join the Confederacy

                Kansas enters the Union as a free state

No sooner had the Mexican War ended than the tensions and hostilities between the North and the South began to claim the nation's attention. Certainly this had been brewing for quite some time. But the Mexican War unleashed a torrent of pent-up frustrations and anxieties on both sides of the Mason-Dixon Line and, in the process, set the country on the path to the most disastrous and destructive confrontation in its history.

The Deep-Rooted Sectional Differences

Both the North and South were highly complicated societies with a variety of dissenters. Only a minority of northerners were abolitionists, and many considered such people fanatics or meddlers. The North also contained many "doughfaces"—a name disparagingly given by John Randolph of Virginia to northern congressmen who voted for extending slavery into the territories. The South, too, was divided somewhat, as it included a few who urged industrialization and manufacturing development in the region. Among the small farmers in upland and backcountry areas there were some who despised slavery and the planter class. One such person was Hinton R. Helper, a small farmer from North Carolina who authored *The Impending Crisis of the South* (1857). Helper was hailed in the North and denounced in the South, since he sought to show not only that slavery economically unprofitable but that it was ruinous to the nonslaveholding whites of the South as well. Indeed, to Helper, slavery was "the root of all the shame, poverty, ignorance, tyranny, and imbecility of the South."

Despite internal divisions, however, there gradually emerged two distinct sectional outlooks which progressively intensified and became more antagonistic. Southern leaders glorified in their agricultural society based on slavery. They condemned dissent and resisted any changes to their world. While not all southerners condoned these attitudes, their opposition was nevertheless a silent one, as it became virtually impossible for dissenters to speak out against the overwhelming weight of majority opinion.

In the North there likewise developed a distinctive ideology, though it developed more slowly and never became so widely accepted as the South's. At the heart of the emerging northern ethos was freedom: freedom to engage in social experiments, freedom to criticize and dissent, freedom to migrate, freedom to attempt upward social mobility. Though freedom, of course, represented different things to different people, there occurred in the North an increasing consensus on "free" values and attitudes.

Besides differences in values and attitudes, economic issues served as a wedge between the sections. Tariffs, federal appropriations, and internal improvement subsidies always created sectional tensions during congressional debates. The industrial, commercial North and the agricultural South seemingly were becoming economically incompatible by the end of the Mexican War.

The desire for a transcontinental railroad exacerbated an already bad situation. By the early 1850s most Americans, regardless of section, strongly supported the concept of a railroad connecting the populated portions of the country with the recently acquired western territories. Southerners, however, wanted a route that would link New Orleans with San Diego or Memphis with San Francisco while northerners demanded that the railroad connect Chicago or Milwaukee with either San Francisco or Puget Sound.

As a result of the constant quarreling, nothing was accomplished in regard to the transcontinental railroad. One remaining boundary dispute, though, was resolved at least in part because of the railroad issue. In 1853, James Gadsden, American minister to Mexico, was authorized by the prosouthern president Franklin Pierce to purchase from Mexico a small piece of territory which now comprises the southern parts of Arizona and of New Mexico. In fact, this land rounded out the present-day continental limits of the United States. The land was particularly sought by southerners for their desired transcontinental railroad route, and they were able to get the Senate to ratify the Gadsden Purchase (1854). After the area was purchased, however, northern senators were able to veto the southern route for the railroad.

Sectional conflict over economic issues, then, was a real issue but it was not enough to cause a civil war, for it had existed prior to 1840 and continued after 1865. Back in 1832 with the nullification crisis, disunionist sentiment was strong only in South Carolina, though the whole South was presumably hurt by the "Tariff of Abominations." A generation later, eleven southern states left the Union when they perceived an apparent threat to their rights.

Clearly, something else must have intervened to forge a stronger bond of southern unity and a stronger sense of shared interests. In 1860, general southern differences and grievances, not those exclusively economic in nature, led to the crisis. And beneath them all lay another, more fundamental factor that would prove to be the fatal one: slavery.

In the final analysis, it was slavery that defined the South. Diverse in climate, crops, and topography, the South got its sense of cohesiveness from its "peculiar institution." As has been shown earlier, after intense attacks on slavery began in the 1830s, southern society closed ranks, hardened its attitudes, and turned on its critics with a fierce counterattack.

Slavery also created a divisive moral issue between the two sections. Long before the eve of the Civil War, the planters had come to consider slavery a positive good that made possible the south's gracious and cultured life. On the other hand, many northerners had increasingly come to see slavery as a sin. To the abolitionists, at least, it was intolerable that society should allow slavery to continue.

Before long, moral indignation against slavery became politicized, and in 1839 the Liberty Party emerged. It was composed mainly of moderate abolitionists who favored political action to stop the "slave power." Though it would only attract a very small minority of northern voters, the Liberty Party would not let America forget about the issue that troubled it most, slavery; nor would it let the major parties evade it.

The Imaginary Dividing Lines

Perhaps if the country had not been confronted time and again after 1846 with the issue of whether new territories should be slave or free, the two sections might have been able to reconcile their differences. Such was not to be.

Ever since Pennsylvania became the first state to abolish slavery in 1780, Americans had drawn imaginary lines separating those regions where they would permit slavery from those where they would forbid it. Legislative action taken during and after the Revolution reinforced the dividing line between slave and free territory among the thirteen original states at the southern boundary of Pennsylvania. The line was the Mason-Dixon Line, so named for the two English surveyors, Charles Mason and Jeremiah Dixon, who surveyed the disputed boundary between Pennsylvania and Maryland between 1763 and 1768. The Mason-Dixon Line was extended further west between Pennsylvania and Virginia in 1779 and again in 1784.

The Northwest Ordinance of 1787, enacted under the Articles of Confederation, excluded slavery from the unorganized region of the nation west of Pennsylvania and north of the Ohio River. The Missouri Compromise of 1820 excluded slavery north of 36°30' (the southern boundary of Missouri) in the region newly acquired by the Louisiana Purchase.

Thus, the whole nation had been assigned one labor system or another prior to the great expansion of the 1840s. With the acquisition of Oregon and the Mexican cessions, the question over the territorial limits of slavery began to rage and would not be quieted until the nation had fought a civil war.

No one really expected slavery to be successfully transplanted to Oregon since that region seemed totally unsuited for plantation agriculture. But the California and New Mexico region was a different story, and southerners did not want slavery to be legally or arbitrarily denied the chance to develop in the Southwest.

Nevertheless, in August 1846, Congressman David Wilmot of Pennsylvania submitted a resolution requiring that slavery be excluded from every part of the territory acquired from Mexico. Southerners were outraged by this: this Wilmot Proviso seemed a flagrantly unfair attempt to exclude them from the benefits of the common victory over Mexico.

Only a few northerners agreed with the southern claims; most took a different view on the issue. The more vehement abolitionists saw any extension of slavery as a moral wrong.

Others, less moralistic, saw the expansion of slavery into the territories as a threat to free labor.

For months following the introduction of the Wilmot Proviso, the two sections bitterly attacked one another with rhetoric. The Proviso passed the House, but southern strength in the Senate kept it from passing. By no means did this victory quiet the furor. The issue still remained deeply embedded in the minds of both northerners and southerners, and neither would forget the anger engendered by it.

The Election of 1848

Not surprisingly, the Wilmot Proviso greatly affected the presidential election of 1848. Both the Whigs and the Democrats tried to avoid definite and provocative references to the question of slavery in the territories. The Whigs adopted no platform and chose as their presidential candidate Mexican War hero Zachary Taylor, a man with no known political record.

The Democrats were less successful in evading the controversial slavery issue. President Polk, tired and worn from the cares of office and unpopular with his party for his aloof and rigid personality, was passed over for renomination. Instead, the Democratic Party chose Lewis Cass of Michigan, an elderly, honest, loyal party regular who opposed the Wilmot Proviso and favored "popular sovereignty," or "squatter sovereignty." That is, Cass was in favor of letting the residents of an unorganized territory decide for themselves whether slavery would be permitted or excluded.

Vehement abolitionists and even moderates who merely opposed the expansion of slavery found it difficult to accept either Cass or Taylor. The situation was perfect for the emergence of a third party, potential members of which could come from the existing Liberty Party and the antislavery elements of the old political organizations. Late in the campaign, then, the Free-Soil

Party was launched, adopting a platform endorsing the Wilmot Proviso, free homesteads, and a higher tariff. Former president Martin Van Buren was chosen as the Free-Soil candidate.

Van Buren's candidacy took many Democratic votes away from Cass and as a result, Taylor won the election. Still, the Free-Soil Party was able to elect ten members to Congress.

The Taylor Administration

Though a southerner and slaveholder, Taylor proved to be a strong supporter of the Union. From his many years in the Army he had acquired a national outlook and an attachment to the concept of nationalism.

Immediately, Taylor had to confront the problem of providing a civil government for the territories annexed from Mexico, which were being administered by military officials who were responsible to the president. Taylor's solution, and it was a simple one, was statehood for those territories. Statehood, it seemed, would not only provide civil government but also prevent the expected controversy over the expansion of slavery in the territories because a territory upon becoming a state, could do whatever it wanted about slavery.

California needed no encouragement to support Taylor's plan, for the gold rush of 1849 was increasing the population in that region hugely. Taylor urged the Californians to apply directly for admission into the Union as a state, taking the slavery issue out of Congress's hands. This the Californians did, and in 1849, having already elected a state government and representatives to Congress, they sent their application for statehood to Washington.

But the Thirtieth Congress was deeply torn over sectional interests. Indeed, it took sixty-three ballots before Howell Cobb of Georgia was elected Speaker of the House. Northerners and southerners alike treated the question of slavery in California as a battlefield maneuver, and Taylor's scheme did not work. California did not yet become a state.

California, slave or free, was certainly not the only issue causing sectional friction. For years, opponents of slavery had demanded that the slave trade in the District of Columbia be abolished. The nation's capital, they insisted, must not be disgraced by the presence of slave pens and auction blocks.

Southerners responded by fuming over the ineffectiveness of the federal Fugitive Slave Law in existence since 1793. They claimed the South was suffering tremendous financial losses because of northern refusal to cooperate with federal authorities in suppressing the escape of slaves to the North and Canada via the Underground Railroad.

Questions over Texas's still unpaid debt to the Union arose, as it had become a state in 1845 owing millions of dollars to the United States government. Texas claimed the portion of New Mexico east of the Rio Grande, although the national government had assigned this region to New Mexico. Texas resented this action and also the government's refusal to assume the Texas war debt. Southern proslavery extremists supported the Texan claims, while northerners upheld that of the New Mexicans.

The status of a government for New Mexico remained unresolved. Would it or would it not permit slavery? Did Congress have the right to decide? Or should the people in the territory decide for themselves, as Lewis Cass had suggested? Without doubt, all of these issues encouraged and intensified the sectional hostilities already running rampant in Congress.

The Compromise of 1850

Under the leadership of two nationalists, Congress set about to settle the burning sectional issues. The aging Henry Clay, now seventy-three years old, a master of compromise, and at the end of his long and illustrious career, was determined to prevent dis-

union. Though a Kentuckian and slaveholder, Clay was a firm
Unionist who refused to see the nation torn apart. So, too, was
the other nationalist, Senator Stephen Douglas of Illinois, thirty-
seven years old and just at the beginning of his career.

Sectional showdown seemed unavoidable, since politicians
on both sides of the Mason-Dixon Line espoused unyielding
positions that prevented compromise. Northerners such as Salmon Chase of Ohio, Charles Sumner of Massachusetts, and William Seward of New York and southerners like John C. Calhoun,
now at age sixty-eight, refused to give any ground on their
respective positions.

Nonetheless, in January 1850, Henry Clay presented a package bill to the Senate designed to settle all the outstanding sectional issues simultaneously. The five separate provisions of
Clay's omnibus bill were these: (1) California was to be admitted
into the Union as a free state; (2) New Mexico was to be given
a territorial government without mention of the slavery issue; (3)
in return for limiting its western boundary, Texas's outstanding
debts would be assumed by the federal government; (4) the slave
trade, not slavery, would be abolished in Washington, D.C.; and
(5) Congress would adopt a new, more effective Fugitive Slave
Law.

In the six months of debate that followed this proposal, it became apparent that while many congressmen could support parts
of this bill, few could endorse the thing as a whole, and thus
Clay's package deal was defeated. This occurred despite perhaps the most eloquent, persuasive speech of Senator Daniel
Webster's long career. Although he still maintained White
House ambitions, Webster's "Seventh of March Address" was
an attempt to calm angry sectional passions by encouraging
northern moderates to support the compromise, even at the risk
of alienating those filled with the strong antislavery sentiment of
his native New England.

Suddenly, on July 9, 1850, President Taylor died. Taylor

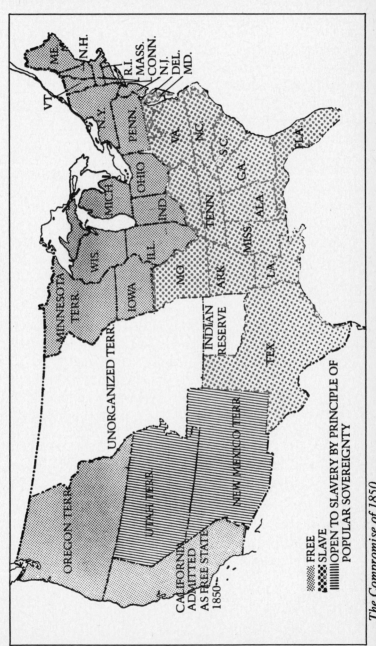

The Compromise of 1850

had labored behind the scenes on Clay's proposals in ways that southerners interpreted as hostile to their section. His death elevated Vice President Millard Fillmore of New York to the presidency. A practical politician who understood the importance of compromise in statecraft, Fillmore appeared more conciliatory to the south than Taylor had been.

With Fillmore's blessings and the work of Douglas, Clay's package was broken up into separate components that were voted upon individually. By mid-September the series of measures had been enacted by both houses of Congress and signed by the president as the Compromise of 1850.

Though northerners disliked the new Fugitive Slave Act and the organization of both New Mexico and Utah territories without slavery exclusion clauses and southerners disliked California's admission as a free state and the bill ending the slave trade in the District of Columbia, the Union was preserved, at least for the time being. What Clay could not accomplish with one single bill had now been achieved by five separate ones.

Soon after the passage of the compromise measures, a convention of slave states met in Nashville, Tennessee, to discuss the Compromise of 1850. Though they adjourned without taking strong disunionist action, their meeting served as an ominous portent of things to come.

The Fugitive Slave Law of 1850

It quickly became apparent that extremists on both sides were dissatisfied with the Compromise. As the months passed, it appeared not only that it had not put an end to sectional discord, but that at least one aspect of the Compromise, the Fugitive Slave Law of 1850, was inflaming sectional animosity even further.

The new law deprived suspected runaway slaves of virtually every right normally granted to those accused of violating the law. Indeed, all a slaveowner had to do was submit an affidavit to a federal commissioner to initiate a claim. While his case was being considered, the accused runaway was detained and denied a trial by jury. The law also stipulated that state officials and private citizens must assist the federal authorities in capturing fugitives. Anyone who refused to cooperate could be fined or imprisoned. In essence, then, the law made every American a potential slavecatcher.

This law generated a great deal of hostility in the north and turned moderates into vehement antislavery advocates. Mob action often prevented the return of fugitive slaves to their masters, and fugitives were given shelter and food in many northern homes, while slave hunters were attacked.

So aroused were some parts of the North that several state legislatures passed "Personal Liberty Laws" making it a crime for state officials to assist slaveowners and federal authorities in recovering fugitives. In effect, these northern states were nullifying a federal law that they found offensive in much the same fashion as South Carolina had done in 1832 with the tariff.

That fact notwithstanding, southerners were outraged by the action of northerners. They accused the North of violating its part of the Compromise of 1850. Ironically, by demanding a stronger federal law and denouncing northern states' efforts to nullify a locally distasteful measure, southerners were implicitly repudiating their states' rights position. Sectional relations were again dangerously strained.

One northerner, particularly outraged at the slave system, taxed relations between the two sections even more. In 1852, Harriet Beecher Stowe published *Uncle Tom's Cabin,* the most effective of all abolitionist propaganda. Stowe belonged to a famous New England ministerial family—her father and seven brothers were preachers—and she had married a minister. For several years she had lived in Cincinnati and from there had made trips into Kentucky to view slavery and plantation life.

Stowe's novel, written after she and her husband had left Cincinnati for Maine, was an indictment of slavery though not of slaveholders; the villain of it, Simon Legree, was from New England. *Uncle Tom's Cabin* sold more than three hundred thousand copies in its first year. When it came to the stage as a play, it reached millions more.

In the North and in Europe, *Uncle Tom's Cabin* was hailed as a masterpiece. In the South, it was despised, since it aroused such strong sympathy for slaves and such utter detestation of slavery.

Uncle Tom's Cabin heightened sectional tensions and brought confrontation that much closer. Indeed, when Abraham Lincoln met Harriet Beecher Stowe some years later during the Civil War he is alleged to have said, "So this is the little lady who wrote the big book that caused the big war!"

From Bad to Worse

After the Compromise of 1850 the nation lost three of its elder statesmen when John C. Calhoun died in 1850 and Henry Clay and Daniel Webster both died in 1852. It was being left to a new generation of leaders to attempt to bridge the ever-growing schism between the North and the South.

In January 1854, sectional angers were again aroused when Senator Stephen Douglas proposed to establish territorial government in the Nebraska country, part of the old Louisiana Purchase, on the basis of popular sovereignty. The Kansas-Nebraska Act, as it was known, sought to divide Nebraska country into two territories.

By allowing popular sovereignty to decide whether or not slavery would be allowed in these two territories, Douglas's bill would also signal the repeal of the 1820 Missouri Compromise provision that prohibited slavery in the Louisiana Purchase north of 36°30′. In this regard, the South might look forward to at least one slave state's joining the Union from an area where slavery had long been expressly prohibited.

Douglas's motive for this proposal was his interest in organizing and developing Nebraska country so it might accommodate a transcontinental railroad route. But, of course, Douglas did not want just any route; rather, the senator wanted the railroad to take a central route connecting his home town of Chicago with California. Thus, his state of Illinois would benefit from the increased trade and wealth that would inevitably follow the railroad.

Douglas's ambitions, though, could never be fulfilled without southern support in Congress. This is why he expressly included repeal of the Missouri Compromise as part of his bill. Southerners had come to resent deeply any attempt to exclude them and their property from territory acquired by expenditures from the common treasury or won by common sacrifice.

Although many southerners disliked popular sovereignty and would have preferred a constitutional amendment guaranteeing that slavery could exist in the territories, popular sovereignty was, after all, better than nothing in this matter that to the southerners was very important.

Realistically, the Kansas-Nebraska area seemed unsuited for plantation agriculture, and the 1860 census was to show that after being open to slavery for six years, Kansas had but two slaves. But symbolically, the Kansas-Nebraska Act was volatile. It mattered little that slavery was never likely to flourish on the prairies. Northerners became outraged at the very possibility. Douglas had completely underestimated the popular response to his bill.

For four turbulent months Congress debated the Kansas-Nebraska Bill. Douglas, however, had a friend in President Franklin Pierce. Nominated in 1852 by the Democrats when they could not agree on any of their front-runners, Pierce went on to victory by defeating the Whig candidate, Mexican War hero General Winfield Scott. Another northerner inclined to favor the South, Pierce threw his weight behind the bill and pressured reluctant northern congressmen to support it as well. The president's intervention proved crucial and the bill passed in May 1854 by a congressional majority which was primarily southern in composition.

Pierce and the Southerners

Pierce also attempted to assist the south by securing lands in Central America suitable for slavery. Largely influenced by his secretary of war, Jefferson Davis, Pierce recognized the government in Nicaragua that was under control of William Walker, a southerner and self-appointed dictator.

In 1854, with almost sixty followers, Walker landed in Nicaragua, and by the following year, he had established himself as dictator of that country. Walker had the support of an American company that was trying to secure a route across Central America to the goldfields of California. Walker had more ambitious plans: to create and lead a new nation consisting of all the countries of Central America and Cuba. Most of Walker's supporters simply wanted to bring Nicaragua into the Union as a slave state.

In 1856 Walker announced the reestablishment of slavery in Nicaragua, received recognition for his government from the Pierce administration, and even won an endorsement from the Democratic Party in its platform. By 1857, however, Walker had alienated the neighboring countries, and he was driven out of power. In 1860, he was executed by a Honduran firing squad.

The Pierce administration tried to obtain Cuba as well. Pierce instructed Pierre Soulé, American minister to Spain, to attempt "to detach that island from the Spanish dominion." After failing in his initial try to purchase Cuba, Soulé collaborated with two other American proslavery ministers, James Buchanan, the

United States minister to England, and John Y. Mason, an American diplomat in France, in issuing the Ostend Manifesto in 1854.

The Ostend Manifesto stated that if Spain should persist in refusing to sell Cuba and if any disturbances there were deemed threatening to the security of the United States, America would be justified in "wresting" it from Spain. In November 1854, when the document became known in Washington, Pierce came under severe attack from northern antislavery forces. His opponents claimed that the president was acting as a pawn for the South by conspiring to bring in a new slave state even at the risk of war with Spain. In the end, the Ostend Manifesto was dropped, but it was not soon forgotten.

The Disintegration of National Political Parties

The sectional issues put an enormous strain on the nation's two major political parties. Already the northern and southern Whigs were badly divided over the slavery issue and it had cost them the presidential election of 1852. Further, the Kansas-Nebraska Act destroyed the Whig Party everywhere in the South except in the border states. And the deaths of Clay and Webster had left the Whigs without their traditional leaders.

Similarly, the Democratic Party split over slavery when northern Democrats bitterly attacked the administration's support of Douglas and Kansas-Nebraska. In many northern states, Democrats met at conventions and passed resolutions condemning Douglas's bill.

Soon, the Whig Party began to crumble, as northern Whigs, more strongly antislavery then their Democratic counterparts, were less willing or able to compromise with the southern members of their own party. For a while, many Whigs took refuge in the American party, dubbed the Know-Nothing Party by Horace

Greeley, an antiforeign political group dedicated to excluding nonnatives and Catholics from public office.

In 1854 the Know-Nothings cut sharply into Whig strength in the North, and it temporarily looked as if they would be the successors to the Whigs. Because of their hatred of foreigners and their religious bigotry, the Know-Nothings both attracted and repelled many voters.

Ultimately, all antislavery and anti-Kansas-Nebraska groups united under the banner of the newly named Republican Party. Originating in a series of spontaneous meetings in the Northwest and Northeast, the groups first united under the name Republican at a February 1854 meeting in Ripon, Wisconsin. The movement soon grew in strength, as many northern Whigs and northern Democrats were drawn to the new party by its central principle of free soil. Indeed, for the moment the Republican Party was a one-idea organization; its only platform was opposition to the expansion of slavery into the territories.

"Bleeding Kansas"

The rise of the Republican Party was accelerated by the outbreak of vicious guerrilla warfare in Kansas. Within weeks of the passage of Douglas's Kansas-Nebraska Bill, advocates and opponents of slavery were at war with one another in Kansas territory. Ambushes, arson, and murder were common. The rest of the nation absorbed in shock the events in "Bleeding Kansas," as one newspaper described it.

Friends and opponents of slavery competed for government control in Kansas. Outsiders exacerbated the situation. For example, the New England Emigrant Aid Company, founded by Eli Thayer, raised funds and sent thousands of antislavery advocates to Kansas. Most of these emigrants came armed with Sharps rifles, called "Beecher's Bibles" after the prominent antislavery minister Henry Ward Beecher.

Such efforts by the free-soilers only encouraged large numbers of proslavery Missourians to cross the border into Kansas. Called by their adversaries "border ruffians," the Missourians were mostly white yeoman farmers.

In 1855, the proslavery group seized control of the Kansas government by a rigged election to the territorial legislature and promptly adopted a drastic slave code. Although there were probably only some fifteen hundred legal votes in the territory, over six thousand votes were counted in the election. Nevertheless, anxious to give the South what it wanted, President Pierce encouraged the proslavery group in the election and adoption of this code.

Antislavery forces rebelled and late in 1855 they called a convention at Topeka, adopted a constitution outlawing slavery and ratified it in a popular vote in which proslavery men refused to participate. Pierce called their movement unlawful and declared that the federal government would support only the proslavery territorial legislature. Despite the president's decree, there were now two rival governments in Kansas, one claiming to represent a slave state, the other a free one.

Among those who turned to violence in Kansas was John Brown. Born in Connecticut, Brown spent most of his life wandering from place to place unsuccessfully trying to make a living and establish a home. By the time he reached Kansas in 1855, with five sons, Brown was an embittered and angry man. A fanatical abolitionist who identified his own sufferings with those of the slaves, Brown considered himself as an avenging God's instrument to destroy slavery.

In Kansas, Brown and his sons immediately aligned themselves with the antislavery forces. Estimating that five antislavery men had been killed already in Lawrence, Kansas, he decided to take revenge. He gathered six followers and in one night murdered five proslavery settlers at Pottawatomie Creek in 1856. The episode touched off a virtual civil war in Kansas.

In May 1856, violence spread to the nation's capital—and indeed the United States Capitol—when the staunch antislavery Senator Charles Sumner of Massachusetts delivered a blistering denunciation of the South in a speech entitled "The Crime against Kansas." In his speech Sumner attacked President Pierce and others, but he saved his sharpest criticism for Senator Andrew Butler of South Carolina for his support of slavery.

Particularly outraged by Sumner's speech was Butler's nephew, Preston Brooks, a member of the House of Representatives from South Carolina. Brooks was determined to chastise Sumner publicly and physically, a method very much in line with the nineteenth-century southern code of ethics and honor. Approaching Sumner at his desk when the Senate adjourned, Brooks proceeded to beat him with a cane until Sumner fell to the floor in bloody unconsciousness.

The injured senator stayed out of the Senate for four years, and during his absence, Massachusetts refused to elect a successor. Northern newspapers referred to the incident as an extension of the events occurring in Kansas, allegorically calling it "Bleeding Sumner." Brooks, censured by the House, resigned and stood for reelection. He was returned by an almost unanimous vote, and shortly after his arrival he began to receive canes as gifts from friendly supporters all over the south!

The violence in Congress, like that in Kansas, was symbolic. It clearly demonstrated that Americans were no longer able to settle their sectional differences by the conventional political processes of debate and the ballot. And the two sections moved further apart.

The Election of 1856

"Bleeding Kansas," the Brooks-Sumner affair, and *Uncle Tom's Cabin* all encouraged northern recruits to the Republican Party, and consequently, it remained a strictly northern party. A few Republicans were "radical" abolitionists; that is, they were morally opposed to slavery anywhere at any time. Most could tolerate slavery but believed that the federal government could and should prevent it from expanding. These Republicans hoped that slavery, if contained, would eventually die.

Some Republicans were actually indifferent to the fate of slavery. So long as the western territories remained white and open to free labor, these Republicans were content. In this regard, they were often as hostile to the slaves as to the slaveholders.

The Republicans ran their first presidential candidate in 1856 when they nominated military man and western explorer John C. Frémont, who had no previous political record to embarrass the new party. The Republican Party platform called for the exclusion from the western territories of "those twin relics of barbarism, polygamy [practiced by the Mormons] and slavery."

The Democrats chose former Pennsylvania senator James Buchanan, largely because alone among prominent Democrats he had been out of the country, serving as ambassador to England, during the worst of "Bleeding Kansas." Thus, he could not be associated with any atrocities that had occurred in the West. The Democratic platform endorsed the Kansas-Nebraska Act and defended popular sovereignty.

The Know-Nothing Party nominated former president Millard Fillmore. At its convention, many northern delegates withdrew because the platform was not sufficiently firm in opposing the expansion of slavery in the territories.

Many voters, fearing that by supporting the Republicans, a purely sectional party, they would be encouraging disunion, cast their ballots for Buchanan, and he was elected president. Buchanan carried all of the slave states except Maryland, and he also won five northern states. Frémont, though, made a respectable showing with the American people, as his popular-vote total was only five hundred thousand less than Buchanan's.

Buchanan was simply the wrong man at the wrong time. Basically, he was indecisive and weak, and his appointments of many southerners and doughface northerners to his cabinet merely exacerbated an already tense situation. His solution to the problems he encountered seemed to be a simple one: give the South what it wanted.

The Dred Scott Decision

Two days after taking the oath of office, Buchanan was faced with a Supreme Court decision that further split the nation. With the assistance of antislavery groups, Dred Scott, a Missouri slave and once the property of an Army surgeon, had sued for his freedom. Scott's suit rested on the contention that he had been taken by his master to the free territory of Minnesota and had lived there long enough to qualify him for freedom. Since 1820, the Minnesota region had been closed to slavery by the Missouri Compromise.

Of the nine justices, five were southerners, and in the majority opinion Chief Justice Roger B. Taney declared that as a slave Scott had no legal rights since he was not a citizen. In addition, Taney said it made no difference that Scott had resided in a free territory since slaves were property and the Constitution protected a man's right to his property. According to the high court, Congress possessed no authority to pass a law prohibiting slavery in the territories, and depriving persons of their slave property. The Missouri Compromise, therefore, had been unconstitutional.

Few decisions in Supreme Court history would create the furor of the Dred Scott decision. President Buchanan endorsed the decision, an act that elated southerners while outraging northerners. Southerners felt that legal sanction was finally given the expansion of slavery, while Republicans feared that their attempts to restrict slavery and forbid it in the territories had now been dealt a death blow.

Buchanan and Kansas

When, in 1857, Buchanan accepted a proslavery constitution adopted in Kansas, he alienated northerners even more. The Lecompton Constitution, as it was called, was exclusively written and voted on by proslavery forces and so did not represent the majority opinion in Kansas. In fact, free-soilers and antislavery forces had boycotted the referendum on it and called for its rejection. Despite advice to the contrary, Buchanan recommended that Congress accept the Lecompton Constitution as a basis for admitting Kansas into the Union as a slave state.

With objections coming from the Republicans, as well as from Stephen Douglas and other western Democrats who saw the Lecompton Constitution as a perversion of popular sovereignty, the document was blocked in Congress. To avert any further dissension in the Democratic Party, a compromise measure, the English Bill, was offered and passed in 1858. The bill provided that the Lecompton Constitution be submitted to the people of Kansas for a third time. With antislavery forces voting this time, it was decisively rejected. But not until the closing hours of the Buchanan administration, in 1861, when a number of southern states had seceded, would Kansas enter the Union as a free state.

The Lincoln-Douglas Debates

Buchanan's indecisiveness encouraged Democrats to look forward to replacing him on the 1860 presidential ticket. Stephen Douglas was the obvious front-runner for that spot. Before he could be considered presidential timber, however, Douglas first had to be reelected to his Senate seat in 1858.

His opponent in the election was an exceptionally able campaigner, Abraham Lincoln, an Illinois lawyer. Lincoln had been a Whig, but reluctantly joined the Republicans after passage of the Kansas-Nebraska Act. Lincoln might have forever remained a local politician had he not been selected to run against Douglas.

The 1858 Illinois senatorial contest attracted national attention, for to remain a strong presidential contender, Douglas had to defeat Lincoln decisively and prove his strength at home. People from all over the nation watched to see what would happen as the two candidates traveled throughout the state campaigning. The election campaign was made all the more intriguing by its format. Because he was not as well known, Lincoln challenged Douglas to a series of debates. The "Little Giant" accepted Lincoln's challenge and the two candidates argued their cases in every congressional district in the state.

Throughout the Lincoln-Douglas debates, Douglas defended popular sovereignty, while Lincoln opposed slavery on moral, political, and economic grounds. But Lincoln was also opposed to the radical antislavery solution of abolishing slavery immediately wherever it existed. He advocated preventing slavery from expanding in the hope that it would eventually die a natural death in the southern states.

In the debate at Freeport, Lincoln posed a question that made this meeting historically the most significant of all the debates. Lincoln asked Douglas what was left of his popular-sovereignty policy now that the Dred Scott decision had declared that only the people of a state, not a territory, could exclude slavery.

Lincoln's query was a loaded one, for no matter how Douglas answered it, he would lose something. If the Little Giant disavowed popular sovereignty, he would no doubt be defeated for reelection and ruin his political career. But if he reaffirmed his theory, southern Democrats would certainly be offended, the party schism deepened, and his chances of obtaining the Democratic presidential nomination in 1860 damaged if not actually destroyed.

Undaunted, Douglas did not dodge the question put to him. He replied that no matter what the Supreme Court said, a territorial government could still exclude slavery merely by refusing to pass a slave code to protect the institution within its jurisdiction. Without such a form of protection—"local police regulations," as Douglas called them—the institution of slavery could not survive a day, he said.

Douglas's reply became known as the Freeport Doctrine or, in the south, the Freeport Heresy. It seriously offended southerners, who considered it just another way to frustrate their gains from the Dred Scott decision. Still, Douglas won the senatorial seat from Illinois in 1858. More significant, however, was that out of this contest Abraham Lincoln had emerged as a national figure. "Old Abe" was now in the running for the Republican Party's top position.

The Raid on Harpers Ferry

Before the presidential election of 1860, the nation witnessed another act of violence, and again it was led by John Brown.

After the Pottawatomie massacre Brown left Kansas and traveled east. Still convinced that he was God's instrument to destroy slavery, he decided to transfer his activities to the South itself. With encouragement and financial aid from such eastern abolitionists as Gerrit Smith and Amos A. Lawrence, Brown concocted a wild scheme to liberate the slaves.

His plan was to seize a mountain fortress in Virginia from which he could launch raids to free the slaves in the surrounding areas. He would arm the newly freed slaves and organize them into a militia of sorts and then force the south into conceding emancipation.

Because he needed guns, Brown decided upon Harpers Ferry, Virginia (now part of West Virginia), where a United

States arsenal was located, for his base of operations. In October 1859, leading nineteen supporters, Brown descended upon the town and captured the arsenal. However, slaves in neighboring Maryland and in Virginia did not rise in insurrection at the news of Brown's attack. Instead, almost immediately Brown was attacked by citizens and local militia companies, who were soon reinforced by a detachment of United States Marines sent to the scene by the federal government.

Led by Colonel Robert E. Lee, the military forces quickly killed ten of Brown's fellow conspirators. With little other recourse, Brown surrendered. Along with six of his followers, Brown was tried in a Virginia court for treason against the state, convicted, and sentenced to death by hanging.

Probably no single event had as much an influence as the Brown raid in convincing southerners that they were unsafe in the Union. Brown's execution raised sectional feelings to a new, fevered pitch. When Brown was eulogized as a martyr and hero in the North, southern slaveowners, who lived in constant fear of slave insurrection, called home their sons from schools and colleges in the North and, with other white southerners, braced themselves for the worst. They did not have long to wait.

The Election of 1860

By the time of the presidential election of 1860, Americans were more deeply divided than ever before. In April 1860, at their nominating convention in Charleston, South Carolina, in the heart of secession country, the Democrats failed to nominate a candidate after sixty ballots. Led by southerners like William Yancey of Alabama, many southern Democrats concluded that there was no hope for the south in the Union. To them, Stephen Douglas's popular-sovereignty platform no longer seemed right. With this in mind, Yancey and fifty other proslavery men walked

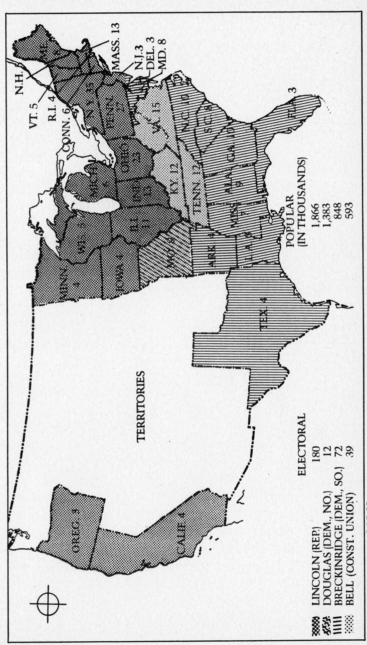

The Election of 1860

	ELECTORAL		POPULAR (IN THOUSANDS)
LINCOLN (REP.)	180		1,866
DOUGLAS (DEM., NO.)	12		1,383
BRECKINRIDGE (DEM., SO.)	72		848
BELL (CONST. UNION)	39		593

N.H.
VT. 5
R.I. 4
CONN. 6
MASS. 13
N.J. 3
DEL. 3
MD. 8
VA. 15
N.C. 10
S.C. 8
GA. 10
ALA. 9
MISS. 7
LA. 6
TENN. 12
KY. 12
FLA. 3
ARK. 4
TEX. 4
MINN. 4
IOWA 4
MO. 9
OREG. 3
CALIF. 4

TERRITORIES

out of the convention. The Democrats adjourned to meet again six weeks later in Baltimore.

In Baltimore most of the southerners reappeared only to walk out again. This time, however, northern Democrats succeeded in nominating Douglas on a platform calling for popular sovereignty. Meeting on their own in Richmond, the southern Democrats nominated Vice President of the United States John C. Breckinridge of Kentucky on a platform that demanded federal protection of slavery in the territories. The Democrats now had two sectional candidates clearly reflecting, in many ways, the mood of the nation.

When the Republicans met in Chicago, Senator William Seward of New York seemed the front-runner. But Seward was too radical, and in his speeches he frightened the moderate Republicans, who feared he might alienate the sections even more. In one speech in particular, Seward had declared that the North and South were engaged in "an irrepressible conflict" that must end with the United States' becoming "entirely a slave-holding nation, or entirely a free-labor nation."

The Republicans realized that they would need much moderate northern support to win, and they simply could not nominate a man such as Seward, who had so flagrantly challenged the South. The Republicans found their moderate candidate on the third ballot in Abraham Lincoln. Radical enough to please the antislavery faction of the party but conservative enough to satisfy the former Whigs, Lincoln appeared to be the ideal candidate. The Republican Party platform demanded the limitation of slavery though it did not specify how it was to be achieved. It also deplored disunion, attacked the fanaticism of John Brown, and endorsed the right of each state to control its local institutions, including slavery. The Republican Party platform also endorsed such measures as a high tariff, internal improvements, a homestead bill, and a Pacific railroad to be built with federal financial assistance.

A fourth party, the Constitutional Union Party, entered the 1860 presidential contest as well. Although it appeared as a new organization, most of its members were in fact elder statesmen and former Whigs. The nominee of this party was John Bell of Tennessee, who ran on a platform that called for the undying support of the Constitution, the Union, and the enforcement of the laws of the land.

With only 39 percent of the nation's popular vote, Abraham Lincoln hardly received a resounding mandate. However, Lincoln received a clear majority of the electoral votes; he took 180 by carrying every free state except New Jersey. Douglas received the second highest popular vote but received only 12 electoral votes because in every state except Missouri he finished second to someone else. Breckinridge took the deep South with 72 electoral votes. The Constitutional Union Party secured many votes in the border states.

The South Secedes

Fearing that Lincoln's election would mean immediate hostility and danger to it, the South took action. Led by the "Fire-eaters"—those favoring secession—South Carolina called a secession convention one month after the election. By unanimous vote, the convention dissolved its ties with the Union and South Carolina had seceded.

In rapid fashion six more southern states—Mississippi, Florida, Alabama, Georgia, Louisiana, and Texas—joined South Carolina. Though there were a few southerners who opposed secession or thought it best to wait for unified action, the secessionists prevailed. By February 1, 1861, the entire deep South was out of the Union, and Lincoln had not even been inaugurated.

The self-proclaimed independent southern state governments began to seize such federal property as customhouses, post offices, mints, hospitals, arsenals, and forts. Southern military men began to resign their commissions with the federal government and cast their lots with their home states. In Washington, southern congressmen resigned one by one.

In February, the seceded states sent delegates to Montgomery, Alabama, and established the Confederate States of America. They chose as president Jefferson Davis of Mississippi and as vice president Alexander Stephens of Georgia. The delegates also adopted a form of government that in many ways resembled the federal government. The Confederate Constitution was modeled after the Constitution of the United States. However, it declared slavery protected everywhere by law and forbade government bounties, subsidies, and protective tariffs.

The lame-duck Buchanan administration did little to help the crisis. While not believing in secession, neither did the president feel compelled to take coercive measures to save the Union. He feared that any action on his part might drive out of the Union the eight remaining slave states of Virginia, Arkansas, Tennessee, Maryland, North Carolina, Kentucky, Missouri, and Delaware. Strongly influenced by his southern advisers, Buchanan did nothing and instead blamed the Republicans, now called "Black Republicans" in the South, for the crisis.

Republicans themselves found that they were divided. Some were happy finally to be rid of the trouble-making slave states; others, fearing for the fate of the country, wanted the president-elect to make some conciliatory gesture to the south to bring it back. Lincoln refused this. He would protect slavery where it existed but he would not allow it to expand and violate his party's platform.

In Congress, meanwhile, desperate efforts were being made to mend the Union. In December of 1860 Senator John J. Crittenden of Kentucky had proposed to extend the Missouri Compromise line of 36°30′ north latitude to the west coast. Like all other plans, this one failed. Republicans refused to remove the restrictions on expansion of slavery, and those southerners who remained insisted on no limitations whatsoever to slavery.

With each passing day the crisis deepened. Interest soon became focused exclusively on the two remaining military posts in Confederate territory still in Union hands: Fort Sumter in Charleston harbor and Fort Pickens at Pensacola, Florida. Their status, like so many issues during the past fifteen years, had become emotion-laden and charged with tremendous symbolic importance. Even President Buchanan was unwilling to give up the forts, though he had done little to prevent other seizures of federal property.

In January, Buchanan had sent the merchant steamer *Star of the West* with provisions and two hundred men to reinforce Major Robert Anderson, who was in command of the federal garrison at Fort Sumter. The ship was fired on by Confederates and turned back leaving Anderson's troops in desperate straits with few supplies.

Nothing was settled when Abraham Lincoln took office on March 4, 1861. His inaugural speech was conciliatory in tone. He would not insist on delivering the federal mails if the south "repelled" such service, nor would he appoint "obnoxious strangers" to federal offices in the south. On the other hand, he promised to "hold, occupy, and possess the property and places belonging to the government." To do otherwise would be to recognize the independence of the Confederacy.

Appreciating the serious needs of the soldiers at Fort Sumter, Lincoln dispatched a ship of supplies after carefully informing the South Carolina authorities. Troops or munitions would be sent, Lincoln said, only if the Confederates offered resistance.

This decision placed the Confederates in a dilemma. If they permitted the expedition to land, they would be bowing tamely to federal authority; their people would not believe that they meant to sustain secession. Their only alternative, then, was to attack the fort before supplies arrived—in effect to declare war.

The Confederate officials in Montgomery debated hours before they directed General Pierre G. T. Beauregard, in charge of the Confederate forces at Charleston, to demand the surrender of the fort. When the demand was rejected the Confederate troops attacked. The siege lasted two days, April 12 and 13, 1861, before—weary, exhausted, and without supplies—the Federals surrendered.

War had finally come. Lincoln moved to increase the size of the federal army and called upon the states to furnish troops to restore the Union. This quickly led to the secession of four more slave states—Virginia on April 17, Arkansas on May 6, North Carolina on May 20, and Tennessee on June 8. The Confederacy was now eleven states. The mountain counties in northwestern Virginia refused to accept the decision of their state, established their own "loyal" government, and two years later, in 1863, would secure admission into the Union as the new state of West Virginia.

The four remaining slave states of Maryland, Delaware, Missouri, and Kentucky cast their lot cautiously with the Union. Lincoln kept a close eye on them, and in Missouri and Maryland he employed military force to ensure their decision.

The lines had now been drawn for the greatest ordeal in American history.

Since the end of the Mexican War, the issue of slavery in the territories had intruded itself into the American political scene. Indeed, the North and the South at times seemed obsessed with it. Northerners had come to fear an aggressive and demanding slave power that would completely ignore the rights of free men. For their part, southerners had developed a deep psychological stake in their "peculiar institution" and feared social and economic catastrophe if it were to be restricted.

Perhaps if Americans had been able to catch their breath in the 1850s they would have been able to resolve their differences by rational and civil means. But the decade of the 1850s was one of the most turbulent periods in all of American history. No sooner would the country recover from one crisis or controversy than a more intense one would arise. In this environment, both sections began to view issues from uncompromising, life or death perspectives.

Perhaps, too, sectional conflict could have been contained if a new generation of statesmen had emerged, skillful enough to enact compromise. Stephen Douglas might have filled the role vacated by Henry Clay, Daniel Webster or even John C. Calhoun, had he not miscalculated so badly the effects of his Kansas-Nebraska Bill in 1854. His efforts to foster popular sovereignty not only facilitated the coming of war but ruined his political career and credibility as well.

As it was, both North and South blundered into a war that both sides naively and confidently believed would be over shortly. Very soon, history would prove the North and the South devastatingly wrong.

Recommended Reading

William L. Barney, *The Road to Secession: A New Perspective on the Old South* (1972)

William L. Barney, *The Secessionist Impulse: Alabama and Mississippi in 1860* (1974)

Eugene H. Berwanger, *The Frontier against Slavery: Western Anti-Negro Prejudice and the Slavery Extension Controversy* (1967)

Frederick J. Blue, *Free Soilers: Third Party Politics, 1848–1854* (1973)

William R. Brock, *Parties and Political Conscience: American Dilemmas, 1840–1850* (1979)

Stanley W. Campbell, *The Slave Catchers: Enforcement of the Fugitive Slave Law, 1840–1860* (1968)

Stephen A. Channing, *Crisis of Fear: Secession in South Carolina* (1970)

William J. Cooper, *The South and the Politics of Slavery, 1828–1865* (1978)

Avery O. Craven, *The Growth of Southern Nationalism, 1848–1861* (1953)

Richard N. Current, *Lincoln and the First Shot* (1963)

David Donald, *Charles Sumner and the Coming of the Civil War* (1960)

Don E. Fehrenbacher, *The Dred Scott Case: Its Significance in American Law and Politics* (1978)

Don E. Fehrenbacher, *Prelude to Greatness: Lincoln in the 1850s* (1962)

Eric Foner, *Free Soil, Free Labor, and Free Men: The Ideology of the Republican Party before the Civil War* (1970)

Eric Foner, *Politics and Ideology in the Age of the Civil War* (1980)

Paul W. Gates, *Fifty Million Acres: Conflicts Over Kansas Land Policy, 1854–1890* (1954)

Holman Hamilton, *Prologue to Conflict: The Crisis and Compromise of 1850* (1964)

Michael Holt, *The Political Crisis of the 1850s* (1978)

Robert W. Johannsen, *Stephen A. Douglas* (1973)

Michael Johnson, *Toward a Patriarchal Society: The Secession of Georgia* (1977)

James C. Malin, *John Brown and the Legend of Fifty-Six* (1970)

James C. Malin, *The Nebraska Question: 1852–1854* (1953)

Robert E. May, *The Southern Dream of a Caribbean Empire, 1854–1861* (1973)

C. W. Morrison, *Democratic Politics and Sectionalism: The Wilmot Proviso Controversy* (1967)

Allen Nevins, *Ordeal of the Union* (2 vols., 1947)

Stephen B. Oates, *To Purge This Land with Blood: A Biography of John Brown* (1970)

Merrill D. Peterson, *The Great Triumvirate: Clay, Webster, and Calhoun* (1987)

David Potter, *The Impending Crisis, 1848–1861* (1976)

Basil Rauch, *American Interest in Cuba, 1848–1855* (1948)

James A. Rawley, *Race and Politics: "Bleeding Kansas" and the Coming of the Civil War* (1969)

Joseph G. Rayback, *Free Soil: The Election of 1848* (1970)

Richard Sewell, *Ballots for Freedom: Anti-Slavery Politics in the United States, 1847–1860* (1974)

Jason H. Silverman, *Unwelcome Guests: Canada West's Response to American Fugitive Slaves, 1800–1865* (1985)

Kenneth Stampp, *And the War Came: The North and the Secession Crisis, 1860–1861* (1950)

Harriet Beecher Stowe, *Uncle Tom's Cabin* (1852, 1964)

J. Mills Thornton III, *Politics and Power in a Slave Society: Alabama, 1800–1860* (1978)

Ralph Wooster, *The Secession Conventions of the South* (1962)

CHAPTER 15

The Crisis of the Union

Time Line

1861	The opening battle of the Civil War, First Bull Run, is fought
	President Lincoln implements a naval blockade of the Confederacy
	The *Trent* affair occurs
1862	Union general George McClellan abandons his Peninsula Campaign to capture Richmond after a victorious but costly Confederate counterattack led by Robert E. Lee

Union general Ulysses S. Grant is stopped in his western campaign at the Battle of Shiloh Church

Union troops are defeated at the Second Battle of Bull Run

The Confederates are stopped at the Battle of Antietam

The *Monitor* and the *Merrimac* battle to a draw at Hampton Roads

Both the federal and Confederate governments are forced to resort to conscription to maintain their ranks

The U.S. Congress passes the Pacific Railway Act, the Morrill Land Grant College Act, and the Homestead Act

Black troops are organized to fight for the Union cause

1863   The Emancipation Proclamation goes into effect

The Confederates defeat the Union army at the Battle of Chancellorsville, but Confederate general Thomas J. "Stonewall" Jackson is accidentally killed by one of his own men

Confederate general Robert E. Lee's northern advance is stopped at the Battle of Gettysburg

The Union army captures Vicksburg

1863–1864	The U.S. Congress passes the National Bank Acts, creating the National Banking System
1864	Union general William T. Sherman captures Atlanta and marches on to the Atlantic coast
	Abraham Lincoln is reelected president
1865	The U.S. Congress creates the Bureau of Internal Revenue and establishes America's first income tax
	Robert E. Lee surrenders the Confederate army to Ulysses Grant at Appomattox Courthouse
	Confederate president Jefferson Davis flees Richmond and is captured in Georgia
	Abraham Lincoln is assassinated by John Wilkes Booth at Ford's Theater; Vice President Andrew Johnson accedes to the presidency

And the war came. Certainly, few Americans realized that they were about to endure four of the bloodiest, most bitter years in the nation's history. Little did northerners or southerners know that their respective governments would spend billions of dollars on arms, munitions, supplies, and services for the military. Outside of the fighting, however, the Civil War marked a watershed in American history—the transition from a sleepy, rural America to an industrialized, urbanized one characterized by great technological advancements. And of course, the war destroyed slavery.

An almost festive atmosphere suffused the opening weeks of the war. But quite soon, the naiveté that made this possible would wear off for everyone.

The War Potential of Each Adversary

With 9 million people, the seceded states had less than one-half the population of the North. Furthermore, 3.5 million of its people were blacks, whom southerners were unwilling to arm. In the North were twenty-three states with a population of approximately 22 million.

Economically, in 1860 the Confederate States of America had only eighteen thousand manufacturing establishments, employing 110,000 workers. The North had more than one hundred thousand factories and shops, with 1,330,000 employees. New York, Massachusetts, and Pennsylvania each surpassed the entire industrial output of the South.

The transportation system of the North was far superior to that of the South. The North had more and better inland water transportation such as steamboats and barges. It also had more surfaced roads and more wagons and pack animals. In the North there were approximately 20,000 miles of railroad track, while the South, containing at least as large a land area, had only 10,000 miles. Too, there were many areas without rail connections between key locations in the South. Consequently, supplies had to be detoured long distances or transported by wagon between railroad depots in the South. As the war dragged on, the Confederate railroad system steadily deteriorated, and by the last eighteen months of the struggle it had virtually collapsed.

Such facts would give the impression that the South possessed absolutely no chance of winning the war. That, however, would be a major misconception. For the most part, the South fought a defensive war in its own country and was in command of interior lines. The invading armies from the North were forced to maintain long lines of communication, to supply themselves in areas where transportation was quite difficult, and to garrison occupied and hostile regions.

The North also had to do much more than capture the Confederate capital or defeat the enemy's armies. It had to thoroughly convince the southern civilian population that the war was hopeless by conquering and holding most of the Confederacy. On the other hand, the South was fighting for something very concrete and easily understood by its populace: independence. The South had no aggressive ambition to take the North. Strategically, then, the Confederacy merely had to survive to win, while the North had to conquer. The Confederacy could therefore fight a less demanding and less expensive defensive war. By contrast, the North had to accept the high cost of attack.

Southerners believed that as northern armies pushed further and further into the South, they would experience growing difficulties and fatigue. If only the war's price could be made high enough to the North, southerners contended, their independence could be guaranteed.

Secession deprived the United States Army of one-third of its officers. Many fine and talented officers took commissions in the Confederate army. Thus military leadership was relatively equal in the early going. Southerners firmly believed, though, that at the level of the common soldier, they were more skilled at fighting than their northern counterparts. Being an outdoor people accustomed to hunting and fishing, they were sure that "Johnny Reb" knew how to use rifles and endure physical hardship much better than "Billy Yank."

The Two War Presidents

Without question, the Union's greatest single asset was Abraham Lincoln, a pragmatic and realistic politician. He managed to make the right political decisions and deal adroitly with conservatives and radicals alike. Despite governors jealously protecting their own powers and military men scornful of his policy, Lincoln was able to handle all dilemmas. He curtailed civil liberties when he felt it was necessary to prevent disorder and dissent. He also carefully dealt with the border states so they would not enter the Confederate camp.

Militarily, Lincoln made mistakes but was capable of learning from his mistakes. Recognizing talent, he ultimately allowed men like General Ulysses S. Grant and General William T. Sherman to manage the Union armies for him. The combination of their talents went a long way toward Union victory.

Lincoln's choices for his cabinet were on the whole sound. William Seward as secretary of state, Gideon Welles as secretary of the navy, Salmon P. Chase as secretary of the treasury, and Edwin Stanton as secretary of war, all proved to be more distinguished and skillful than their southern counterparts. Here, Lincoln quickly learned from his mistakes. The president's initial appointment to head the War Department, Simon Cameron, turned out to be corrupt and incompetent. Discovering his error, Lincoln immediately shipped Cameron off to Russia as American minister and replaced him with the caustic and nettlesome, but eminently qualified Stanton. In the end, each man in Lincoln's cabinet was so jealous of his colleagues' authority that he had little time to subvert the president's powers.

Lincoln's greatest success, though, was as a symbol of the Union's determination to survive. A master of English prose, he turned out major state papers and addresses that rank among the most inspiring evocations of the democratic spirit. The war could easily have been perceived as a war of conquest not unlike the British effort to suppress the colonists over eighty years before; Lincoln transformed it into a struggle embodying the noblest aspirations of the American people. Indeed, the president persuaded his fellow citizens that the Union was humanity's "last, best hope." If it should be defeated, democracy would fail and tyranny would triumph.

Lincoln's counterpart, Jefferson Davis, was an experienced military man, a former United States senator from Mississippi, and had been secretary of war in the Pierce administration. He was honest, courageous, and intelligent, but he was also obsessed with trivialities and so involved himself in insignificant and time-consuming details. Unlike Lincoln, Davis was argumentative, insensitive to public opinion, and far too sensitive to criticism. Of the two leaders, we must conclude that Davis was the less effective.

The Fighting Begins

After raising armies, both sides believed they would win in short order. In fact, enthusiasm and a sense of frivolity accompanied the opening battle. In July 1861, at the First Battle of Bull Run, 20 miles south of Washington, many sightseers observed the fighting from vantage points in the countryside while picnicking.

Yet the struggle at Bull Run resulted in the rout of federal troops under the command of General Irvin McDowell, and necessity of more adequate planning and preparation, and less pomp and ceremony, was impressed upon both the North and the South by this battle.

Following Bull Run, George B. McClellan, fresh from victory in West Virginia, was given command of the Army of the Potomac. In preparation for his Peninsula Campaign (March to July 1862)—an advance upon the Confederate capital of Richmond, Virginia (made the capital in May 1861 because Montgomery, Alabama, was too far from the Confederate war front—McClellan delayed considerably by reorganizing, drilling, and reequipping the Union army. Finally ordered by Lincoln to set his army in motion, McClellan approached Richmond by way of Fort Monroe and the peninsula between the York and James rivers. Proceeding all too cautiously, he waited in vain for reinforcements outside of Richmond before launching an offensive. At Malvern Hill, McClellan successfully met a Confederate counteroffensive. After the battle, however, the Union general concluded his position was untenable and abandoned his long anticipated campaign just as Robert E. Lee took command of the Confederate troops.

In the West, Union forces under the command of George H. Thomas and Ulysses S. Grant were enjoying better luck. In January, Thomas defeated the Confederates in the Battle of Mill Springs in Kentucky. Several weeks later Grant captured Fort Donelson in Tennessee, taking fourteen thousand Confederate prisoners. Shortly thereafter, Nashville fell to the Union army. At the Battle of Shiloh Church (April 1862), though, Confederate General Albert Sidney Johnston stopped Grant's advance after two days of bloody fighting.

In July 1862, McClellan was removed from command of the Army of the Potomac. After General John Pope suffered a disastrous defeat at the hands of Thomas J. "Stonewall" Jackson in the Second Battle of Bull Run (August 1862), however, the former leader of the northern army was recalled. McClellan stopped Lee in Maryland at the Battle of Antietam (September 1862) but lost the opportunity of decisively defeating the far smaller Confederate force.

In November, Lincoln again replaced McClellan. Giving the command to Ambrose Burnside, though, proved to be unwise. In December 1862, at Fredericksburg, Virginia, the new Union commander's decisions resulted in the virtual slaughter of his troops.

Lincoln replaced Burnside with Joseph J. Hooker, who quickly demonstrated that he was no better than his predecessor. At the Battle of Chancellorsville (May 1863), Hooker's army was thoroughly defeated by Lee and Jackson. The only consolation for the Union to come from this battle was that Stonewall Jackson, one of the Confederacy's most skillful generals and a considerable thorn in the North's side, was accidentally killed by one of his own men.

The Naval War

Shortly after the outbreak of hostilities in April 1861, Lincoln had implemented a blockade of the Atlantic coast from South Carolina to Florida in an attempt to starve the Confederacy into submission. Lincoln recognized that the South had no navy and virtually no merchant marine from which a navy could be improvised. On the other hand, the North was constantly expanding its naval squadrons under the watchful eye of Secretary of the Navy Gideon Welles. By the fall of 1862, the North controlled all important southern ports except Wilmington, North Carolina, Charleston, South Carolina, and Mobile, Alabama. And Confederate blockade-runners were finding it increasingly difficult to carry on their trade through ports in the West Indies with the blockade tightening around them.

The Confederates made a daring attempt to break the blockade when they reconstructed the frigate *Merrimac* as an ironclad and sent it to Hampton Roads, Virginia, in March 1862, to demolish the wooden ships of the Union navy. The *Merrimac* might have accomplished its goal had it not been for the appearance of another ironclad, the *Monitor,* built for the United States government. Although neither ship could claim victory the Confederate attempt to break the blockade was thwarted. The *Merrimac* was retired, never again to challenge federal naval supremacy. Henceforth, however, wooden ships would seem obsolete.

The steady pressure brought on by the Union blockade slowly starved the south. Rations were reduced; clothing, shoes, and medicines were lacking; the Confederate transportation system broke down for want of replacement parts; and general destitution made support of the armies in the field increasingly difficult.

The Social Effects of the War

The war dragged on, and by mid-1862 neither the Union nor Confederate ranks could any longer be filled by hopes of glory. Bitter fighting, growing casualty lists, and news of danger, anguish, and the hard work of soldiering dampened youthful enthusiasm. Fewer and fewer volunteers turned up at the recruiting offices. As a result, both governments resorted to conscription—the first in American history.

Their respective draft laws contained many inequities. The Confederate measure provided that anyone who supervised twenty slaves or more, whether as owner or as overseer, was exempt from service. The Union law enabled a man to avoid service if he could find and pay for a substitute or give the government $300.

The exemptions in both conscription systems were defended on the grounds of national interest or compassion. In truth, however, both draft laws favored the affluent over the ordinary man and encouraged critics in the North and South to charge that the war was "a rich man's war and a poor man's fight."

In the North particularly, opposition to the draft took violent forms. The culmination was four days of rioting, looting, arson, and attacks on blacks and abolitionists in New York City in July 1863. The riots were so serious that Union troops had to be called in from the battlefields to suppress them.

Conscription was a unique manifestation of expanded central governmental power. The three previous American wars had been fought by volunteers. Now, under the strain of this war, both Union and Confederate governments had assumed a prerogative never claimed before, the right to compel men to risk their lives for the state.

Paying for the war was a major challenge to both governments, and in 1861, Americans did not pay heavy taxes. In the Confederacy, the government could not bring itself to initiate an income tax to finance its war effort. But the war exacted a tremendous cost from both governments. At one point in the war, the Union treasury was spending $2 million a day on munitions, supplies, war matériel, military pay, and other expenses.

Unable to secure loans from foreign and domestic sources and unwilling to tax, the Confederate government in 1863 began to infringe upon the sacred rights of property and bypass private enterprise as a means of financing its war effort. The Confederate Congress authorized the impressment of slaves for the building of fortifications and for other government work as needed. It also empowered the government to assign soldiers to work in crucial war factories. The government in Richmond regimented agriculture: in April 1863 it assumed the authority to take from each farmer one-tenth of all major crops he produced.

In the North, by 1865 Congress had imposed taxes on hundreds of items, created a Bureau of Internal Revenue, and established America's first income tax. With access to the markets of Europe, the gold of the West, and most of the country's banking capital, the Union was in much better financial shape than the South, and in some ways its financial power even grew during the Civil War, making it much easier for the North to borrow to finance its war effort.

Under the National Bank Acts of 1863 and 1864, the North created the National Banking System, which lasted without serious modification until 1913, and through it issued paper money with better financial backing than the South's. The North was thus able to avoid the massive inflation plaguing the South because of the low value of Confederate money.

This was no mean feat. By late 1864, northern price levels were only about two and a half times those of the prewar period, while in the South prices had risen to fifty times their 1860 levels. During 1863–1864 flour sold in the South for $300 a barrel; broadcloth, for $125 a yard; chickens, for $35 a pair; beef, for $5 a pound; and men's shoes, for $125 a pair. Many southerners, particularly those who lived in towns or who had fixed incomes, could not pay these prices. Forced to do without, these Confederates simply lost their will to endure or win.

The expansion of the Union government's power in financial areas was matched, if not exceeded, by its intrusion into transportation. In 1861, the Union had 22,000 or so miles of railroad track. This constituted the most extensive railroad network in the world, but not as yet an integrated system. Many smaller communities remained without railroad connections, and varying track gauges prevented rapid through traffic on many routes. The most obvious deficiency of all was the lack of rail connections to the west coast.

During the war the Union reduced these shortcomings. Most importantly, with the South out of the Union, Congress passed the Pacific Railway Act of 1862, a measure to subsidize a transcontinental railroad. Immediately after the war ended, crews were laying track across the plains and mountains at a furious pace.

The Lincoln administration pursued a vigorous and successful policy of controlling and coordinating the existing railroads to meet war needs. After May 1862, the railroads operated under governmental supervision, and 650 miles of new track were constructed to link existing routes. The Union government's increased role in transportation enabled the railroads to accomplish marvels in moving northern troops and supplies throughout the war.

On the other hand, the Davis administration failed to mobilize southern railroads for the Confederate war effort. Due to the lack of personnel and material, the Confederacy did little to prevent locomotives from breaking down and tracks from wearing out. Many small private companies continued to determine rail rates and make other significant decisions affecting the southern economy throughout the war. Because of the ineffective rail service, southern troops were often shoeless, hungry, and ragged toward the end of the war while Confederate warehouses remained filled with supplies and clothing.

The needs of war greatly expanded the federal government. In 1861 the Union had 40,000 civil service employees; by 1865 there were 195,000, a fivefold increase to accommodate the enlarged government functions. As the Union's government expanded, its economy grew as well. Increased production in industry and manufacturing made the northern standard of living actually improve.

Agricultural decline in the South due to invading armies, breakdown of transportation, and the erosion of the slave labor system was matched by a steadily improving agriculture in the North. This was evidenced by the creation in 1861 of the Department of Agriculture within the Patent Office; the Morrill Land Grant College Act (1862), which set aside several million acres of federal land for support of agricultural and industrial higher education; and the Homestead Act (1862), which provided that any citizen (or alien declaring intention to become one) who was head of a family and over twenty-one might claim 160 acres of land on the surveyed portion of the public domain.

The Homestead Act especially encouraged settlement in the West and the growth of small farms. This was because after adding improvements and paying a nominal registration fee and local taxes, the homesteader would become owner of the land.

Protest and Dissent During the War

The Union government was often intolerant of dissent and indifferent to civil liberties. Ironically, repression was stronger in the North, which had a tradition of intellectual freedom, than in the South, which had one of intolerance.

Dissent in the North ranged from mild disagreement with Lincoln's policies to violent opposition that bordered on treason. The War Democrats often disagreed with Lincoln over the best ways of obtaining victory, but they followed the lead of Stephen Douglas in offering their unwavering support to the Union. After Douglas died in June 1861, the War Democrats continued to support the Union throughout the war.

The Peace Democrats, or Copperheads, as their detractors called them, were far more critical of the Lincoln administration. They favored a negotiated peace with the South; either Lincoln should allow the South back into the Union with its rights and institutions guaranteed, or he should permit it to leave without further war and bloodshed.

The Peace Democrats became more numerous as the war continued and southern victories grew fewer. Most of their support was in the Midwest. Led by men like Clement Vallandigham and George Pendleton of Ohio and Daniel Voorhees of Indiana, they vehemently objected to the increased powers of the federal government and the expanded role of the president. They also resisted every attempt to make abolition a part of the Union cause, and they assailed the administration's efforts to curtail the civil liberties of whites.

In the border states of Delaware, Kentucky, Missouri, and Maryland, anti-Union sentiment was frequently intense. Occasionally, these states themselves became literal battlegrounds between pro-Union and pro-Confederate groups. Neighbor fought neighbor with a viciousness that sometimes transcended anything found on the battlefields. In Missouri, for instance, full-scale guerrilla war broke out between Unionists and Confederate sympathizers. Throughout these states Union commanders frequently used severe and arbitrary methods that further alienated the pro-southern populace and fostered even greater discontent.

Ultimately, President Lincoln had to determine how much dissent was permissible in a nation threatened with dissolution. Certainly, Lincoln was not a harsh man; he was deeply compassionate and strongly committed to free speech. But the president reasoned his first responsibility was to preserve the Union.

Within his own party, Lincoln had to contend with radicals who believed the president was not being firm enough with the South. They particularly attacked his refusal to use the war as an opportunity to destroy slavery and his reluctance to employ blacks in the armed forces. Republican conservatives maintained just the opposite: the war to restore the Union must not be "abolitionized." According to these Republicans, to attack slavery would not only force the border states out of the Union but strengthen the southern determination to resist as well. Lincoln balanced all wings of his party by listening to them, making them feel they had made a significant contribution, and then heeding their advice only when he agreed with it.

Dealing with dissenters outside the Republican Party, however, was more difficult. Lincoln's most outspoken critic was Clement Vallandigham, and the Ohioan proved to be a constant irritant to the president. In 1863, Vallandigham was arrested by General Ambrose Burnside for defying a military order against "declaring sympathy for the enemy." Tried by a military commission, Vallandigham was convicted of disloyalty and attempting to subvert the federal government. The entire affair became a major embarrassment for Lincoln when Vallandigham became a free-speech symbol in the North. To detach himself from the mess, Lincoln eventually freed Vallandigham from jail but banished him to the Confederacy.

Vallandigham was but one of many dissenters the president faced. Lincoln suspended *habeas corpus*, the traditional protection of accused parties against arbitrary imprisonment, in areas where disloyalty seemed to endanger the war effort. He also endorsed congressional enactments imposing severe penalties on persons guilty of treason or conspiracy to commit treason. In September 1863, Lincoln signed a sweeping order making subject to martial law anyone who sought to discourage enlistment, came out against the draft, or engaged in other disloyal practices.

Yet at no time did Lincoln feel comfortable with what he felt compelled to do, and he frequently restrained excesses committed by his subordinates. One such incident occurred when the overzealous General Burnside closed the Democratic *Chicago Times* for supporting Vallandigham. Realizing that such action was unnecessary, the president promptly reopened the paper.

"King Cotton" Diplomacy

Southern leaders saw cotton as their best diplomatic weapon. The textile industry, contended the Confederates, was fundamental to the economies of England and France, which depended upon the South for the lion's share of their cotton. The South was convinced that to deprive Europe of its cotton would mean the financial collapse of the Continent. Toward this end, the southern states embargoed the export of cotton and patriotic Confederates pressured planters to curtail the amount of cotton they planted. Some planters even burned their cotton to create an artificial scarcity. This campaign cut the South's 1862 output to a third of its prewar volume. Pushed to their economic limits, the Europeans would have to intervene on the side of the South, it was naively assumed.

The diplomacy based on "King Cotton" never paid off in the way its advocates had envisioned. In 1861, English manufacturers had a surplus of cotton on hand. Thereafter, when the supply became increasingly small, a few mills were indeed forced to close. Both England and France, however, were able to avoid a complete shutdown of their textile industries by relying upon new suppliers of cotton, most notably Egypt and India.

No European nation extended diplomatic recognition to the Confederacy, and though at times, England and France offered to mediate in the American crisis, they never moved to intervene in the war. This was because neither of the European nations could afford to take the chance unless the Confederacy seemed on the verge of winning, and the South never approached the prospect of certain victory.

The North also had a distinct advantage that its southern adversary lacked: the prospect of emancipation. Although they might be indifferent to the concept of southern independence, the British middle and working classes could not in all good conscience support the slave regime. If the North could convince the British people of its antislavery intentions, London would certainly find it difficult to intervene on behalf of the Confederacy.

Still, the South won several of the early diplomatic rounds. Late in 1861, John Slidell and James M. Mason, Confederate ministers to France and England respectively, ran the Union blockade and reached Havana. There they boarded the *Trent*, a British steamer bound for Europe. On November 7, Captain Charles Wilkes of the U.S.S. *San Jacinto* intercepted the *Trent*, arrested Slidell and Mason, and took them to Boston. The British were outraged and demanded the two Confederates' release, an official apology, and reparations. Lincoln and his secretary of state, William Seward, delayed acting on this situation for a time and then released Slidell and Mason with an apology.

The *Trent* affair worked to the advantage of the South. Early in 1862, the British government gave the Confederacy permission to use British shipyards to build and outfit six cruisers including the *Alabama*, the *Florida*, and the *Shenandoah*. As another residual effect of the *Trent* affair, London allowed the Confederate navy to contract with Laird, a shipbuilding company in Scotland, for the purchase of several powerful ironclad Laird Rams, ships with pointed prows which could be used for ramming and sinking Union vessels and thus breaking the blockade.

But thanks to the efforts of Richard Cobden and John Bright, two British antislavery friends of the United States, and Lincoln's minister to England, Charles Francis Adams, the tide of diplomatic opinion soon turned. In October 1863, the British government seized the Laird Rams before the south could take delivery, and the threat to the Union blockade was ended.

The Emancipation Proclamation

Lincoln tried to avoid the issue of slavery. So long as there was any possibility that the border slave states might join the South, Lincoln believed that he must focus public opinion on reuniting the nation and not on ending the "peculiar institution." Thus, Lincoln constantly tried to restrain those military and civilian leaders who sought to use the war to destroy slavery.

Many prominent northern blacks like Frederick Douglass joined white abolitionists in asserting that the war was a struggle over slavery. To win it, they insisted, the Union must fight to end enslavement. "The very stomach of this rebellion," wrote Douglass, "is the negro in the condition of a slave. Arrest that hoe in the hands of the negro and you smite the rebellion in the very seat of its life."

Douglass was right. In the South, even with the absence from the farms and plantations of thousands of young white men, the black population did not rebel and liberate itself. In many ways, work went on as normal. But this fact should not be misunderstood. The slaves refused to rebel because they recognized that there was little chance for a successful uprising in as heavily armed and militarized a community as the wartime south. When Union armies advanced into the Confederacy, black refugees flocked to their lines.

At first, Union officials did not know what to do with these refugees. Called by General Benjamin Butler the "contraband of war," blacks were put to work as free laborers on military fortifications. Recognizing an obvious need for the protection of the blacks, many different factions soon demanded an overall policy in this regard.

Lincoln originally hoped that compensated emancipation and colonization in either Africa or Latin America would suffice. Blacks, however, were hostile to the notion of colonization, and in the border states slaveholders proved unwilling to consider freeing their slaves even if paid.

The alternative was simply abolishing slavery, an institution deeply embedded in American life and representing $4 billion worth of private property. At first, Lincoln was reluctant to take that step.

The strong likelihood that the destruction of slavery would shorten the war finally convinced the president that abolition by federal proclamation was an action he must take. Lincoln was influenced in making this decision by three powerful considerations. First was the reliance of the Confederacy upon slave labor. Lincoln hoped that if southern blacks knew that the federal government intended to free them, they might cease to be a source of strength for the South. Second was the potential value of black soldiers. If the North could exploit this human resource, perhaps it could counterbalance the immediate battlefield losses and declining enthusiasm of white volunteers. Slave refugees might flock to the Union army, Lincoln thought, if they were promised freedom in exchange for military service. Finally, there was a distinct moral advantage to turning the war for the Union into a war for human freedom. The president shrewdly concluded that if the Union cause was identified with the end of slavery, it would be quite difficult for any European nation to provide assistance to the Confederacy.

Lincoln waited for an opportune time to make his announcement concerning emancipation, fearing that if he made it at the wrong moment it would be construed as an act of desperation. Finally, on September 22, 1862, after the northern victory at Antietam, he issued a preliminary emancipation proclamation declaring that on January 1, 1863, in every part of the South still in rebellion, all slaves would be "thenceforward and forever free."

The Emancipation Proclamation took effect as scheduled, on New Year's Day 1863. In actuality, it affected only those areas where federal law could not be enforced: the Confederacy. It made no reference to slavery in the border states, and had the Union lost the war, it would have become a symbol of futility. But such was not to be. Although slavery would not be legally abolished across the land until the ratification of the Thirteenth Amendment to the Constitution in 1865, the Emancipation Proclamation effectively sounded the death knell of slavery all over the United States.

War's Effects Behind the Lines

On the civilian front, the war caused pronounced changes. We have already seen in part how southerners experienced great hardships. As prices rose, transportation broke down, and as the northern blockade strengthened its stranglehold, Confederate living standards deteriorated. Indeed, food riots occurred in such cities as Mobile (1863) due to impoverished conditions. Throughout the entire South, tea and coffee, both imported items, became rare, forcing the Confederates to use parched wheat, corn, peanuts, and even acorns as substitutes.

When commodities were available, because of severe inflation they often sold at prices far beyond the means of the average consumer. During the course of the war, the price of bacon increased sixfold, flour came to cost seven times more, and tea came to cost twelve times what it did in 1860. Certainly, deprivation and hunger hurt southern morale and led to an increase in anti-Confederate sentiment.

Even at the outset of the war, there existed a significant degree of Unionist sentiment in the hill country and in isolated sections, all over the South. In the mountainous western counties of Virginia, anti-Confederate feeling resulted in the establishment of a separate state government with its capital at Wheeling. In June 1863, Lincoln admitted its fifty rebellious counties into the Union as the new state of West Virginia.

As military and civilian conditions deteriorated in the Confederacy, southern Unionists and dissenters became more open in their opposition to continuing the war. They were soon attacking southern leadership and insisting that local and state needs came before those of the new nation.

Governors Joseph E. Brown of Georgia and Zebulon Vance of North Carolina, in particular, frustrated the Davis administration at every turn when they felt that the rights and prerogatives of their states were being ignored by Confederate authorities. In order to meet their local needs, they refused to contribute men, money, and supplies to the central government, severely hurting the Confederate war effort.

As living conditions worsened in the South, they improved in the north. By 1863, the North generally was prosperous. Businesses stimulated by war orders and agriculture stimulated by increased demands both reached high production levels and, in turn, poured more money back into the economy.

Northern women actually benefited from the war. Before 1861, employment opportunities for women had been limited. With the absence of thousands of men now in Union armies, traditional sex barriers weakened. Many women joined the vastly expanded War and Treasury Departments as secretaries, copyists, and clerks. The number of female factory operatives, schoolteachers, and clerical workers for private businesses also increased.

One of the most significant developments for women was the creation of a female nursing profession. Through the efforts of women like Clara Barton and Dorothea Dix, hundreds of women were employed in medical capacities with the Union army by the end of the war.

After the war, some of these employment gains were nullified when government departments contracted and men returned to civilian life. But women had indeed made gains in the north. Clara Barton, who would found the American Red Cross some twenty years after the Civil War, perceptively observed that by war's end "woman was at least fifty years in advance of the normal position which continued peace . . . would have assigned her."

In the Confederate army, women had no role as nurses. That is not to say that Confederate women did not contribute. They took on clerical, farming, and schoolteaching jobs formerly reserved for men, and worked in the farm fields to help meet the labor shortage. Without doubt, southern women contributed a great deal to the Confederate cause and their patriotism and sacrifice were undeniable.

Black and Ethnic Soldiers

Two sources of northern strength, foreigners and blacks, were largely denied the South. In fact, about 25 percent of the Union troops were foreign-born, mostly German or Irish. Although several thousand foreign-born young men did fight for the Confederacy, most European immigrants had avoided the South before 1861, and unlike the North, the Confederacy received few, if any, new arrivals after the war began.

Despite much race prejudice, with growing resistance to white volunteerism, black troops were recruited by the northern army. Most of these soldiers were northern free blacks or former southern slaves.

Organized in August 1862, black troops, always under the command of a white officer and usually treated as second-class troops in matters of pay, bounties for service, and other benefits, fought with much valor for the Union cause. In March 1863, Lincoln called the black troops "very important, if not indispensable" to the Union war effort. By 1865, the Union had enrolled over 178,000 black soldiers.

The impressive performance of the black and foreign-born Union troops had positive effects upon racial and ethnic attitudes in the North. Nativism declined somewhat, and although racial bigotry continued, the legal and social position of blacks improved. A few northern states repealed their laws discriminating against free blacks or denying them the right to reside within their borders. Several cities ceased their practice of segregating blacks on streetcars or in schools. The racial and ethnic attitudes of northern Americans still had a very long way to go, but the exemplary record of minority troops forced at least a few people to reconsider their beliefs.

The Turning Points of the War

Until the middle of 1863 it still seemed possible for the South to obtain a victory. Lee's defeat of Hooker at Chancellorsville in May, even though it had resulted in the death of Stonewall Jackson, had served to encourage the south. Lee was now determined to assume the offensive. If he could take the war to the North, Lee reasoned, and threaten Washington, D.C., or capture a major city like Philadelphia, he might destroy northern morale and force a negotiated peace. Early in the summer (June 15) Lee's Army of northern Virginia crossed the Potomac River and headed northward into the Cumberland Valley of Pennsylvania.

Lee's northern advance alarmed Lincoln, who quickly replaced the unsuccessful Hooker with Major General George G. Meade as the commander of the Army of the Potomac. For the first three days of July, Meade and Lee clashed at Gettysburg, a little village 50 miles from the state capital at Harrisburg. The fighting was exceptionally bloody, much of it hand to hand.

The battle was indecisive until, on the last day, the Confederates launched ten thousand men under General George Pickett against the Union forces perched on ominously named Cemetery Ridge. This daring ploy almost worked, but after furious fighting the Union held its position.

Pickett's Charge was the last burst of Confederate strength. Lee expected Meade to counterattack, but his Union counterpart commanded an army as exhausted and crippled as the Confederates. Seeing his chance to flee, Lee ordered a general retreat. Soon, the Army of northern Virginia was back in the Old Dominion never again to venture north.

Lee's defeat at Gettysburg coincided with Grant's capture of Vicksburg, Mississippi, after a long and costly siege. In the fall of 1863, Grant and General George H. Thomas won the battles of Lookout Mountain and Missionary Ridge and, by so doing, pushed the Confederates out of war-ravaged Tennessee.

Grant was called to assume command of all the northern troops, and he returned east in March 1864. In the following months he determined that the only way to break the Confederate back was to launch a war of attrition. This he did, and while the gains in ground during this campaign were negligible, the losses on both sides were staggering. In the battles of the Wilderness (May 5 to 7), Spotsylvania Court House (May 8 to 19), and Cold Harbor (June 1 to 3), Grant pressed stubbornly on toward Richmond at tremendous cost. In a month of fighting he lost a total of fifty-five thousand men—killed, wounded, and captured—and Lee lost thirty-one thousand. Nevertheless, the North, exhausted and weary though it may have been, had reserves in manpower; the South did not and the end was in sight.

The Election of 1864

Even though the nation was in the midst of war, a presidential election still occurred in 1864. The Republicans again went with Lincoln and chose as his running mate Andrew Johnson, a Tennessee Unionist. The Democrats chose George McClellan, who had been the first commander of all the northern troops, and George H. Pendleton of Ohio. Neither man was an extreme Copperhead but both favored a negotiated peace with the South and hoped to ride a wave of discouragement that followed Confederate victories during the late summer and fall of 1864.

After three long years of war, Lincoln himself was pessimistic about his prospects of being returned to office. Indeed, the president believed that it was "exceedingly probable that this Administration will not be reelected."

Fortunately for Lincoln, however, General William T. Sherman's capture of Atlanta in September 1864 once again brightened the prospects of Union victory. One hundred thousand strong, Sherman's army marched almost unopposed across Georgia, toward the Atlantic Ocean, and in the process inaugurated a new kind of warfare. The prophet of modern total war, Sherman waged war against the civilian population of the south, intending to break the Confederacy of its will to endure. His army marched on a 60-mile front, destroying property and supplies that might be used by the Confederate forces. By December, Sherman was at Savannah and his victories cut the already divided South into more pieces.

With northern morale revived, Lincoln swept the electoral college in November and won a popular majority of four hundred thousand votes over McClellan.

The Death of the Confederacy

Shortly after Lincoln's reelection, the Confederacy began to crumble. After Savannah, Sherman headed toward South Carolina, still facing slight opposition and still destroying the enemy's property as he went. When he advanced into North Carolina, the Confederate government pieced together a small army of thirty thousand under Joseph E. Johnston to oppose him, but they could do little more than delay Sherman's march.

In April 1865, Grant finally forced Lee out of Petersburg and Richmond, Virginia. Lee moved westward with his army now shrunk to twenty-five thousand. Realizing that his men were hungry, demoralized, and on the verge of being surrounded, Lee asked Grant for peace terms on April 7, 1865. Two days later, on April 9, the war-weary generals met and agreed on surrender terms at the crossroads hamlet of Appomattox Courthouse.

Grant was generous. The Confederate officers and men were to be released on their promise not to take up arms again. The Confederates would surrender all weapons and war matériel, but the men could keep their personal equipment, including their horses and mules. In short order, twenty-five thousand Confederates laid down their arms.

In North Carolina, Johnston reached the same conclusion as Lee, and on April 18, he surrendered to Sherman near Durham. Jefferson Davis, defiant to the end and unable to recognize defeat, fled southward, and was captured in Georgia.

The war was over. The losses were staggering: 618,000 Americans (360,000 of the North and 258,000 of the South) had died in the four years of bloody fighting.

Five days after the war ended, with the problems of reconstructing the Union now on his mind, Lincoln took a night off and went with his wife Mary and some friends to see the British play *Our American Cousin* at Ford's Theater. The actor and Confederate sympathizer John Wilkes Booth entered the presidential box during the play and shot Lincoln once. The president languished through the night and died early the next morning on April 15.

Booth and a few other disgruntled southerners had concocted a plot to destroy the man they held responsible for the fall of the Confederacy. To throw the federal government into chaos, they also planned to assassinate Secretary of State William Seward,

Vice President Andrew Johnson, and other top Union officials. After escaping, Booth was cornered in a barn in Virginia and either shot himself or was shot by a zealous Union soldier before disclosing the full conspiracy. What was without doubt was that he had assassinated the president, and with Lincoln's death went any hopes for a peaceful and efficient reconstruction of the Union.

What had all the death and destruction accomplished? Certainly the Civil War ended any future threat of national dissolution at the hands of armed internal forces. Never again, not even during periods of intense sectional discord, would any part of the United States threaten to secede.

The war also brought more social and economic coherence to the nation as a whole. It facilitated the building of a transcontinental railroad and the creation of a national banking system making possible a new national currency.

Most significant of all, the war destroyed slavery. But by no means did it end problems between the two races. Racism and discrimination would continue into the present day. But the Civil War did obliterate an institution that rigidly relegated an entire race of people to an inferior and grossly exploited status. And with the demise of the "peculiar institution" came eventual reform and improvement.

As we shall see in the next chapter, American society after the Civil War failed terribly in its bid to make good on the promise of racial equality. This fact cannot be denied. Few critics of American race relations, though, no matter how harsh, can deny that the Civil War's greatest legacy, the destruction of slavery, was the necessary first step toward racial equality.

Recommended Reading

Thomas B. Alexander and Richard Beringer, *The Anatomy of the Confederate Congress* (1972)

Michael Barton, *Good Men: The Character of Civil War Soldiers* (1981)

Richard Beringer, Herman Hattaway, Archer Jones, and William Still, *Why the South Lost the Civil War* (1986)

Bruce Catton, *Glory Road* (1952)

Bruce Catton, *Mr. Lincoln's Army* (1951)

Bruce Catton, *A Stillness at Appomattox* (1956)

Thomas L. Connelly and Archer Jones, *The Politics of Command* (1973)

Adrian Cook, *The Armies of the Streets* (1974)

Dudley T. Cornish, *The Sable Arm: Black Troops in the Union Army, 1861–1865* (1953)

Lawanda Cox, *Lincoln and Black Freedom: A Study in Presidential Leadership* (1981)

David P. Crook, *Diplomacy during the Civil War* (1975)

Richard N. Current, *The Lincoln Nobody Knows* (1958)

David Donald, ed., *Why the North Won the Civil War* (1960)

Martin Duberman, *Charles Francis Adams, 1807–1886* (1960)

Robert F. Durden, *The Gray and the Black* (1972)

Clement Eaton, *A History of the Southern Confederacy* (1954)

Clement Eaton, *Jefferson Davis* (1977)

Norman B. Ferris, *The Trent Affair* (1977)

Emerson D. Fite, *Social and Industrial Conditions in the North during the Civil War* (1910)

Shelby Foote, *The Civil War*, 3 vols. (1958–1973)

John Hope Franklin, *The Emancipation Proclamation* (1963)

George M. Fredrickson, *The Inner Civil War* (1965)

Douglass S. Freeman, *Lee: A Biography*, 4 vols. (1934–1935)

Paul Gates, *Agriculture and the Civil War* (1965)

Herman Hattaway and Archer Jones, *How the North Won: A Military History of the Civil War* (1983)

Virgil C. Jones, *The Civil War at Sea*, 3 vols. (1960–1962)

Frank L. Klement, *The Copperheads in the Middle West* (1960)

Margaret K. Leech, *Reveille in Washington, 1860–1865* (1941)

Lloyd Lewis, *Sherman: Fighting Prophet* (1932)

Gerald F. Linderman, *Embattled Courage: The Experience of Combat in the American Civil War* (1987)

Ella Lonn, *Foreigners in the Confederacy* (1940)

Ella Lonn, *Foreigners in the Union Army and Navy* (1951)

William S. McFeely, *Grant: A Biography* (1981)

James M. McPherson, *Battle Cry of Freedom: The Civil War Era* (1988)

James M. McPherson, ed., *The Negro's Civil War* (1965)

Grady McWhinney and Perry Jameson, *Attack and Die* (1982)

Allan Nevins, *The War for the Union*, 4 vols. (1959–1971)

Benjamin P. Quarles, *The Negro and the Civil War* (1953)

Charles P. Roland, *The Confederacy* (1960)

Benjamin P. Thomas, *Abraham Lincoln* (1952)

Emory M. Thomas, *The Confederate Nation, 1861–1865* (1979)

Emory M. Thomas, *The Confederacy as a Revolutionary Experience* (1971)

Glyndon G. Van Deusen, *William Henry Seward* (1967)

Bell I. Wiley, *Confederate Women* (1975)

Bell I. Wiley, *The Life of Billy Yank: The Common Soldier of the Union* (1952)

Bell I. Wiley, *The Life of Johnny Reb: The Common Soldier of the Confederacy* (1943)

Kenneth P. Williams, *Lincoln Finds a General*, 5 vols. (1949–1959)

T. Harry Williams, *Lincoln and His Generals* (1952)

CHAPTER 16

Reconstructing the Union

Time Line

1863	President Lincoln issues his Ten Percent Plan to readmit Confederate states into the Union
1864	Congress passes the Wade-Davis Bill, its own Reconstruction program; Lincoln pocket-vetoes it
1865	The Thirteenth Amendment to the Constitution, abolishing slavery, is ratified
	President Andrew Johnson reveals his Reconstruction plans while Congress is adjourned

The Freedmen's Bureau is established

"Johnson governments" in the South establish strict black codes

Congress refuses to seat the southern delegations elected under the Johnson Reconstruction plan

Congress establishes the Joint Committee on Reconstruction

1866   Congress proposes the Fourteenth Amendment to the Constitution, defining U.S. citizenship as including blacks; it is ratified two years later (1868)

The Ku Klux Klan is formed by a group of young Confederate veterans

Tennessee is readmitted to the Union .

1867   Over President Johnson's veto, Congress passes the first two Reconstruction Acts

President Johnson suspends from office Secretary of War Edwin Stanton in apparent defiance of the Tenure of Office Act

1868   The House of Representatives passes a resolution to impeach President Johnson

Johnson is acquitted of impeachment charges in the Senate by one vote

Ulysses S. Grant is elected president

Arkansas, North Carolina, South Carolina, Alabama, Florida, and Louisiana are readmitted to the Union

1870	The Fifteenth Amendment to the Constitution, specifying the right of black men to vote, is ratified
	Virginia, Mississippi, Texas, and Georgia rejoin the Union
1870–1871	Congress passes three "force bills" declaring the Ku Klux Klan's terrorist activity illegal
1872	Ulysses S. Grant is reelected president
	Grant's administration is plagued by one scandal after another, starting with the Crédit Mobilier
1875	Congress passes the Civil Rights Act
1876	The presidential election between Democrat Samuel Tilden and Republican Rutherford B. Hayes is thrown into the House of Representatives for resolution
1877	The Compromise of 1877 gives the presidency to Hayes and ends Reconstruction by removing all federal troops from the South

---

The war was over. Or was it? The battlefield fighting ended with the surrender of the Confederate army at Appomattox. But bitter political wrangling would ensue for the next twelve years. When the smoke cleared, a president was impeached and race relations in the South were almost as poisoned as they had been during the antebellum period. From most standpoints, the Reconstruction period was unsuccessful. Indeed, a Rip Van Winkle who went to sleep in the South in 1857 and awakened in 1877 might conceivably believe that he had not missed very much. We must now turn our attention to what went wrong and what was the legacy of that failure.

The Aftermath of War

After the Civil War, the South lay in ruins. The South had absorbed the brunt of the fighting and places like interior South Carolina, which had been hit hard by General Sherman's army, "looked for many miles," as one Union soldier wrote home, "like a broad black streak of ruin and desolation." In Virginia's Shenandoah Valley, scarcely a farm animal remained alive. Southern cities as well were devastated. Columbia, capital of South Carolina, consisted of a blackened wasteland with barely a building standing in the business district. Atlanta, Richmond, Selma, and other southern urban areas experienced similar fates and would require massive rebuilding.

Yet the physical destruction was but the tip of the iceberg. Human losses were staggering. Of the South's white male population of two and a half million in 1860, a quarter million, or about 10 percent, had died of battle wounds or disease. Most were young and had represented the South's future. Of those who survived, some were maimed and many others emotionally scarred. "A more completely crushed country I have seldom witnessed," a Yankee officer wrote the United States attorney general.

The South's banking system, based on now worthless Confederate bonds, had collapsed. Personal savings had been wiped out when the Confederate currency lost its value. Perhaps even more traumatic, the region's labor system was destroyed. Slavery as an economic system, and as a social one, was dead, but no one knew what the alternative would be. Many blacks remained on the farms and plantations and continued to plant, cultivate, or harvest. Thousands of others, whether to taste their newborn freedom or search for long-lost relatives, traveled the roads or headed for the cities, abandoning the land that had traditionally sustained the South's economy.

The physical and institutional destruction of war was equaled by the psychological damage. People both north and south of the Mason-Dixon Line harbored deep resentments. After struggling for independence for four years, white southerners could not help feeling angry and disappointed. Northerners would not easily forget the sacrifices and losses they suffered in suppressing what they considered to be a treasonous rebellion.

The American people, then, faced the formidable tasks of restoring the nation and healing physical, political, and emotional wounds of the war. For the next twelve years, until 1877, Reconstruction would dominate the political and intellectual life of all Americans. It would be a time of great upheaval and controversy.

Presidential Reconstruction

Even before Lee's surrender at Appomattox in 1865, the Union government had begun to consider the question of Reconstruction. As northern victories increased, Lincoln was confronted with the problem of how to govern the conquered territory. Martial law could suffice for a time, but it flagrantly contradicted the American tradition of civilian rule.

It seemed, at first, that an expeditious reconciliation was possible. Former Confederate soldiers were inclined to accept their defeat and abstain from further resistance. Most former slaves hoped to live harmoniously with southern whites. They eagerly desired and anticipated acquiring the land that they tilled, but they did not aspire to any violent retribution against their former masters.

For their part, northerners had accomplished their initial war objectives: the defeat of the South and destruction of the "slave power." They had even made slavery unconstitutional by the adoption of the Thirteenth Amendment to the Constitution which went into effect on December 18, 1865. While a few northerners insisted on some punishment of the South to pay for the 360,000 Union deaths, most took a more compassionate view, believing instead that nearly 260,000 Confederate deaths and the surrender had been payment enough.

Lincoln initiated the process of Reconstruction while the war was still being fought. Whenever federal troops occupied significant areas in the South, the president enacted a policy of moderation and reconciliation in the hope of restoring the Union as quickly as possible.

In December 1863, Lincoln issued his Ten Percent Plan. This plan provided amnesty to all southerners (with a few exceptions) who took an oath of allegiance to the Constitution and the Union. It stated that, in any Confederate state, when the number of citizens equal to 10 percent of those who had voted in the presidential election of 1860 took this oath, the military authority could then establish a state government.

Lincoln's plan encountered opposition in Congress from his own party, and it was eventually defeated. A group of radical Republicans, led by Senator Charles Sumner of Massachusetts and Representative Thaddeus Stevens of Pennsylvania, opposed it strenuously. They believed the plan was too lenient, and allowed the South readmission into the Union too easily. The majority of radical Republicans considered the Confederacy the sole cause of the Civil War, and felt they must be made to pay for it.

The radical Republicans were united in their belief that the former slaves must be given the right to vote. Without it, they reasoned, the new freedmen could not enjoy genuine independence from their ex-masters. In this vein, all the radicals contended that the federal government must do something to ensure the freedmen's vote. What the radicals disagreed on was whether the vote was all that the former slaves needed to be free. For example, Charles Sumner believed that black suffrage alone would be sufficient to remake the South, while Thaddeus Stevens asserted that the redistribution of land to the freedmen was required as well.

The moderate Republicans, who formed the majority of the party, did not agree with the radicals that the federal government should ensure black voting. Along with the radicals, though, they believed that Lincoln should punish the South, guarantee the abolition of slavery, and establish the Republican Party in the South.

In July 1864, the Republican Congress, to advance its own Reconstruction program and to reestablish its authority, passed the Wade-Davis Bill. The bill asserted that Congress, not the president, was primarily responsible for Reconstruction. In regard to the South, Congress assumed the constitutional interpretation, promoted by Thaddeus Stevens, that the seceded states had actually left the Union and were now no more than conquered territory.

The Wade-Davis Bill stated that before a new southern state government could be formed, a majority of white male citizens must pledge their support to the United States Constitution. In addition, each state must write a new constitution, and only those who had taken an ironclad oath that they had never taken up arms against the United States or voluntarily aided the Confederacy could participate in its writing. The new state constitutions had to abolish slavery, disfranchise Confederate civil and military leaders, and repudiate war debts.

The Wade-Davis Bill was more stringent a bill than he had wanted, so Lincoln pocket-vetoed it, holding the bill unsigned until Congress adjourned. Tennessee, Arkansas, Virginia, and Louisiana, however, chose to enter the Union on Lincoln's Ten Percent Plan terms, and so the president restored them to the Union. But this was only temporary.

Lincoln's assassination profoundly altered the course of Reconstruction and made an already difficult task seemingly impossible. The Civil War had expanded presidential power beyond any previous American experience, and now Congress began to become extremely jealous of its prerogatives. Lincoln's successor, Vice President Andrew Johnson, lacked the compromising skills necessary to coexist with Congress, and consequently, he mismanaged much of the situation.

Johnson grew up as a poor southerner, developing much of the antiblack and antiaristocratic sentiments of the areas in which he was raised, North Carolina and Tennessee. This goes far to explain his insensitivity to the plight of blacks and his initial hostility to the southern planter class. Johnson was also a rigid man who lashed out at his opponents. His stubbornness would often force his opponents into positions more extreme than the ones from which they had started. Perhaps more than any other factor, Johnson's inability to compromise discouraged the moderates in Congress and eventually drove them into the radical camp.

Paradoxically, Johnson initially seemed to get along with his party members. In fact, first impressions were favorable. Radicals believed he would be tougher on the South than Lincoln after Johnson said in a speech that "treason . . . must be made infamous and traitors . . . punished." Congressman George W. Julian went so far as to say that "the accession of Johnson will prove a Godsend to the country."

Johnson's first act of Reconstruction was to extend pardons to large groups of southerners who were willing to take an oath of loyalty to the Union. Excluded from the pardon was the planter class, defined as all those whose taxable property was worth more than $20,000. Those excluded could apply individually and directly to the president, but the radicals did not expect Johnson to be lenient. The power of the pardon was an important one because unpardoned southerners could not vote,

hold office, or reacquire property seized by the federal government during the war.

During Johnson's first eight months in office, Congress was
not in session. Lincoln was assassinated in April and Congress
was not scheduled to convene until December, so Johnson had a
free hand in formulating policy. Given the tension existing between the executive and legislative branches of government, a
wiser man might have called the congressmen into session to
consult them on Reconstruction, but Johnson did not.

Without Congress's input, Johnson revealed his Reconstruction plans. For each former Confederate state the president
would appoint a provisional governor who would then call a state
convention composed of delegates who had taken the required
loyalty oath. Besides recommending to these conventions that
they repudiate their Confederate war debts and that educated
blacks be given the vote, Johnson gave the state conventions almost complete latitude in deciding what sort of governments
they wanted. Once they had complied with these relatively
lenient conditions, the states would be readmitted into the Union.
Naively, Johnson assumed Congress would accept the results of
his plans when it met in December.

Shortly thereafter, each unreconstructed southern state followed Johnson's instructions. Every state except South Carolina
repudiated its war debt, but while each state acknowledged the
end of slavery, none made a concession toward black voting.
Still, the states held elections for both state and national offices.
Satisfied that the southern states met his conditions, Johnson
recognized the newly created state governments in the South.

The "Johnson Governments"

In the months that followed, the "Johnson governments" experienced no restraint from Washington. Their activities during
this period deeply dismayed many northerners, strengthened the

hand of the radicals, and destroyed any possibility that Congress would accept Johnson's Reconstruction policy.

Basically, two aspects of the Johnson governments alienated and angered northern Republicans. First, in their elections for state and federal offices, southern voters turned overwhelmingly to former Confederates for their leadership. Indeed, about eighty high-ranking Confederates, even Alexander H. Stephens, former vice president of the Confederate States of America, were elected to the upcoming Congress. Most of these men had received individual pardons from Johnson.

Second, the southern state governments not only refused to give blacks the vote but made the status of blacks in postbellum society inferior in other ways. They established black codes that extended some rights to blacks previously denied, such as legalized marriage; the ability to buy, own, and transfer property; and the ability to appear, plead, and testify in courts. But these black codes basically relegated the freedmen to a position of legal inferiority to whites. For example, blacks could not enter into work contracts freely, were subjected to elaborate regulations supervised by a judge, were threatened with severe vagrancy laws if not gainfully employed and could be imprisoned or sentenced to hard labor, were forbidden to carry firearms, received more severe sentences for similar crimes than whites, and were restricted as to where they could live and own property.

Many northerners believed these codes were no better than the antebellum slave codes. Congress was outraged when it received reports from white southern Unionists that the former secessionists were bragging about once again holding the upper hand and making life difficult for their opponents.

Congressional Reconstruction

By the time Congress convened in December 1865, Johnson had exhausted the patience of the Republican majority, radicals and moderates alike. When the southern delegations appeared in Washington seeking admission to Congress, the Republicans refused to seat them and determined to take over the task of Reconstruction themselves.

Congress then quickly established the Joint Committee on Reconstruction—fifteen senators and representatives, of whom three were Democrats—to oversee all measures having to do with restoring the South to the Union. The committee was headed by Thaddeus Stevens of Pennsylvania and soon became a vehicle for the radicals.

The first act of congressional Reconstruction was a bill to extend the life of the Freedmen's Bureau and broaden its authority. Established in March 1865, the bureau provided aid for refugees both white and black. Among other responsibilities, it distributed rations, found employment for freedmen, transported home those displaced by the war, and established hospitals and schools. In enlarging the bureau's scope, Congress gave it "military power and jurisdiction" over all cases involving discrimination against freedmen.

Congress considered the Freedmen's Bureau Bill a mild measure justified by the South's apparent stubbornness, but Johnson vetoed it. The president said it gave the bureau too much power in legal matters. Congress interpreted the veto as an expression of Johnson's resistance to a strict Reconstruction policy and as an attempt by him to retain executive control of Reconstruction.

From that point on, Johnson and Congress were in tense opposition over Reconstruction. When moderate Lyman Trumbull of Illinois introduced a bill calling for defining United States citizenship as including blacks, Republicans endorsed it, but Johnson responded with another veto. This alienated all Republicans, who believed the president had gone too far, and his veto was quickly overridden. In addition, Johnson had squandered any hope of receiving support from the moderate Republicans.

Assuming the initiative, Congress proposed the Fourteenth Amendment to the Constitution, which did define United States citizenship as including blacks and which would guarantee that individual rights could not be taken away by the states. That this amendment was necessary was obvious; the Thirteenth Amendment (December 1865) had confirmed Lincoln's Emancipation Proclamation and officially abolished slavery, but it did nothing to make freedmen equal to whites under the law.

Nevertheless, the Fourteenth Amendment was not all that it could have been. Congress had the opportunity to end all political discrimination on racial grounds. Instead, it gave way to conservative opinion and northern racial prejudice by passing a diluted measure. Instead of giving the vote to all men, it merely declared that whenever a state denied any portion of its adult male population the right to vote, the representation of that state in Congress would be reduced proportionately.

Under the Fourteenth Amendment the South, with its large black population, should have had a compelling incentive to grant black men full voting rights, while the northern states, with few black residents, could continue to deny them their rights without serious penalty. However, not until the adoption of the Fifteenth Amendment (1870) was "race, color, or previous condition of servitude" eliminated as grounds for denying any male the vote.

Congress, in an effort to force southern states to ratify the Fourteenth Amendment, made it a condition for being readmitted and put much pressure on the South to adopt it. Still, it would take two more years of political fighting, until 1868, for the Fourteenth Amendment to become part of the Constitution.

Not surprisingly, Johnson furiously attacked the Fourteenth Amendment, despite its moderation, and blamed it on the radicals. Disregarding precedent, the president campaigned personally in the off-year congressional elections of 1866 in hopes of defeating the radicals. Throughout the country Johnson charged that Congress had acted illegally by approving the Fourteenth Amendment without the representation of all the southern states. Further, he declared that southerners were the "loyal" ones while the radical Republicans in Congress were the "real traitors."

The outcome of the 1866 elections was a humiliating defeat for President Johnson. The Republicans won a three-to-one majority in Congress. They gained control of every northern state and the states of West Virginia, Missouri, and recently readmitted Tennessee. The Republican-dominated Congress was now veto-proof.

The new Congress quickly took advantage of its mandate. In March 1867, over Johnson's veto, the first two Reconstruction Acts were passed, declaring Johnson's governments in the South invalid and dividing the South into five military districts, each to be supervised by a general and each subject to martial law. The generals were to oversee the writing of new southern state constitutions in which blacks must be allowed to participate. Any new constitution must support the principle that black men could vote but former Confederates could not. When these new state constitutions had been adopted, when a majority of southern states had ratified the Fourteenth Amendment, and when the amendment had become part of the federal Constitution, then those states that had complied with this process would be allowed to seat their delegations in Congress.

At every opportunity Johnson did what he could to undermine the Reconstruction Acts. Reluctantly, Congress concluded its only alternative was impeachment. Yet the congressmen still needed convincing evidence against the president. Johnson supplied them with it in August 1867, when, during a congressional recess, he suspended from office the radical Republican secretary of war Edwin Stanton. This appeared to be in violation of the Tenure of Office Act passed earlier in the year by Congress to prevent Johnson from dismissing any appointed official who favored congressional policies over his own. The Tenure of Office Act required congressional consent to the removal of any official whose initial appointment had needed congressional approval.

The president restored Stanton in January 1868 when the Senate refused to accept his removal, but a month later Johnson fired Stanton again. This defiance seemed to provide the grounds for impeachment that had not existed before. On February 24, 1868, the House passed a resolution to impeach the president.

With the Senate presiding, the impeachment trial of Andrew Johnson became the show trial of the century. The major charge against the president was the "unlawful" removal of Stanton. Johnson was ably defended by Attorney General Henry Stanbery, who contended that Stanton was not covered by the Tenure of Office Act since Lincoln had appointed him, not Johnson. Furthermore, Stanbery maintained, the law was, in all likelihood, unconstitutional. And finally, Stanton, who had barricaded himself in the War Department and refused to leave, was technically still in office, so no law had been broken.

The trial lasted ten weeks and was the talk of Washington and the country. Republicans insisted that acquittal would be a victory for traitors and rebels. Democrats and Johnson's few supporters claimed that conviction would mean that Congress had successfully usurped the power of the executive branch.

When the vote finally came on May 26, 1868, Johnson was acquitted by one vote. He finished out his term still stubborn and opposing the radicals whenever he could. Nevertheless, the impeachment and trial, albeit unsuccessful, had minimized the president's influence. Until he left office, Johnson would very much be a lame-duck president.

The South Reconstructed

In the presidential election of 1868 the Republicans chose war hero Ulysses S. Grant on a platform that promised justice for both southern Unionists and freedmen and peace between the sections. Grant's Democratic opponent was the wartime governor of New York, Horatio Seymour, who ran on a platform that demanded the restoration of "home rule" to the South. After a bitter campaign centering around Reconstruction policy and Seymour's record as governor (he had been a Peace Democrat), Grant carried twenty-six states and Seymour only eight. But in popular votes, Grant received merely 310,000 more than Seymour.

By the time of Grant's inauguration in 1869, the southern governments organized under the congressional Reconstruction Acts, composed of white and black Republicans and decidedly radical in temper, had been admitted to the Union, and the Fourteenth Amendment had been added to the Constitution. In a strictly technical sense, all southern states had been "reconstructed" with the exception of Virginia, Mississippi, Texas, and Georgia, which would not rejoin the Union until 1870. And there were changes aplenty in the South.

Physical reconstruction and repair of the South was proceeding at an amazing pace. Southern railroads were being rebuilt and extended. Indeed, between 1865 and 1879, some 7,000 miles of track were added to the southern network of railroads. Needed capital was supplied by investors in the North and in Great Britain who anticipated a more favorable southern business climate. Southern state governments, as well, invested in business ventures, and the rebound of industry and transportation was impressive.

In agriculture, corn and cotton still continued to be the chief elements in the southern economy. By 1878, the South's cotton production had risen almost to its prewar peak. Thereafter, it grew steadily, and by the 1890s the South was producing twice as many bales of cotton as it had in 1859.

Experiments also occurred in the postwar South to create a black yeomanry by giving freedmen confiscated Confederate land. Radical Republicans, led by Thaddeus Stevens, believed that only landowning could protect blacks against exploitation and keep them from being reenslaved. This experiment, however, unrealistically raised black expectations. The freedmen believed that the government intended to give them "40 acres and a mule," and were deeply disappointed when it proved untrue. In short, a large black landowning class never materialized. What land was given over to blacks was isolated and infertile, and few if any black families were able to make a success farming on it.

Congress might have heeded Stevens's advice and turned over all confiscated Confederate land to the freedmen. But in the end, the radical Republicans were not so very radical after all. Their respect for private property, even that of the former rebels, simply took precedence over their concern for the freedmen. Most of the radicals, in fact, were certain that the ballot offered sufficient protection to the freedmen and there was no need for a social revolution.

Though few southern blacks ever became yeoman farmers, they did remain on the land, and the new system that emerged was tenantry. Tenantry took many forms and included whites as well as blacks. Thousands of Confederate privates returned home, not to become successful planters, but rather to become tenants on land owned by former slaveholders. In return for working a portion of the land, tenants might pay rent either in cash or in a percentage of the crop, usually cotton. Though the system was certainly not as desirable as ownership, a black tenant was at least free from constant supervision and sometimes could save enough to buy land.

The greatest number of tenant farmers were "sharecroppers," who turned over their crops to the landowners in exchange for a percentage of the profits. Linked to this system was the crop-lien arrangement of credit where a storekeeper, who was sometimes the landlord, would extend credit to the tenant for supplies during the growing season. When harvest came and the cotton was sold, the tenant would repay the debt.

However, the storekeepers kept the books, and this gave dishonest ones an excellent opportunity to cheat the sharecroppers, an opportunity that all too many of them exploited. If a tenant could not meet his debt, he could not change the merchant with whom he dealt. Instead, the sharecropper remained perennially tied to the merchant almost like a serf from the medieval period.

The freedmen's fate after the Civil War, then, represents largely an opportunity lost. This is not to say, of course, that freedom was no better than slavery. Some blacks managed to become landowners despite all the obstacles. Most were released from the degradation of stifling personal supervision by whites. And economically, blacks were better off as sharecroppers than as slaves. Nevertheless, with the system considerably stacked against them, the majority of blacks were not able to lift themselves above poverty. Whereas the South might have become a region of prosperous small farms run by blacks and whites alike, Dixie remained dominated by a planter elite resting predominantly upon a black labor force.

Too, segregation remained an overwhelming characteristic of life in the South. In 1875, Congress passed a strongly worded Civil Rights Act guaranteeing to all persons, regardless of race, "the full and equal enjoyment of all the accommodations . . . of inns, public conveyances . . . theaters, and other places of amusement." Separation, discrimination, and inequality, however, persisted throughout the South. In most southern communities, trains, buses, and theaters had white and black sections.

The greatest failure of Reconstruction was political. Giving the freedmen the vote went against traditional southern attitudes. Respecting blacks as political equals and even, in the case of black officials, as superiors was completely alien to the established values and customs of the white South.

Yet the southern state governments established under the Reconstruction Acts of 1867 assigned to blacks important participatory roles. Blacks voted in the elections supervised by the five regional military commanders, and many were returned to office as members of the state legislatures and in other official capacities. In Alabama, Florida, South Carolina, Mississippi, and Louisiana, where blacks constituted a majority of all registered voters, they contributed significantly to Republican victories. Blacks held positions of importance in all Reconstruction governments, although the number of black officeholders was never commensurate with their presence among the population as a whole.

Black political leaders came primarily from an elite class that had been freed before the Civil War. Some of these leaders were even the sons of planters who had provided them with an education. Blanche K. Bruce, one of the two black U.S. senators from Mississippi, had received tutoring on the plantation of his white father. The other black senator from Mississippi was Hiram Revels, who matriculated for two years in a Quaker seminary in Liberty, Indiana, before completing his formal education at Knox College in Illinois. P. B. S. Pinchback, the black lieutenant governor of Louisiana, had begun his formal schooling in Cincinnati, having been sent there at age nine by his planter father. Bruce, Revels, and Pinchback, as well as the other black artisans, shopkeepers, ministers, and teachers who held office in the Reconstruction South, emphasized the importance of black suffrage and the need for public improvement of all kinds, especially of schools and roads.

The impressive efforts of the black legislators notwithstanding, black people did not dominate the radical state regimes that congressional Reconstruction brought to power. Rather, whites controlled the reconstructed state governments, holding the vast majority of state offices. They were a considerably diverse group. Among them were nonslaveholding whites, labeled "scalawags" by their Democratic opponents. Some were wealthy individuals, often former Whigs, who sought southern industrial development. Still others were migrants from the North, whom the Democrats called "carpetbaggers." In fact, carpetbaggers held more than half the governorships and almost half the congressional positions.

While some carpetbaggers aspired only to achieve great personal wealth, most usually made long-term commitments to southern society. A majority were former Union army officers who brought far more with them than carpetbags in which to carry off the wealth of the South; they brought capital and skills to invest in the South's future. Many were college graduates and such professionals as lawyers, engineers, and teachers. The scalawags were poorer but often owned their own farms. They had wished to see a South free of a slaveowning aristocracy and usually had opposed or refused to support the Confederacy.

In general, the Republican-dominated southern state governments were remarkably honest and effective. They spent huge sums of money on rebuilding and internal improvements. They assisted railroads and industry. They set up the South's first state-supported school systems and sharply increased public spending for poor relief, prisons, and state hospitals. Although it still lagged far behind the North in providing social services, under Republican rule the South did make marked progress.

The new Republican governments in the South were also more democratic than previous ones. In the state constitutions adopted under congressional Reconstruction, many appointive positions were made elective. Yeoman farmer regions were better represented in the legislature than they were before the war, and whites who had not previously met old property qualifications were given the vote. The number of crimes punishable by death was reduced, and married women received more control over their property, as they had in the North before 1860.

The South Redeemed

Despite the improvements made by these governments, many white southerners despised the Republican regimes as expensive and Yankee-inspired. The governments represented a new order, especially in race relations, and after 250 years of regarding blacks as inferior, the white South could not accept any changes that declared the legal equality of blacks.

Opposition to the Republican rule in the South steadily grew. In the end, the champions of these governments could not match the organization, experience, and ruthlessness of the fierce defenders of the Old South who hoped to "redeem" the South from "Black Republicanism."

A major weapon of the "redeemers" was the Ku Klux Klan. Formed in 1866 by a group of young Confederate veterans primarily as a social club, the Klan quickly became an antiblack, anti-Republican organization. In the beginning, it used fear and superstition to intimidate blacks. Later the members resorted to more violent methods. They burned black homes, attacked black militiamen, ambushed both white and black Republican leaders, and lynched blacks accused of crimes.

At the height of its activity in the late 1860s, the Klan went virtually unchecked. Then in 1870 and 1871, Congress passed three "force bills" declaring the Klan's terrorist activity illegal. Intended to support the Republican Reconstruction programs, the bills gave the president the authority to prosecute in federal courts anyone preventing a qualified person from voting. As a result of the vigorous prosecution of these laws, the Klan temporarily declined.

Southern white conservatives, however, persisted in their determination to regain control of the South. They intimidated white Republicans and isolated them from the mainstream of southern civilization. In turn, out of frustration, desperation, and fear, many southern whites abandoned the Republicans and turned to the safer and more accepted Democratic Party.

Blacks who continued to vote Republican were denied jobs or fired from those they had. Against the more stubborn black Republicans, violence was threatened and used.

These tactics worked. Slowly, the Democrats "redeemed" the southern states, so that by 1876 only Louisiana, Florida, and South Carolina remained under Republican administrations. And the reason the Republicans stayed in power in these three states was simple: they were protected there by federal troops.

Obviously, the southern Democratic redeemers were effective. But if the commitment of northerners to Republican rule in the South had not been waning, it is doubtful that the redeemers would have been so successful. The decline of this northern conviction had several sources. More and more Republicans had come to believe that the defense of black equality was merely an excuse for continued domination by the corrupt wing of their party. Whenever a new scandal was uncovered in the Grant administration, and there were many, its significance would be minimized by an appeal to Republican unity against the former rebels, a process generally called "waving the bloody shirt."

The all-consuming problems of the blacks and their southern oppressors always seemed to justify any Republican activity. By the mid-1870s, many who had once supported the Republican Party had concluded that abandoning the blacks and their friends in the South would be better than abandoning the country as a whole.

Quite simply, Grant's years in office had hurt the Republican Party. Although he had defeated Horace Greeley for reelection in 1872, Grant's second term was scandal-ridden. The financial scandal that left an indelible mark of corruption on Grant's administration—its first big scandal, which broke in 1872—centered around the Crédit Mobilier construction company. The Crédit Mobilier acted as the construction company for the Union Pacific Railroad, which was heavily financed by the government. With this in mind, the Crédit Mobilier charged the railroad huge sums for its services. A clique consisting of the major stockholders in both corporations skimmed $23 million in profits from the railroad company. Several congressmen were sold stock in Crédit Mobilier by Oakes Ames, a member of the Pacific Railroad Committee in the House, in an effort to stave off an investigation of the company. Then a Senate investigating committee implicated Grant's vice president, Schuyler Colfax, in the scam.

One dreary episode followed another during Grant's second term. Benjamin H. Bristow, secretary of the treasury, discovered that some of his officials and a group of distillers operating as a "whiskey ring" were bilking the government out of millions in taxes by filing false reports. Among the prominent Republicans involved was the president's close friend and private secretary, Orville E. Babcock. Grant vehemently defended Babcock and appointed him to another office, and to avoid further accusations, he eased Bristow out of the cabinet. In the "Salary Grab Act" (1873), Congress raised the salaries of its own members 50 percent and made the increase retroactive for two years, thus giving each member of Congress a considerable windfall. Increases were also provided for the president, cabinet members, and the Supreme Court. This act was considered yet another scandal condoned by President Grant.

Finally, Grant's secretary of war, William W. Belknap, was charged with receiving bribes from a trader at one of the Army posts who wanted to retain his profitable job. Belknap was impeached by the House of Representatives but was not convicted by the Senate. He had quickly resigned, and the Senate held no jurisdiction over a cabinet officer who had resigned.

If the performance of Grant's administration was not sufficient to weaken northern commitments, fatigue and racism also contributed to the federal abandonment of black equality. For how long, many northerners asked, should the nation invest time, energy, and money in sustaining a system that clearly the "best elements" of southern society opposed? These northerners came to believe that blacks would never make good citizens and there was no point in continuing the futile battle. Such arguments were reinforced by a growing attitude among northern commercial and industrial groups that peace in the South would be better for business than the political turbulence that had constantly agitated the nation.

The Election of 1876

The end of Reconstruction came in 1876. In the presidential election of that year, the Democrats nominated Samuel Tilden, governor of New York and a symbol of honest government. Their platform promised to withdraw federal troops from the South and endorsed traditional Democratic low-tariff, small-government policies. The Republicans nominated Governor Rutherford B. Hayes of Ohio, also a symbol of honest government, on a platform that stated they would never abandon the black man and would continue to support a protective tariff.

The results of the election were so close that they were challenged. The Democrats claimed they had won the states of New York, New Jersey, Connecticut, Indiana, and the entire South. The Republicans insisted that the "unredeemed" states of Florida, Louisiana, and South Carolina belonged to them. They also challenged one Democratic vote in Oregon, where electors had split between the two candidates.

As in 1824, the election was thrown into the House of

Representatives for resolution. For the next four months political turmoil prevailed as the legislators tried to settle the issue before inauguration day in March 1877.

Both sides resorted to every weapon in the dispute. Propaganda, legal maneuvering, congressional commissions, and threats of violence all clouded the political atmosphere during the fall and winter. A hidden but crucially important issue behind the scenes was the railroads. The Republicans favored huge land grants for completion of the national rail network; the Democrats did not.

At the time of this election a major land grant of considerable importance to southern commercial and business interests was being considered in Congress. The Texas and Pacific Railroad, which would benefit from this grant, was supposed to connect New Orleans and other important southern cities with the Pacific coast. This rail link, it was generally believed, would bring wealth to many communities in the South.

A Democratic administration, of course, would remove the troops from the remaining "unredeemed" states and end Reconstruction. But it would also oppose the Texas and Pacific Railroad project, it was believed, since the Democrats, as a rule, disliked federal aid. This reasoning apparently prompted key southern leaders, many of them former Whigs with little love lost for the Democrats, to bargain with the Republicans. In exchange for an assurance from the Republicans that they would remove the federal troops from the South, appoint southerners to important governmental positions, and support a Texas and Pacific land grant, southerners in the House of Representatives agreed to throw their support to Hayes.

This bargain, known as the Compromise of 1877, gave Hayes the election. Shortly after Hayes took the oath of office in March 1877, becoming the nineteenth president of the United States, the last federal troops were withdrawn from the South. This removal of the troops was a symbol that the national govern-

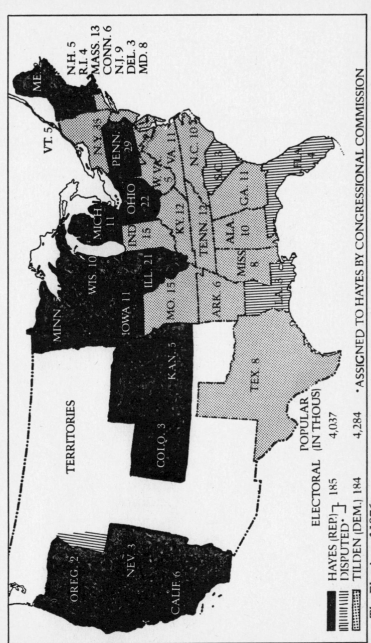

The Election of 1876

ME. 2
VT. 5
N.H. 5
R.I. 4
MASS. 13
CONN. 6
N.J. 9
DEL. 3
MD. 8

N.Y. 35
PENN. 29
OHIO 22
MICH. 11
IND. 15
ILL. 21
WIS. 10
IOWA 11
MINN. 5
MO. 15
KAN. 5
COLO. 3
TERRITORIES
OREG. 3
NEV. 3
CALIF. 6
KY. 12
W.VA. 5
VA. 11
N.C. 10
S.C. 7
GA. 11
TENN. 12
ALA. 10
MISS. 8
LA. 8
ARK. 6
TEX. 8

HAYES (REP.) ⎤ 185
DISPUTED · ⎦
TILDEN (DEM.) 184

ELECTORAL

POPULAR
(IN THOUS)
4,037
4,284

· ASSIGNED TO HAYES BY CONGRESSIONAL COMMISSION

ment was giving up on its attempt to control southern politics
and to determine the place of blacks in southern society. The
white southern conservative regimes had indeed accomplished a
major triumph. The South was now "redeemed" and
Reconstruction was over.

*By many standards, Reconstruction was a failure. While it
did materially repair the devastated South, it did not resolve the
problems of the freedmen. In the end, it almost reduced them to
slaves again. True, there were some tangible gains made. The
Fourteenth and Fifteenth Amendments became part of the Constitution and in the twentieth century would serve as the foundation for a "second Reconstruction." That would occur in the
1950s and 1960s.*

*Still, the failure to correct or replace the "peculiar institu-
tion" with a more equitable labor system laid the seeds for racial problems well into the next century. Instead of a prosperous
black yeomanry, the South would have a large class of impoverished sharecroppers tied forever to the land in an indebted
condition. Following the return to conservative rule, the freedmen lost whatever political independence they had gained. Instead of political democracy, Reconstruction bequeathed the
South a legacy of fraud, intimidation, and gross racial exclusion.
Instead of spurring economic growth and development,
Reconstruction kept the South poor. On every economic in-
dicator—literacy, per capita income, sanitation, infant mortality, and housing—the South lagged, and would continue to lag,
behind the rest of the nation.*

*Meanwhile the remainder of the nation was turning away
from the chronic problems of the South to what many Americans
considered to be a more pressing concern. The South and
Reconstruction faded into unpleasant memories as most of the*

country enjoyed a period of economic expansion that would far surpass anything in the past.

Recommended Reading

Richard Abbott, *The Republican Party and the South, 1855–1877* (1986)

Howard Beale, *The Critical Year* (1930)

Herman Belz, *Reconstructing the Union* (1969)

Michael L. Benedict, *A Compromise of Principle: Congressional Republicans and Reconstruction* (1974)

Michael L. Benedict, *The Impeachment of Andrew Johnson* (1973)

George R. Bentley, *A History of the Freedmen's Bureau* (1955)

Eugene H. Berwanger, *The West and Reconstruction* (1981)

Claude Bowers, *The Tragic Era* (1929)

William R. Brock, *An American Crisis* (1963)

Fawn Brodie, *Thaddeus Stevens* (1959)

Dan Carter, *When the War Was Over: The Failure of Self-Reconstruction in the South, 1865–1867* (1985)

LaWanda Cox and John Cox, *Politics, Principles, and Prejudice, 1865–1866: Dilemma of Reconstruction America* (1963)

Robert Cruden, *The Negro in Reconstruction* (1969)

David Donald, *Charles Sumner and the Rights of Man* (1970)

David Donald, *The Politics of Reconstruction* (1965)

William A. Dunning, *Reconstruction, Political and Economic, 1865–1877* (1907)

Clement Eaton, *The Waning of the Old South Civilization, 1860–1880* (1968)

John Hope Franklin, *Reconstruction after the Civil War* (1961)

William Gillette, *Retreat from Reconstruction, 1869–1879* (1979)

Herbert Gutman, *The Black Family in Slavery and Freedom, 1750–1925* (1976)

William B. Hesseltine, *Lincoln's Plan of Reconstruction* (1960)

Gerald Jaynes, *Branches without Roots: The Genesis of the Black Working Class in the American South, 1862–1882* (1986)

Leon Litwack, *Been in the Storm So Long: The Aftermath of Slavery* (1980)

Peyton McCrary, *Abraham Lincoln and Reconstruction* (1978)

William S. McFeely, *Grant* (1981)

William S. McFeely, *Yankee Stepfather: O. O. Howard and the Freedmen* (1968)

Eric L. McKitrick, *Andrew Johnson and Reconstruction* (1960)

Robert C. Morris, *Reading, 'Riting, and Reconstruction: The Education of Freedmen in the South, 1861–1870* (1981)

Claude F. Oubre, *Forty Acres and a Mule* (1978)

Phillip S. Paludan, *A Covenant with Death* (1975)

Rembert W. Patrick, *The Reconstruction of the Nation* (1967)

Michael Perman, *Emancipation and Reconstruction, 1862–1979* (1987)

Michael Perman, *Reunion without Compromise* (1973)

Michael Perman, *The Road to Redemption* (1984)

Keith Polakoff, *The Politics of Inertia: The Election of 1876 and the End of Reconstruction* (1973)

Roger Ransom and Richard Sutch, *One Kind of Freedom: The Economic Consequences of Emancipation* (1977)

James L. Roark, *Masters without Slaves* (1977)

Willie Lee Rose, *Rehearsal for Reconstruction: The Port Royal Experiment* (1964)

Terry Seip, *The South Returns to Congress* (1983)

Kenneth Stampp, *The Era of Reconstruction, 1865–1877* (1965)

Albion W. Tourgee, *A Fool's Errand: A Novel of the South during Reconstruction* (1879, 1966)

Hans L. Trefousse, *Impeachment of a President* (1975)

Hans L. Trefousse, *The Radical Republicans* (1969)

Allen W. Trelease, *White Terror: The Ku Klux Klan Conspiracy and Southern Reconstruction* (1971)

Joel Williamson, *After Slavery: The Negro in South Carolina during Reconstruction, 1861–1877* (1964)

C. Vann Woodward, *Reunion and Reaction: The Compromise of 1877 and the End of Reconstruction* (1951)

C. Vann Woodward, *The Strange Career of Jim Crow* (1974)

APPENDIX 1

The Declaration of
Independence

The original spelling, capitalization, and punctuation have been retained in this version.

In Congess, July 4, 1776, the unanimous Declaration of the thirteen United States of America.

When, in the Course of human events, it becomes necessary for one people to dissolve the political bands which have connected them with another, and to assume, among the Powers of the earth, the separate and equal station to which the Laws of Nature and of Nature's God entitle them, a decent respect to the opinions of mankind requires that they should declare the causes which impel them to the separation.

We hold these truths to be self-evident, that all men are created equal, that they are endowed by their Creator with certain unalienable Rights, that among these, are Life, Liberty, and the pursuit of Happiness. That, to secure these rights, Governments are instituted among Men, deriving their just Powers from the consent of the governed. That, whenever any form of Government becomes destructive of these ends, it is the Right of the People to alter or to abolish it, and to institute new Government, laying its foundation on such Principles, and organizing its Powers in such form, as to them shall seem most likely to effect their Safety and Happiness. Prudence, indeed, will dictate that Governments long established should not be changed for light and transient causes; and, accordingly, all experience hath shewn, that mankind are more disposed to suffer, while evils are sufferable, than to right themselves by abolishing the forms to which they are accustomed. But, when a long train of abuses and usurpations, pursuing invariably the same Object, evinces a design to reduce them under absolute Despotism, it is their right, it is their duty, to throw off such Government, and to provide new Guards for their future Security. Such has been the patient sufferance of these Colonies; and such is now the necessity which constrains them to alter their former Systems of Government. The history of the present King of Great Britain is a history of repeated injuries and usurpations, all having in direct object the establishment of an absolute Tyranny over these States. To prove this, let Facts be submitted to a candid world.

He has refused his Assent to Laws, the most wholesome and necessary for the public good.

He has forbidden his Governors to pass Laws of immediate and pressing importance, unless suspended in their operation till his Assent should be obtained; and when so suspended, he has utterly neglected to attend to them.

He has refused to pass other Laws for the accommodation of large districts of People, unless those people would relinquish the right of Representation in the legislature; a right inestimable to them and formidable to tyrants only.

He has called together legislative bodies at places unusual, uncomfortable, and distant from the depository of their Public Records, for the sole Purpose of fatiguing them into compliance with his measures.

He has dissolved Representative Houses repeatedly, for opposing, with manly firmness, his invasions on the rights of the People.

He has refused for a long time, after such dissolutions, to cause others to be elected; whereby the Legislative Powers, incapable of Annihilation, have returned to the People at large for their exercise; the State remaining in the mean time exposed to all dangers of invasion from without, and convulsions within.

He has endeavoured to prevent the Population of these States; for that purpose obstructing the Laws for Naturalization of Foreigners; refusing to pass others to encourage their migrations hither, and raising the conditions of new Appropriations of Lands.

He has obstructed the Administration of Justice, by refusing his Assent to Laws for establishing judiciary Powers.

He has made Judges dependent on his Will alone, for the tenure of their offices, and the amount and payment of their salaries.

He has erected a multitude of New Offices, and sent hither swarms of Officers to harrass our People, and eat out their substance.

He has kept among us, in times of Peace, Standing Armies, without the Consent of our legislatures.

He has affected to render the Military independent of and superior to the Civil Power.

He has combined with others to subject us to a jurisdiction foreign to our constitution, and unacknowledged by our laws; giving his Assent to their Acts of pretended Legislation;

For quartering large bodies of armed troops among us:

For protecting them, by a mock Trial, from Punishment for

any Murders which they should commit on the Inhabitants of these States:

For cutting off our Trade with all parts of the world:

For imposing Taxes on us without our Consent:

For depriving us, in many cases, of the benefits of Trial by Jury:

For transporting us beyond Seas to be tried for pretended offences:

For abolishing the free System of English Laws in a neighbouring province, establishing therein an Arbitrary government, and enlarging its Boundaries, so as to render it at once an example and fit instrument for introducing the same absolute rule into these Colonies:

For taking away our Charters, abolishing our most valuable Laws, and altering fundamentally the Forms of our Governments:

For suspending our own Legislatures, and declaring themselves invested with Power to legislate for us in all cases whatsoever.

He has abdicated Government here, by declaring us out of his protection, and waging War against us.

He plundered our seas, ravaged our Coasts, burnt our towns, and destroyed the Lives of our People.

He is at this time transporting large Armies of foreign Mercenaries to compleat the works of death, desolation and tyranny, already begun with circumstances of Cruelty and perfidy scarcely paralleled in the most barbarous ages, and totally unworthy the Head of a civilized nation.

He has constrained our fellow Citizens, taken Captive on the high Seas, to bear Arms against their Country, to become the executioners of their friends and Brethren, or to fall themselves by their Hands.

He has excited domestic insurrections amongst us, and has endeavoured to bring on the inhabitants of our frontiers, the merciless Indian Savages, whose known rule of warfare, is an undistinguished destruction of all ages, sexes, and conditions.

In every stage of these Oppressions, We have Petitioned for Redress, in the most humble terms: Our repeated Petitions have been answered only by repeated injury. A Prince, whose character is thus marked by every act which may define a Tyrant, is unfit to be the ruler of a free People.

Nor have We been wanting in attentions to our British brethren. We have warned them from time to time of attempts by their legislature to extend an unwarrantable jurisdiction over us. We have reminded them of the circumstances of our emigration and settlement here. We have appealed to their native justice and magnanimity, and we have conjured them, by the ties of our common kindred, to disavow these usurpations, which, would inevitably interrupt our connexions and correspondence. They too have been deaf to the voice of justice and consanguinity. We must, therefore, acquiesce in the necessity, which denounces our Separation, and hold them, as we hold the rest of mankind, Enemies in War, in Peace Friends.

WE, THEREFORE, the Representatives of the UNITED STATES OF AMERICA, in GENERAL CONGRESS assembled, appealing to the Supreme Judge of the World for the rectitude of our intentions, DO, in the Name, and by Authority of the good People of these Colonies, solemnly PUBLISH and DECLARE, That these United Colonies are, and of Right ought to be FREE AND INDEPENDENT STATES; that they are Absolved from all Allegiance to the British Crown, and that all political connexion between them and the State of Great Britain, is and ought to be totally dissolved; and that, as FREE and INDEPENDENT STATES, they have full Power to levy War, conclude Peace, contract Alliances, establish Commerce, and to do all other Acts and Things which INDEPENDENT STATES may of right do. AND for the support of this Declaration, with a firm reliance on the protection of divine Providence, we mutually pledge to each other our Lives, our Fortunes, and our sacred Honour.

APPENDIX 2

The Constitution of the United States of America

The original spelling, capitalization, and punctuation have been retained in this version.

We the People of the United States, in Order to form a more perfect Union, establish Justice, insure domestic Tranquility, provide for the common defence, promote the general Welfare, and secure the Blessings of Liberty to ourselves and our Posterity, do ordain and establish this CONSTITUTION for the United States of America.

Article I

Section 1. All legislative Powers herein granted shall be vested in a Congress of the United States, which shall consist of a Senate and House of Representatives.

Section 2. The House of Representatives shall be composed of Members chosen every second Year by the People of the several States, and the Electors in each State shall have the Qualifications requisite for Electors of the most numerous Branch of the State Legislature.

No Person shall be a Representative who shall not have attained to the Age of twenty-five Years, and been seven Years a Citizen of the United States, and who shall not, when elected, be an Inhabitant of that state in which he shall be chosen.

Representatives and direct Taxes shall be apportioned among the several States which may be included within this Union, according to their respective Numbers, which shall be determined by adding to the whole Number of free Persons, including those bound to Service for a Term of Years, and excluding Indians not taxed, three fifths of all other Persons. The actual Enumeration shall be made within three Years after the first Meeting of the Congress of the United States, and within every subsequent Term of ten Years, in such Manner as they shall by Law direct. The Number of Representatives shall not exceed one for every thirty Thousand, but each State shall have at Least one Representative; and until such enumeration shall be made, the State of New Hampshire shall be entitled to chuse three, Massachusetts eight, Rhode-Island and Providence Plantations one, Connecticut five, New York six, New Jersey four, Pennsylvania eight, Delaware one, Maryland six, Virginia ten, North Carolina five, South Carolina five, and Georgia three.

When vacancies happen in the Representation from any State, the Executive Authority thereof shall issue Writs of Election to fill such Vacancies.

The House of Representatives shall chuse their Speaker and other Officers; and shall have the sole Power of Impeachment.

Section 3. The Senate of the United States shall be composed of two Senators from each State, chosen by the Legislature thereof, for six Years; and each Senator shall have one Vote.

Immediately after they shall be assembled in Consequence of the first Election, they shall be divided as equally as may be into three Classes. The Seats of the Senators of the first Class shall be vacated at the Expiration of the second Year, of the second Class at the Expiration of the fourth Year, and of the third Class at the Expiration of the sixth Year, so that one-third may be chosen every second Year; and if Vacancies happen by Resignation, or otherwise, during the Recess of the Legislature of any State, the Executive thereof may make temporary Appointments until the next Meeting of the Legislature, which shall then fill such Vacancies.

No Person shall be a Senator who shall not have attained to the Age of thirty Years, and been nine Years a Citizen of the United States, and who shall not, when elected, be an Inhabitant of that State for which he shall be chosen.

The Vice President of the United States shall be President of the Senate, but shall have no vote, unless they be equally divided.

The Senate shall chuse their other Officers, and also a President pro tempore, in the absence of the Vice President, or when he shall exercise the Office of the President of the United States.

The Senate shall have the sole Power to try all Impeachments. When sitting for that purpose they shall be on Oath or Affirmation. When the President of the United States is tried, the Chief Justice shall preside: And no person shall be convicted without the Concurrence of two thirds of the Members present.

Judgment in Cases of Impeachment shall not extend further than to removal from Office, and disqualification to hold and enjoy any Office of honor, Trust, or Profit under the United States: but the Party convicted shall nevertheless be liable and subject to Indictment, Trial, Judgment, and Punishment, according to Law.

Section 4. The Times, Places and Manner of holding Elections for Senators and Representatives, shall be prescribed in each State by the Legislature thereof; but the Congress may at any time by Law make or alter such Regulations, except as to the Places of Chusing Senators.

The Congress shall assemble at least once in every Year, and such Meeting shall be on the first Monday in December, unless they shall by Law appoint a different Day.

Section 5. Each House shall be the Judge of the Elections, Returns and Qualifications of its own Members, and a Majority of each shall constitute a Quorum to do Business; but a smaller number may adjourn from day to day, and may be authorized to compel the Attendance of absent Members, in such Manner, and under such Penalties, as each House may provide.

Each House may determine the Rules of its Proceedings, punish its Members for disorderly Behaviour, and, with the Concurrence of two thirds, expel a Member.

Each House shall keep a Journal of its Proceedings, and from time to time publish the same, excepting such Parts as may in their Judgment require Secrecy; and the Yeas and Nays of the Members of either House on any question shall, at the Desire of one fifth of those Present, be entered on the Journal.

Neither House, during the Session of Congress, shall, without the Consent of the other, adjourn for more than three days, nor to any other Place than that in which the two Houses shall be sitting.

Section 6. The Senators and Representatives shall receive a Compensation for their Services, to be ascertained by Law, and paid out of the Treasury of the United States. They shall in all Cases, except Treason, Felony, and Breach of the Peace, be privileged from Arrest during their Attendance at the Session of their respective Houses, and in going to and returning from the same; and for any Speech or Debate in either House, they shall not be questioned in any other Place.

No Senator or Representative shall, during the Time for which he was elected, be appointed to any civil Office under the Authority of the United States, which shall have been created, or the Emoluments whereof shall have been increased, during such time; and no Person holding any Office under the United States shall be a Member of either House during his continuance in Office.

Section 7. All Bills for raising Revenue shall originate in the House of Representatives; but the Senate may propose or concur with Amendments as on other bills.

Every Bill which shall have passed the House of Representatives and the Senate, shall, before it become a Law, be presented to the President of the United States; If he approve he shall sign it, but if not he shall return it, with his Objections, to that House in which it shall have originated, who shall enter the objections at large on their Journal, and proceed to reconsider it. If after such Reconsideration two thirds of that House shall agree to pass the bill, it shall be sent, together with the Objections, to the other House, by which it shall likewise be reconsidered, and if approved by two thirds of that House, it shall become a Law. But in all such Cases the Votes of both Houses shall be determined by Yeas and Nays, and the Names of the Persons voting for and against the Bill shall be entered on the Journal of each House respectively. If any Bill shall not be returned by the President within ten Days (Sundays excepted) after it shall have been presented to him, the Same shall be a Law, in like Manner as if he had signed it, unless the Congress by their Adjournment prevent its Return, in which Case it shall not be a Law.

Every Order, Resolution, or Vote to which the Concurrence of the Senate and House of Representatives may be necessary (except on a question of Adjournment) shall be presented to the President of the United States; and before the Same shall take Effect, shall be approved by him, or being disapproved by him, shall be repassed by two thirds of the Senate and House of Representatives, according to the Rules and Limitations prescribed in the Case of a Bill.

Section 8. The Congress shall have Power To lay and collect Taxes, Duties, Imposts and Excises, to pay the Debts and provide for the common Defence and general Welfare of the United States; but all Duties, and Excises shall be uniform throughout the United States;

To borrow money on the credit of the United States;

To regulate Commerce with foreign Nations, and among the several States, and with the Indian Tribes;

To establish an uniform rule of Naturalization, and uniform Laws on the subject of Bankruptcies throughout the United States;

To coin Money, regulate the Value thereof, and of foreign Coin, and fix the Standard of Weights and measures;

To provide for the Punishment of counterfeiting the Securities and current Coin of the United States;

To establish Post Offices and post Roads;

To promote the Progress of Science and useful Arts, by securing for limited Times to Authors and Inventors the exclusive Right to their respective Writings and Discoveries;

To constitute Tribunals inferior to the Supreme Court;

To define and punish Piracies and Felonies committed on the high Seas, and Offenses against the Law of Nations;

To declare War, grant Letters of Marque and Reprisal, and make Rules concerning Captures on Land and Water;

To raise and support Armies, but no Appropriation of Money to that Use shall be for a longer Term than two Years;

To provide and maintain a Navy;

To make Rules for the Government and Regulation of the land and naval forces;

To provide for calling forth the Militia to execute the Laws of the Union, suppress Insurrections and repel Invasions;

To provide for organizing, arming, and disciplining the Militia, and for governing such Part of them as may be employed in Service of the United States, reserving to the States respectively, the Appointment of the Officers, and the Authority of training the Militia according to the discipline prescribed by Congress;

To exercise exclusive Legislation in all Cases whatsoever, over such District (not exceeding ten Miles square) as may, by Cession of particular States, and the acceptance of Congress, become the Seat of the Government of the United States, and to exercise like Authority over all Places purchased by the Consent of the Legislature of the State in which the Same shall be, for the Erection of Forts, Magazines, Arsenals, Dock-yards, and other needful Building;—And

To make all Laws which shall be necessary and proper for carrying into Execution the foregoing Powers, and all other Powers vested by this Constitution in the Government of the United States, or in any Department or Officer thereof.

Section 9. The Migration or Importation of such Persons as any of the States now existing shall think proper to admit, shall not be prohibited by the Congress prior to the Year one thousand eight hundred and eight, but a tax or duty may be imposed on such Importation, not exceeding ten dollars for each Person.

The privilege of the Writ of Habeas Corpus shall not be suspended, unless when in Cases of Rebellion or Invasion the public Safety may require it.

No bill of Attainder or ex post facto Law shall be passed.

No capitation, or other direct, Tax shall be laid unless in Proportion to the Census or Enumeration herein before directed to be taken.

No Tax or Duty shall be laid on Articles exported from any State.

No Preference shall be given by any Regulation of Commerce or Revenue to the Ports of one State over those of another: nor shall Vessels bound to, or from, one State, be obliged to enter, clear, or pay Duties in another.

No Money shall be drawn from the Treasury, but in Consequence of Appropriations made by Law; and a regular Statement and Account of the Receipts and Expenditures of all public Money shall be published from time to time.

No Title of Nobility shall be granted by the United States: And no Person holding any Office of Profit or Trust under them, shall, without the Consent of the Congress, accept of any present, Emolument, Office, or Title, of any kind whatever, from any King, Prince, or foreign State.

Section 10. No State shall enter into any Treaty, Alliance, or Confederation; grant Letters of Marque and Reprisal; coin Money; emit Bills of Credit; make any Thing but gold and silver Coin a Tender in Payment of Debts; pass any Bill Attainder, ex post facto Law, or Law impairing the Obligation of Contracts, or grant any title of Nobility.

No State shall, without the Consent of the Congress, lay any Imposts or Duties on Imports or Exports, except what may be absolutely necessary for executing its inspection Laws; and the net Produce of all Duties and Imposts, laid by any State on Imports or Exports, shall be for the use of the Treasury of the United States; and all such Laws shall be subject to the Revision and Control of the Congress.

No state shall, without the Consent of Congress, lay any duty of Tonnage, keep Troops, or Ships of War in time of Peace, enter into any Agreement or Compact with another State, or with a foreign Power, or engage in War, unless actually invaded, or in such imminent Danger as will not admit of delay.

Article II

Section 1. The executive Power shall be vested in a President of the United States of America. He shall hold his Office during the Term of four years, and, together with the Vice president, chosen for the same Term, be elected, as follows:

Each State shall appoint, such Manner as the legislature thereof may direct, a Number of Electors, equal to the whole

Number of Senators and Representatives to which the State may be entitled in the Congress: but no Senator or Representative, or Person holding an Office of Trust or Profit under the United States, shall be appointed an Elector.

[The Electors shall meet in their respective States, and vote by Ballot for two persons, of whom one at least shall not be an Inhabitant of the same State with themselves. And they shall make a List of all the Persons voted for, and of the Number of Votes for each; which List they shall sign and certify, and transmit sealed to the Seat of the Government of the United States, directed to the President of the Senate. The President of the Senate shall, in the Presence of the Senate and House of Representatives, open all the Certificates, and the Votes shall then be counted. The Person having the greatest Number of Votes shall be the President, if such Number be a Majority of the whole Number of Electors appointed; and if there be more than one who have such Majority, and have an equal Number of Votes, then the House of Representatives shall immediately chuse by Ballot one of them for President; and if no Person have a majority, then from the five highest on the List the said House shall in like Manner chuse the President. But in chusing the President, the Votes shall be taken by States, the Representation from each State having one Vote; a quorum for this Purpose shall consist of a Member or Members from two-thirds of the States, and a Majority of all the states shall be necessary to a Choice. In every Case, after the Choice of the President, the Person having the greatest Number of Votes of the Electors shall be the Vice President. But if there should remain two or more who have equal votes, the Senate shall chuse from them by Ballot the Vice President.]

The Congress may determine the Time of chusing the Electors, and the Day on which they shall give their Votes; which Day shall be the same throughout the United States.

No person except a natural-born Citizen, or a Citizen of the

United States, at the time of the Adoption of this Constitution, shall be eligible to the Office of President; neither shall any Person be eligible to that Office who shall not have attained to the Age of thirty-five Years, and been fourteen Years a Resident within the United States.

In Case of the Removal of the President from Office, or of his Death, Resignation, or Inability to discharge the Powers and Duties of the said Office, the same shall devolve on the Vice President, and the Congress may by Law provide for the Case of Removal, Death, Resignation, or Inability, both of the President and Vice President, declaring what Officer shall then act as President, and such Officer shall act accordingly, until the disability be removed or a President shall be elected.

The President shall, at stated Times, receive for his Services a Compensation, which shall neither be increased nor diminished during the Period for which he shall have been elected, and he shall not receive within that Period any other Emolument from the United States, or any of them.

Before he enter on the execution of his Office, he shall take the following Oath or Affirmation:—"I do solemnly swear (or affirm) that I will faithfully execute the Office of President of the United States, and will, to the best of my Ability, preserve, protect, and defend the Constitution of the United States."

Section 2. The President shall be Commander in Chief of the Army and Navy of the United States, and of the Militia of the several States, when called into the actual Service of the United States; he may require the Opinion, in writing, of the principal Officer in each of the executive Departments, upon any subject relating to the Duties of their respective Offices, and he shall have power to Grant Reprieves and Pardons for Offenses against the United States, except in Cases of Impeachment.

He shall have Power, by and with Advice and Consent of the Senate, to make Treaties, provided two thirds of the Senators present concur; and he shall nominate, and by and with the Advice and Consent of the Senate, shall appoint Ambassadors, other public Ministers and Consuls, Judges of the supreme Court, and all other Officers of the United States, whose Appointments are not herein otherwise provided for, and which shall be established by Law: but the Congress may by Law vest the Appointment of such inferior Officers, as they think proper, in the President alone, in the Courts of Law, or in the Heads of Departments.

The President shall have Power to fill up all Vacancies that may happen during the Recess of the Senate, by granting Commissions which shall expire at the End of their next Session.

Section 3. He shall from time to time give to the Congress Information of the State of the Union, and recommend to their Consideration such Measures as he shall judge necessary and expedient; he may, on extraordinary occasions, convene both Houses, or either of them, and in Case of Disagreement between them, with respect to the Time of Adjournment, he may adjourn them to such Time as he shall think proper; he shall receive Ambassadors and other public Ministers; he shall take care that the Laws be faithfully executed, and shall Commission all the Officers of the United States.

Section 4. The President, Vice President and all civil Officers of the United States, shall be removed from Office on Impeachment for, and Conviction of, Treason, Bribery, or other high Crimes and Misdemeanors.

Article III

Section 1. The judicial Power of the United States, shall be vested in one supreme Court, and in such inferior Courts as the Congress may from time to time ordain and establish. The Judges, both of the supreme and inferior Courts, shall hold their Offices during good Behaviour, and shall, at stated Times, receive for their Services, a Compensation, which shall not be diminished during their Continuance in Office.

Section 2. The judicial Power shall extend to all Cases, in Law and Equity, arising under this Constitution, the Laws of the United States, and Treaties made, or which shall be made, under their Authority; — to all Cases affecting Ambassadors, other public Ministers and Consuls;—to all cases of admiralty and maritime Jurisdiction;—to Controversies to which the United States shall be a Party; — to Controversies between two or more States;—between a State and Citizens of another State;—between Citizens of different States:—between Citizens of the same State claiming Land's under Grants of different States, and between a State, or the Citizens thereof, and foreign States, Citizens or Subjects.

In all Cases affecting Ambassadors, other public Ministers and Consuls, and those in which a State shall be Party, the supreme Court shall have original Jurisdiction. In all the other Cases before mentioned, the supreme Court shall have appellate Jurisdiction, both as to Law and Fact, with such Exceptions, and under such Regulations as the Congress shall make.

The trial of all Crimes, except in Cases of Impeachment, shall be by Jury; and such Trial shall be held in the State where the said Crimes shall have been committed; but when not committed within any State, the Trial shall be at such Place or Places as the Congress may by Law have directed.

Section 3. Treason against the United States, shall consist only in levying War against them, or in adhering to their Enemies, giving them Aid and Comfort. No Person shall be convicted of Treason unless on the Testimony of two Witnesses to the same overt Act, or on Confession in open Court.

The Congress shall have Power to declare the Punishment of Treason, but no Attainder of Treason shall work Corruption of Blood, or Forfeiture except during the Life of the Person attained.

Article IV

Section 1. Full Faith and Credit shall be given in each State to the public Acts, Records, and judicial Proceedings of every other State. And the Congress may by general Laws prescribe the Manner in which such Acts, Records and Proceedings shall be proved, and the Effect thereof.

Section 2. The Citizens of each State shall be entitled to all Privileges and Immunities of Citizens in the several States.

A Person charged in any State with Treason, Felony, or other Crime, who shall flee from Justice, and be found in another State, shall on demand of the executive Authority of the State from which he fled, be delivered up, to be removed to the State having Jurisdiction of the Crime.

No Person held to Service or Labour in one State, under the Laws thereof, escaping into another, shall, in Consequence of any Law or Regulation therein, be discharged from such Service or Labour, but shall be delivered up on Claim of the Party to whom such Service or Labour may be due.

Section 3. New States may be admitted by the Congress into this Union; but no new State shall be formed or erected within the Jurisdiction of any other State; nor any State be formed by the Junction of two or more States, or parts of States, without the Consent of the Legislatures of the States concerned as well as of the Congress.

The Congress shall have Power to dispose of and make all needful Rules and Regulations respecting the Territory or other Property belonging to the United States; and nothing in this Constitution shall be so construed as to Prejudice any Claims of the United States or of any particular State.

Section 4. The United States shall guarantee to every State in this union a Republican Form of Government, and shall protect each of them against Invasion; and on Application of the

Legislature, or of the Executive (when the Legislature cannot be convened) against domestic Violence.

Article V

The Congress, whenever two-thirds of both Houses shall deem it necessary, shall propose Amendments to this Constitution, or, on the Application of the Legislatures of two-thirds of the several States, shall call a Convention for proposing Amendments, which, in either Case, shall be valid to all Intents and Purposes, as part of this Constitution, when ratified by the Legislatures of three-fourths of the several States, or by Conventions in three-fourths thereof, as the one or the other Mode of Ratification may be proposed by the Congress; Provided that no Amendment which may be made prior to the Year One thousand eight hundred and eight shall in any Manner affect the first and fourth Clauses in the Ninth Section of the first Article; and that no State, without its Consent, shall be deprived of its equal Suffrage in the Senate.

Article VI

All Debts contracted and Engagements entered into, before the Adoption of this Constitution, shall be as valid against the United States under this Constitution, as under the Confederation.

This Constitution, and the Laws of the United States which shall be made in Pursuance thereof; and all Treaties made, or which shall be made, under the Authority of the United States, shall be the supreme Law of the Land; and the Judges in every State shall be bound thereby, any Thing in the Constitution or Laws of any State to the Contrary notwithstanding.

The Senators and Representatives before mentioned, and the Members of the several State Legislatures, and all executive and judicial Officers, both of the United States and of the several

States, shall be bound by Oath or Affirmation to support this Constitution; but no religious Test shall ever be required as a qualification to any Office or public Trust under the United States.

Article VII

The Ratification of the Conventions of nine States shall be sufficient for the Establishment of this Constitution between the States so ratifying the same.

Done in Convention by the Unanimous Consent of the States present the Seventeenth Day of September in the Year of our Lord one thousand seven hundred and Eighty seven, and of the Independence of the United States of America the Twelfth. In Witness whereof We have hereunto subscribed our Names.

Articles in Addition to, and Amendment of, the Constitution of the United States of America, Proposed by Congress, and Ratified by the Legislatures of the Several States, Pursuant to the Fifth Article of the Original Constitution.

[The first ten amendments went into effect in 1791]

Amendment I

Congress shall make no law respecting an establishment of religion, or prohibiting the free exercise thereof; or abridging the freedom of speech, or of the press; or the right of the people peaceably to assemble, and to petition the Government for a redress of grievances.

Amendment II

A well regulated Militia, being necessary to the security of a free State, the right of the people to keep and bear Arms shall not be infringed.

Amendment III

No Soldier shall, in time of peace, be quartered in any house, without the consent of the Owner, nor in time of War, but in a manner to be prescribed by law.

Amendment IV

The right of the people to be secure in their persons, houses, papers, and effects, against unreasonable searches and seizures, shall not be violated, and no Warrants shall issue, but upon probable cause, supported by Oath or affirmation, and particularly describing the place to be searched, and the persons or things to be seized.

Amendment V

No person shall be held to answer for a capital or otherwise infamous crime, unless on a presentment or indictment of a Grand Jury, except in cases arising in the land or naval forces, or in the Militia, when in actual service in time of War or public danger; nor shall any person be subject for the same offence to be twice put in jeopardy of life or limb; nor shall be compelled in any criminal case to be a witness against himself, nor be deprived of life, liberty, or property, without due process of law; nor shall private property be taken for public use, without just compensation.

Amendment VI

In all criminal prosecutions, the accused shall enjoy the right to a speedy and public trial, by an impartial jury of the State and district wherein the crime shall have been committed, which district shall have been previously ascertained by law, and to be informed of the nature and cause of the accusation; to be confronted with the witnesses against him; to have compulsory process for obtaining witnesses in his favour, and to have the Assistance of Counsel for defence.

Amendment VII

In suits at common law where the value in controversy shall exceed twenty dollars, the right of trial by jury, shall be preserved, and no fact tried by a jury shall be otherwise reexamined in any Court of the United States, than according to the rules of the common law.

Amendment VIII

Excessive bail shall not be required, nor excessive fines imposed, nor cruel and unusual punishments inflicted.

Amendment IX

The enumeration in the Constitution, of certain rights, shall not be construed to deny or disparage others retained by the people.

Amendment X

The powers not delegated to the United States by the Constitution, nor prohibited by it to the States, are reserved to the States respectively, or to the people.

Amendment XI (1798)

The Judicial power of the United States shall not be construed to extend to any suit in law or equity, commenced or prosecuted against one of the United States by Citizens of another State, or by Citizens or Subjects of any Foreign State.

Amendment XII (1804)

The Electors shall meet in their respective States and vote by ballot for President and Vice-President, one of whom, at least, shall not be an inhabitant of the same State with themselves; they shall name in their ballots the person voted for as President, and in distinct ballots the person voted for as Vice-President, and they shall make distinct lists of all persons voted for as President, and of all persons voted for as Vice-President, and of the number of votes for each, which lists they shall sign and certify, and transmit sealed to the seat of the government of the United States, directed to the President of the Senate;—The President of the Senate shall, in the presence of the Senate and House of Representatives, open all the certificates and the votes shall then be counted; — The person having the greatest number of votes for President, shall be the President, if such number be a majority of the whole number of Electors appointed; and if no person have such majority, then from the persons having the highest numbers not exceeding three on the list of those voted for as President, the House of Representatives shall choose immediately, by ballot, the President. But in choosing the President, the votes shall be taken by states, the representation from each state having one vote; a quorum for this purpose shall consist of a member or members from two-thirds of the states, and a majority of all the states shall be necessary to a choice. And if the House of Representatives shall not choose a President whenever the right of choice shall devolve upon them, before the fourth day of March next following, then the Vice-President shall act as President, as in the case of the death or other constitutional disability of the President.—The person having the greatest number of votes as Vice-President, shall be the Vice-President, if such number be a majority of the whole number of Electors appointed, and if no person have a majority, then from the two highest numbers on the list, the Senate shall choose the Vice-President; a quorum for the purpose shall consist of two-thirds of the whole number of Senators, and a majority of the whole number shall be necessary to a choice. But no person constitutionally ineligible to the office of President shall be eligible to that of Vice-President of the United States.

Amendment XIII (1865)

Section 1. Neither slavery nor involuntary servitude, except as a punishment for crime whereof the party shall have been duly convicted, shall exist within the United States, or any place subject to their jurisdiction.

Section 2. Congress shall have power to enforce this article by appropriate legislation.

Amendment XIV (1868)

Section 1. All persons born or naturalized in the United States, and subject to the jurisdiction thereof, are citizens of the United States and of the State wherein they reside. No State shall make or enforce any law which shall abridge the privileges or immunities of citizens of the United States; nor shall any State deprive any person of life, liberty, or property, without due process of law; nor deny to any person within its jurisdiction the equal protection of the laws.

Section 2. Representatives shall be apportioned among the several States according to their respective numbers, counting the whole number of persons in each State, excluding Indians not taxed. But when the right to vote at any election for the choice of electors for President and Vice-President of the United States, Representatives in Congress, the Executive and Judicial officers of a State, or the members of the Legislature thereof, is denied to any of the male inhabitants of such State, being twenty-one years of age, and citizens of the United States, or in any way abridged, except for participation in rebellion, or other crime, the basis of representation therein shall be reduced in the proportion which the number of such male citizens shall bear to the whole number of male citizens twenty-one years of age in such State.

Section 3. No person shall be a Senator or Representative in Congress, or elector of President and Vice-President, or hold any office, civil or military, under the United States, or under any State, who, having previously taken an oath, as a member of Congress, or as an officer of the United States, or as member of any State legislature, or as an executive or judicial officer of any State, to support the Constitution of the United States, shall have engaged in insurrection or rebellion against the same, or given aid or comfort to the enemies thereof. But Congress may by a vote of two-thirds of each House, remove such disability.

Section 4. The validity of the public debt of the United States, authorized by law, including debts incurred for payment of pensions and bounties for services in suppressing insurrection or rebellion, shall not be questioned. But neither the United States nor any State shall assume or pay any debt or obligation incurred in aid of insurrection or rebellion against the United States, or any claim for the loss or emancipation of any slave; but all such debts, obligations, and claims shall be held illegal and void.

Section 5. The Congress shall have the power to enforce, by appropriate legislation, the provisions of this article.

Amendment XV (1870)

Section 1. The right of citizens of the United States to vote shall not be denied or abridged by the United States or by any State on account of race, color, or previous condition of servitude—

Section 2. The Congress shall have power to enforce this article by appropriate legislation.

Amendment XVI (1913)

The Congress shall have power to lay and collect taxes on incomes, from whatever source derived, without apportionment among the several States, and without regard to any census or enumeration.

Amendment XVII (1913)

The Senate of the United States shall be composed of two Senators from each State, elected by the people thereof, for six years; and each Senator shall have one vote. The electors in each State shall have the qualifications requisite for electors of the most numerous branch of the State legislatures.

When vacancies happen in the representation of any State in the Senate, the executive authority of such State shall issue writs of election to fill such vacancies: *Provided,* That legislature of any State may empower the executive thereof to make temporary appointments until the people fill the vacancies by election as the legislature may direct.

This amendment shall not be so construed as to affect the election or term of any Senator chosen before it becomes valid as part of the Constitution.

Amendment XVIII (1919)

Section 1. After one year from the ratification of this article the manufacture, sale, or transportation of intoxicating liquors within, the importation thereof into, or the exportation thereof from the United States and all territory subject to the jurisdiction thereof for beverage purposes is hereby prohibited.

Section 2. The Congress and the several States shall have concurrent power to enforce this article by appropriate legislation.

Section 3. This article shall be inoperative unless it shall have been ratified as an amendment to the Constitution by the legislatures of the several States, as provided in the Constitution, within seven years from the date of the submission hereof to the States by the Congress.

Amendment XIX (1920)

The right of citizens of the United States to vote shall not be denied or abridged by the United States or by any State on account of sex.

Congress shall have power to enforce this article by appropriate legislation.

Amendment XX (1933)

Section 1. The terms of the President and Vice-President

shall end at noon on the 20th day of January, and the terms of Senators and Representatives at noon on the 3d day of January, of the years in which such terms would have ended if this article had not been ratified; and the terms of their successors shall then begin.

Section 2. The Congress shall assemble at least once in every year, and such meeting shall begin at noon on the 3d day of January, unless they shall by law appoint a different day.

Section 3. If, at the time fixed for the beginning of the term of the President, the President elect shall have died, the Vice-President elect shall become President. If a President shall not have been chosen before the time fixed for the beginning of his term, or if the President elect shall have failed to qualify, then the Vice-President elect shall act as President until a President shall have qualified; and the Congress may by law provide for the case wherein neither a President elect nor a Vice-President elect shall have qualified, declaring who shall then act as President, or the manner in which one who is to act shall be selected, and such person shall act accordingly until a President or Vice-President shall have qualified.

Section 4. The Congress may by law provide for the case of the death of any of the persons from whom the House of Representatives may choose a President whenever the right of choice shall have devolved upon them, and for the case of the death of any of the persons from whom the Senate may choose a Vice-President whenever the right of choice shall have devolved upon them.

Section 5. Sections 1 and 2 shall take effect on the 15th day of October following the ratification of this article.

Section 6. This article shall be inoperative unless it shall have been ratified as an amendment to the Constitution by the legislatures of three-fourths of the several States within seven years from the date of its submission.

Amendment XXI (1933)

Section 1. The eighteenth article of amendment to the Constitution of the United States is hereby repealed.

Section 2. The transportation or importation into any State, Territory, or possession of the United States for delivery or use therein of intoxicating liquors, in violation of the laws thereof, is hereby prohibited.

Section 3. This article shall be inoperative unless it shall have been ratified as an amendment to the Constitution by conventions in the several States, as provided in the Constitution within seven years from the date of the submission hereof to the States by the Congress.

Amendment XXII (1951)

No person shall be elected to the office of the President more than twice, and no person who has held the office of President, or acted as President, for more than two years of a term to which some other person was elected President shall be elected to the office of the President more than once.

But this Article shall not apply to any person holding the office of President when this Article was proposed by the Congress, and shall not prevent any person who may be holding the office of President, or acting as President, during the term within which this article becomes operative from holding the office of President or acting as President during the remainder of such term.

This article shall be inoperative unless it shall have been ratified as an amendment to the Constitution by the legislatures of three-fourths of the several states within seven years from the date of its submission to the states by the Congress.

Amendment XXIII (1961)

Section 1. The District constituting the seat of Government of the United States shall appoint in such manner as the Congress may direct:

A number of electors of President and Vice-President equal to the whole number of Senators and Representatives in Congress to which the District would be entitled if it were a State, but in no event more than the least populous State; they shall be in addition to those appointed by the States, but they shall be considered, for the purposes of the election of President and Vice-President, to be electors appointed by a State; and they shall meet in the District and perform such duties as provided by the twelfth article of amendment.

Section 2. The Congress shall have power to enforce this article by appropriate legislation.

Amendment XXIV (1964)

Section 1. The right of citizens of the United States to vote in any primary or other election for President or Vice President, for electors for President or Vice President, or for Senator or Representative in Congress, shall not be denied or abridged by the United States or any other State by reason of failure to pay any poll tax or other tax.

Section 2. The Congress shall have the power to enforce this article by appropriate legislation.

Amendment XXV (1967)

Section 1. In case of the removal of the President from office or of his death or resignation, the Vice President shall become President.

Section 2. Whenever there is a vacancy in the office of the Vice-President, the President shall nominate a Vice President who shall take office upon confirmation by a majority vote of both Houses of Congress.

Section 3. Whenever the President transmits to the President pro tempore of the Senate and the Speaker of the House of

Representatives his written declaration that he is unable to discharge the powers and duties of his office, and until he transmits to them a written declaration to the contrary, such powers and duties shall be discharged by the Vice President as Acting President.

Section 4. Whenever the Vice-President and a majority of either the principal officers of the executive departments or of such other body as Congress may by law provide, transmit to the President pro tempore of the Senate and the Speaker of the House of Representatives their written declaration that the President is unable to discharge the powers and duties of his office, the Vice President shall immediately assume the powers and duties of the office as Acting President.

Thereafter, when the President transmits to the President pro tempore of the Senate and the Speaker of the House of Representatives his written declaration that no inability exists, he shall resume the powers and duties of his office unless the Vice President and a majority of either the principal officers of the executive departments or of such other body as Congress may by law provide, transmit within four days to the President pro tempore of the Senate and the Speaker of the House of Representatives their written declaration that the President is unable to discharge the powers and duties of his office. Thereupon Congress shall decide the issue, assembling within forty-eight hours for that purpose if not in session, If the Congress, within twenty-one days after receipt of the latter written declaration, or, if Congress is not in session, within twenty-one days after Congress is required to assemble, determines by two-thirds vote of both Houses that the President is unable to discharge the powers and duties of his office, the Vice President shall continue to discharge the same as Acting President; otherwise, the President shall resume the powers and duties of his office.

Amendment XXVI (1971)

Section 1. The right of citizens of the United States, who are eighteen years of age or older, to vote shall not be denied or abridged by the United States or by any State on account of age.

Section 2. The Congress shall have the power to enforce this article by appropriate legislation.

APPENDIX 3

Presidential Elections

Year	Candidate	Parties	Electoral Vote
1789	**George Washington**	No party designations	69
	John Adams		34
	Others		35
1792	**George Washington**	No party designations	132
	John Adams		77
	George Clinton		50
	Others		5
1796	**John Adams**	Federalist	71
	Thomas Jefferson	Democratic-Republican	68
	Thomas Pinckney	Federalist	59
	Aaron Burr	Democratic-Republican	30
	Others		48
1800	**Thomas Jefferson**	Democratic-Republican	73
	Aaron Burr	Democratic-Republican	73
	John Adams	Federalist	65
	Charles C. Pinckney	Federalist	64
	John Jay	Federalist	1
1804	**Thomas Jefferson**	Democratic-Republican	162
	Charles C. Pinckney	Federalist	14

1808	**James Madison**	Democratic-Republican	122
	Charles C. Pinckney	Federalist	47
	George Clinton	Democratic-Republican	6
1812	**James Madison**	Democratic-Republican	128
	DeWitt Clinton	Federalist	89
1816	**James Monroe**	Democratic-Republican	183
	Rufus King	Federalist	34
1820	**James Monroe**	Democratic-Republican	231
	John Quincy Adams	Democratic-Republican	1
1824	**John Quincy Adams**	Democratic-Republican	84
	Andrew Jackson	Democratic-Republican	99
	William Crawford	Democratic-Republican	41
	Henry Clay	Democratic-Republican	37
1828	**Andrew Jackson**	Democratic	178
	John Quincy Adams	National Republican	83
1832	**Andrew Jackson**	Democratic	219
	Henry Clay	National Republican	49
	William Wirt	Anti-Masonic	7
	John Floyd	National Republican	11
1836	**Martin Van Buren**	Democratic	170
	William H. Harrison	Whig	73
	Hugh L. White	Whig	26
	Daniel Webster	Whig	14
	W.P. Mangum	Whig	11
1840	**William H. Harrison**	Whig	234
	Martin Van Buren	Democratic	60
1844	**James K. Polk**	Democratic	170
	Henry Clay	Whig	105
	James G. Birney	Liberty	0
1848	**Zachary Taylor**	Whig	163
	Lewis Cass	Democratic	127
	Martin Van Buren	Free-Soil	0
1852	**Franklin Pierce**	Democratic	254
	Winfield Scott	Whig	42
	John P. Hale	Free-Soil	0
1856	**James Buchanan**	Democratic	174
	John C. Fremont	Republican	114
	Millard Fillmore	American	8
1860	**Abraham Lincoln**	Republican	180
	Stephen A. Douglas	Democratic	12
	John C. Breckinridge	Democratic	72

	John Bell	Constitutional Union	39
1864	**Abraham Lincoln**	Republican	212
	George B. McClellan	Democratic	21
1868	**Ulysses S. Grant**	Republican	214
	Horatio Seymour	Democratic	80
1872	**Ulysses S. Grant**	Republican	286
	Horace Greeley	Democratic; Liberal Republican	66
1876	**Rutherford B. Hayes**	Republican	185
	Samuel J. Tilden	Democratic	184
1880	**James A. Garfield**	Republican	214
	Winfield S. Hancock	Democratic	155
	James B. Weaver	Greenback-Labor	0
1884	**Grover Cleveland**	Democratic	219
	James G. Blaine	Republican	182
	Benjamin F. Butler	Greenback-Labor	0
1888	**Benjamin Harrison**	Republican	233
	Grover Cleveland	Democratic	168
1892	**Grover Cleveland**	Democratic	277
	Benjamin Harrison	Republican	145
	James B. Weaver	Populist	22
1896	**William McKinley**	Republican	271
	William J. Bryan	Democratic; Populist	176
1900	**William McKinley**	Republican	292
	William J. Bryan	Democratic; Populist	155
1904	**Theodore Roosevelt**	Republican	336
	Alton B. Parker	Democratic	140
	Eugene V. Debs	Socialist	0
1908	**William H. Taft**	Republican	321
	William J. Bryan	Democratic	162
	Eugene V. Debs	Socialist	0
1912	**Woodrow Wilson**	Democratic	435
	Theodore Roosevelt	Progressive	88
	William H. Taft	Republican	8
	Eugene V. Debs	Socialist	0
1916	**Woodrow Wilson**	Democratic	277
	Charles E. Hughes	Republican	254
1920	**Warren G. Harding**	Republican	404
	James M. Cox	Democratic	127
	Eugene V. Debs	Socialist	0

1924	**Calvin Coolidge**	Republican	382
	John W. Davis	Democratic	136
	Robert M. LaFollette	Progressive	13
1928	**Herbert C. Hoover**	Republican	444
	Alfred E. Smith	Democratic	87
1932	**Franklin D. Roosevelt**	Democratic	472
	Herbert C. Hoover	Republican	59
	Norman Thomas	Socialist	0
1936	**Franklin D. Roosevelt**	Democratic	523
	Alfred M. Landon	Republican	8
	William Lemke	Union	0
1940	**Franklin D. Roosevelt**	Democratic	449
	Wendell L. Willkie	Republican	82
1944	**Franklin D. Roosevelt**	Democratic	432
	Thomas E. Dewey	Republican	99
1948	**Harry S Truman**	Democratic	303
	Thomas E. Dewey	Republican	189
	J. Strom Thurmond	States' Rights	39
	Henry A. Wallace	Progressive	0
1952	**Dwight D. Eisenhower**	Republican	442
	Adlai E. Stevenson	Democratic	89
1956	**Dwight D. Eisenhower**	Republican	457
	Adlai E. Stevenson	Democratic	73
1960	**John F. Kennedy**	Democratic	303
	Richard M. Nixon	Republican	219
1964	**Lyndon B. Johnson**	Democratic	486
	Barry M. Goldwater	Republican	52
1968	**Richard M. Nixon**	Republican	301
	Hubert H. Humphrey	Democratic	191
	George C. Wallace	American Independent	46
1972	**Richard M. Nixon**	Republican	520
	George S. McGovern	Democratic	17
	Others		1
1976	**Jimmy Carter**	Democratic	297
	Gerald R. Ford	Republican	240
	Others		1
1980	**Ronald Reagan**	Republican	489
	Jimmy Carter	Democratic	49
	John Anderson	Independent	0
1984	**Ronald Reagan**	Republican	525
	Walter Mondale	Democratic	13

APPENDIX 4

Admission of States

Order of Admission	State	Date of Admission
1	Delaware	December 7, 1787
2	Pennsylvania	December 12, 1787
3	New Jersey	December 18, 1787
4	Georgia	January 2, 1788
5	Connecticut	January 9, 1788
6	Massachusetts	February 6, 1788
7	Maryland	April 28, 1788
8	South Carolina	May 23, 1788
9	New Hampshire	June 21, 1788
10	Virginia	June 25, 1788
11	New York	July 26, 1788
12	North Carolina	November 21, 1789
13	Rhode Island	May 29, 1790
14	Vermont	March 4, 1791
15	Kentucky	June 1, 1792
16	Tennesse	June 1, 1796
17	Ohio	March 1, 1803

18	Louisiana	April 30, 1812
19	Indiana	December 11, 1816
20	Mississippi	December 10, 1817
21	Illinois	December 3, 1818
22	Alabama	December 14, 1819
23	Maine	March 15, 1820
24	Missouri	August 10, 1821
25	Arkansas	June 15, 1836
26	Michigan	January 26, 1837
27	Florida	March 3, 1845
28	Texas	December 29, 1845
29	Iowa	December 28, 1846
30	Wisconsin	May 29, 1848
31	California	September 9, 1850
32	Minnesota	May 11, 1858
33	Oregon	February 14, 1859
34	Kansas	January 29, 1861
35	West Virginia	June 30, 1863
36	Nevada	October 31, 1864
37	Nebraska	March 1, 1867
38	Colorado	August 1, 1876
39	North Dakota	November 2, 1889
40	South Dakota	November 2, 1889
41	Montana	November 8, 1889
42	Washington	November 11, 1889
43	Idaho	July 3, 1890
44	Wyoming	July 10, 1890
45	Utah	January 4, 1896
46	Oklahoma	November 16, 1907
47	New Mexico	January 6, 1912
48	Arizona	February 14, 1912
49	Alaska	January 3, 1959
50	Hawaii	August 21, 1959

Index